# GOOD LIFE® SAN FRANCISCO NIGHTLIFE GUIDE

SO-DFJ-629

# CREDITS

**Editor**
Jeremy Chipman

**Copy Editors**
Julie Carlson, Cynthia Rubin, Sharon Silva

**Associate Editor**
Susie Kramer

**Cover Design**
Big Fish Books

**Cover Image**
Jerry Kearns, *Golden Gate,* 1994
Mixed Media, 8⁵⁄₁₆ x 6¹⁵⁄₁₆ inches
Courtesy Modernism Gallery, San Francisco

**Contributors**
Lysa Allman dba Lyman Productions, Arie Atlas, Kristen Bruno,
Beverly Cambron, Holly Erickson, Amanda Freeman, Karen
Godfredsen, Susie Kramer, Nancy Lee, David McFarland,
Maureen McKeon, Lakenda North, Barry Roche, Luna Salaver,
Paul Schmidtberger, Charlie Schroder, Mimi Lathan Towle,
Sean Vitali, Stephanie Vollmer, Raymond R. Watson

Good Life San Francisco Nightlife Guide
ISBN 0-886776-08-3 Softcover.
Copyright © 1998 Good Life Publications. All rights reserved.
Maps © 1998 Good Life Publications. All rights reserved.

Printed in Canada on recycled paper.

Please send all comments, corrections, and additions for
future editions to:

Good Life Publications
580 Washington St. #306
San Francisco, California 94111
(415) 989-1844 or (888) 989-GOOD
(415) 989-3122 fax
comments@goodlifebooks.com

## Special Sales

Good Life guides are available at bulk discounts for conventions, corporate gifts, fundraising sales premiums, and sales promotions. Special editions, including custom covers, excerpts of
existing guides, and corporate imprints, can be created for large
orders. For more information, contact Good Life Publications.

# INTRODUCTION

Looking for a place to drink? To dance? To hear live music? San Francisco, a city with so many restaurants that every resident could sit down simultaneously for a dinner out, has an impressive number of bars and clubs as well. Like the dining scene, however, the City's nightlife is characterized as much by the quality as by the quantity of choices. There are downtown supper clubs where socialites chatter over the clinking of wineglasses. There are neighborhood sports bars full of grown-ups screaming their lungs out for the Niners or Giants. There are elegant ballrooms on Nob Hill and proletarian dives in the Mission. In fact, with bars ranging from the Abbey Tavern to Zeitgeist, every variety of night owl is provided for, whether tastes run upscale or downscale, crowded or quiet, bottled domestic beer or exotic mixed drink, cool jazz or white-hot punk rock.

This book is a subjective and selective look at bars and clubs in San Francisco. It greatly expands on information that first appeared in the Nightlife section of Good Life's *San Francisco Insider's Guide*. Capsule reviews of some 300 bars and clubs are included, arranged in chapters by neighborhood so you can easily plan your pub crawls. Even so, it is merely a sampling of what you can do when the sun goes down (and, on occasion, *before* the sun goes down). We encourage you to be adventurous: each and every neighborhood has at least a few hangouts that are worthy of a visit, and some have so many good ones that you wouldn't need to venture any further. Plenty of slick new nightspots are opening all the time, and plenty of longtime out-of-the way bars are waiting to be rediscovered and appreciated.

Every effort has been made to ensure that the information is up-to-date, but the reality is that the nightlife scene is ever-changing. Dance-oriented nightclubs, which pursue the steadily shifting tastes of their fickle clientele, can change their musical stripes overnight—or simply shut down. Some popular dance nights are known to migrate from one club to another on short notice, so always call ahead. By comparison, bars and pubs are generally more stable and secure in their identity (The Saloon has been at its location since a guy named Lincoln was President) and, by extension, have a reliable, recognizable clientele.

Currently, a cloud of uncertainty hangs over San Francisco's bar industry: the impending citywide ban on smoking in drinking establishments. Slated to become law as early as 1998, it has bar owners panicked, afraid that their customers, unable to fathom enjoying their pint without dragging on a Marlboro, will vanish. But no matter what the future brings, people will always enjoy going out, whether it's across town or across the street, and San Francisco's nightspots will be ready for them.

Whatever your destination, keep in mind that closing time for bars is 2am, with last call usually around 1:30. Some dance clubs stay open much later: indeed, SoMa warehouse raves don't even get rolling until 4am. The legal drinking age in California is 21, and most bars and clubs check ID at the door. Some nightspots, especially those with live entertainment, have "All Ages" nights when the age requirement drops to 18. Folks over 21 can get their hands stamped in order to purchase liquor. Remember, drinking and driving is always a bad idea.

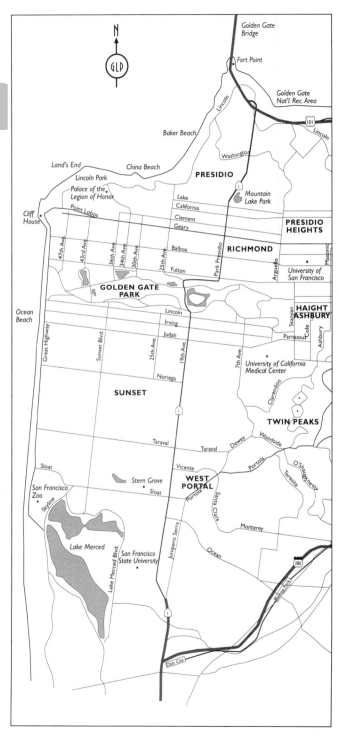

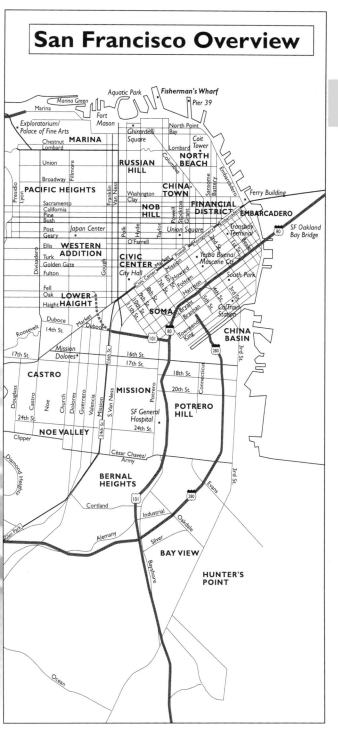

# San Francisco Overview

Marina Green

Aquatic Park

**Fisherman's Wharf**

Pier 39

Marina

Fort Mason

Exploratorium/
Palace of Fine Arts

North Point
Bay

Ghirardelli
Square

Coit
Tower

Chestnut

**MARINA**

Lombard

Lombard

Columbus

**NORTH
BEACH**

Union

Fillmore

**RUSSIAN
HILL**

Broadway

Sansome

Battery

Embarcadero

Presidio

Lyon

**PACIFIC HEIGHTS**

Franklin

Van Ness

**CHINA-
TOWN**

Ferry Building

Sacramento

Washington

California

Clay

**FINANCIAL
DISTRICT**

Grant

Powell

Stockton

**EMBARCADERO**

Pine

**NOB
HILL**

Bush

Polk

Hyde

Taylor

Union Square

**SF Oakland
Bay Bridge**

Post

Japan Center

Geary

O'Farrell

Transbay
Terminal

80

Ellis

**WESTERN
ADDITION**

**CIVIC
CENTER**

Montgomery

Divisadero

Turk

Gough

City Hall

Market

2nd St.

**Yerba Buena/
Moscone Ctr.**

Golden Gate

Civic Center

Powell

Mission

Fulton

Howard

3rd St.

4th St.

5th St.

6th St.

Folsom

Harrison

South Park

Fell

7th St.

8th St.

9th St.

10th St.

11th St.

Oak

**LOWER
HAIGHT**

**SOMA**

Bryant

Cal Train
Station

Haight

Brannan

Duboce

Roosevelt

Market

Duboce

14th St.

101

80

Townsend

King

**CHINA
BASIN**

17th St.

Mission
Dolores

16th St.

16th St.

280

3rd St.

17th St.

**CASTRO**

18th St.

Douglass

Castro

Noe

Church

Dolores

Guerrero

Valencia

Mission

S. Van Ness

Potrero

Connecticut

20th St.

**MISSION**

**POTRERO
HILL**

24th St.

SF General
Hospital

Clipper

**NOE VALLEY**

24th St.

24th St.

Diamond Heights

César Chavez/
Army

**BERNAL
HEIGHTS**

3rd St.

Cortland

101

280

Evans

Glen Park

Industrial

Oakdale

Alemany

Silver

**BAY VIEW**

Bayshore

**HUNTER'S
POINT**

Ocean

5

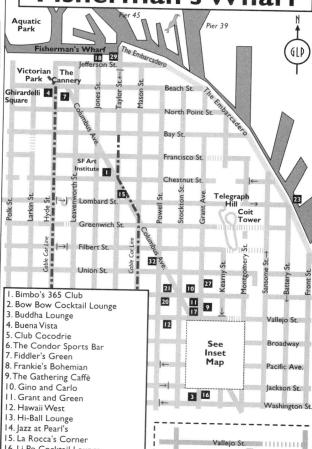

# North Beach
# Chinatown
# Fisherman's Wharf

Aquatic Park

Pier 45

Pier 39

N
GLP

Fisherman's Wharf

Victorian Park

The Cannery

Ghirardelli Square

Jefferson St.

Beach St.

North Point St.

Bay St.

Francisco St.

Columbus Ave.

Jones St.

Taylor St.

Mason St.

The Embarcadero

SF Art Institute

Chestnut St.

Lombard St.

Greenwich St.

Filbert St.

Union St.

Polk St.

Larkin St.

Hyde St.

Leavenworth St.

Cable Car Line

Cable Car Line

Columbus Ave.

Powell St.

Stockton St.

Grant Ave.

Telegraph Hill

Coit Tower

Kearny St.

Montgomery St.

Sansome St.

Battery St.

Front St.

Vallejo St.

Broadway

Pacific Ave.

Jackson St.

Washington St.

See Inset Map

1. Bimbo's 365 Club
2. Bow Bow Cocktail Lounge
3. Buddha Lounge
4. Buena Vista
5. Club Cocodrie
6. The Condor Sports Bar
7. Fiddler's Green
8. Frankie's Bohemian
9. The Gathering Caffè
10. Gino and Carlo
11. Grant and Green
12. Hawaii West
13. Hi-Ball Lounge
14. Jazz at Pearl's
15. La Rocca's Corner
16. Li Po Cocktail Lounge
17. Lost and Found Saloon
18. Lou's Pier 47
19. Mr. Bing's
20. North Star
21. O'Reilly's Irish Bar
22. Palladium
23. Pier 23 Café
24. Purple Onion
25. The Saloon
26. San Francisco Brewing Company
27. Savoy Tivoli
28. Spec's 12 Adler Museum Café
29. Tarantino's
30. Tosca Café
31. Vesuvio Café
32. Washington Sq. Bar & Grill

Vallejo St.

Columbus Ave.

Broadway

Pacific Ave.

Jackson St.

Grant Ave.

Kearny St.

Montgomery St.

The sidewalks of North Beach are heavily populated by out-of-towners, and it's no wonder. This is the historical San Francisco that even the locals can't seem to get enough of: the Barbary Coast and the Beats, with enough of a red-light district left on Broadway to remind everyone what else was (is) popular among consenting adults. At night, Columbus and Grant avenues bustle with activity from the bars and cafés. The crowd is diverse—young and old, American and international—and each spot has a completely different atmosphere. Where else but North Beach could a friendly dive like Specs happily coexist between the mature elegance of Pearl's and Tosca?

The neighborhood may offer unadulterated fun, but keep in mind that parking here is an unadulterated nightmare. If the crowds become too much to take, head down Grant Avenue away from the water, toward the bars of Chinatown, which have as much character as the North Beach ones but are a lot less crowded, even on weekends.

★

## BIMBO'S 365 CLUB
*1025 Columbus Ave. (Chestnut/Francisco), (415) 474-0365*
*Open for performances only*

The living definition of swank, this cavernous nightclub/lounge was hip long before the current Cocktail Nation craze. Founded in 1931 by Agostino "Bimbo" Giontoli and still family-run, Bimbo's exquisite interior features red velvet curtains, a plush black-and-red diamond carpet, a garish nude painting, large candelabras, a giant mirrored disco ball—you get the picture. All this plus a separate barroom with a giant fishbowl and a white-stucco lobby with a plaster mermaid centerpiece. Bimbo's hosts diverse musical events most nights of the week, from avant-garde rock to soul and funk, and on special evenings, the world-famous Dolphina, otherwise known as the Girl in the Fishbowl, makes an appearance. The menu is limited, featuring bottled beer and a few unremarkable victuals, which is why you should order what everyone else orders—cocktails, cocktails, and more cocktails, preferably one of their reliable martinis. If attending a low-volume performance, try to get a spot up front near the stage, where the crowd is more attentive. Toward the back of the room the chatting is so loud you probably wouldn't hear a plane if it landed next to your table. Oh, and a couple more things: Be sure to tip the bathroom steward, and do dress up, even if it's just high casual.

## BOW BOW COCKTAIL LOUNGE
*1155 Grant Ave. (Pacific/Broadway), (415) 421-6730*
*Hours unavailable at presstime*

For more than a decade, owner Candy Wong has presided over this North Beach hole-in-the-wall, a quiet little spot that is frequented by tourists and locals on weekends but is largely empty on weeknights. There are no tables, just a jet-black bar watched over by two red dragons and a plastic Spuds MacKenzie doll.

Both the walls around the bar are mirrored, which creates an interesting, if disconcerting, effect after a couple of drinks. A jukebox in the back plays Sam Cooke on honest-to-goodness 45s, and Candy, a very personable lady with an affinity for makeup, always has one of her two TVs tuned to an old movie. Miller, Bud, and Tsingtao are all available in bottle form. *Note:* As of August 1997, the bar is closed while the building undergoes seismic retrofitting. Call ahead.

## BUDDHA LOUNGE
*901 Grant Ave. (Washington), (415) 362-1792*
*Daily 11am-midnight*

Chinatown bars are unique, and the Buddha Lounge is no exception. It isn't just that the barmaid constantly rearranges the seating arrangements with every new arrival. It isn't that she uses Sunny Delight in place of orange juice to make screwdrivers. It isn't the sign at the back gate that says "To open door: 1) Push; 2) Pull." It isn't the martial arts movies on the overhead TV, the particleboard awning over the bar supported by fake bamboo poles, or the jukebox where Dinah Shore and Bell Biv Devoe play back-to-back. No, what makes this place and all of its neighborhood brethren so unique is that it's still just a bar: a place to be social, sip a cold one, and wonder whose idea it was to put reflecting mirrors behind the bar. Why, exactly, would someone want to *see* themselves getting plastered?

## CLUB COCODRIE
*1024 Kearny St. (Broadway/Pacific), (415) 986-6678*
*Daily 4pm-2am*

Cocodrie deserves your admiration for effort alone: aside from the weekend soundings at the nearby Purple Onion, the streets of North Beach are littered with the carcasses of dead rock clubs (The Stone comes to mind). So this large, open room, done up in office carpeting with walls painted purple and mustard, adds the draw of New Orleans food, free pool during happy hour (all night Sundays to Tuesdays), and cheap pints to its nightly live-music offerings—mostly unsigned local alternative bands preaching to the converted, in other words, their friends. Still, there's only so long you can stare at the alligator heads hanging from behind the bar, and if you really wanted Cajun cuisine you'd be in the French Quarter by now. At some point you'll want to admit you're here for the music, head on over to the world's smallest mosh pit/dance floor at the foot of the tiny black stage, and get to it. Small cover charge.

## THE CONDOR SPORTS BAR
*300 Columbus Ave. (Broadway), (415) 781-8222*
*M-Th 2pm-2am; F-Su noon-2am*

One of the Barbary Coast's most famous (and infamous) strip joints until 1991, the Condor is now a run-of-the-mill brick, wood, and neon sports bar that honors its past with decor featuring artifacts from its former life, including a white player piano hanging from the ceiling and the historic "flashing nipple" signpost that once served as the beacon to North Beach eros. Newspaper articles about the legendary stripper Carol Doda line the walls, and the route to the men's room features a hall-of-fame pantheon of topless women. The bar even serves a cocktail called La Femme in a 22-ounce, nine-inch-tall glass. It's hard to reconcile all this with the current sports bar theme: 18 beers on draft, four pool tables, pinball machines, sports memorabilia, and countless TVs, all of which appeal to coach potatoes who somehow got out of their houses for a few hours. Perhaps sports bars are the strip joints of the 1990s; it's something to ponder if you visit the Condor.

### FIDDLER'S GREEN
*1333 Columbus Ave. (North Point/Beach), (415) 441-9758*
*Daily 9:30am-2am*

This upstairs-downstairs Irish bar attracts ex-pats, North Beach singles, and a smattering of tourists looking for Pier 39. The downstairs bar has a low ceiling, wooden benches, and historical photos of Ireland on the walls. Upstairs is more expansive, with more headroom, more bar space, and a large dance floor. Trainspotting, Thursday night's party during which DJs spin UK house music, is popular. On Friday and Saturday nights, the party spills out onto the front steps. Murphy's and Guinness are among the beers on tap. Full lunch and dinner menus are served.

## Dancing

For a dancer, the Bay Area is dancing heaven. Whether you like hip-hop, salsa, samba, mosh pits, line dancing, or just watching others sweat and gyrate to loud, rhythmic sounds, this is *the* place to be. Few metropolitan areas can boast of such a concentrated variety of clubs for every dancing taste.

Specialty dance sites like **Caribbean Gardens**, 1306 Bayshore Ave., Burlingame, (650) 347-9007, which caters to fans of Latin and Caribbean dance, happily coexist with the eclectic spots that feature a different dance sound for each day of the week; for example, **1015 Folsom,** 1015 Folsom St., SF, (415) 431-1200 or **Bahia Cabana** (see Upper Market bar listing). Of course, there are also clubs featuring the latest in '90s-style dance. The immense, multifaceted **Sound Factory** (see SoMa bar listing), is three clubs in one (techno, old-school funk, and hip-hop), where you can virtually dance the night away—or at least until 4am. If it's authentic '70s funk that suits you, find it live at such dance destinations as **Brennan's**, 4th and University, Berkeley, (510) 841-0960, where bands like Downtown Rhythm cover James Brown and Funkadelic on Saturday nights.

For unique dance mixes, Bay Area DJs sometimes produce their own dance parties at local clubs, usually with just a $5 cover charge. SpinCycle Productions throws a gig twice a year featuring an energetic mix of the latest carnival music: soca, salsa, samba, merengue, and reggae. You can be placed on SpinCycle's mailing list by making your way to jimbo@arana.com on the Internet.

If you don't know how to dance, the Bay Area has scores of good schools that teach technique. For ballroom, swing, and tango, check out **Metronome Ballroom,** 1830 17th St., SF, (415) 252-9000. **Rhythm and Motion**, 1133 Mission St., (415) 621-0643, in San Francisco is a studio that offers a variety of classes, including hip-hop. Some clubs offer salsa lessons whenever they have salsa night, such as **Café du Nord** (see Castro bar listing) on Tuesdays. If you want to learn samba, the San Francisco-based **Escola Nova de Samba** (415) 661-4798 is the oldest active samba school in the United States, plus there are many other Bay Area samba-lesson possibilities.

Lastly, it's always a good idea to pick up one of the local free publications, such as the *Bay Guardian*, *SF Weekly*, or *East Bay Express*, for current listings on special events, DJs, and band information.

### FRANKIE'S BOHEMIAN CAFÉ
*443 Broadway (Kearny/Montgomery), (415) 788-7936*
*Daily noon-midnight*

Spinning DJ beats and featuring three separate bars within this enormous red barn, Frankie's Broadway location has great potential, if only the owners would invest in some wintertime heaters and a summertime ventilation system. As it is, they're still packing them in from Thursday through Saturday nights, when the dance floor is crammed tight and hard-driving rock fills the air. If you're over the age of 25, you might be lonely for similar company. This is strictly a college Greeks and Junior Marina-ites scene, with a corresponding decibel level. Off days, the crowds are slow going. You'll find a dozen beers on tap, and the restaurant serves fair fare with a Euro-Czech twist at reasonable prices.

### THE GATHERING CAFFE
*1326 Grant Ave. (Vallejo/Green), (415) 433-4247*
*Su-Th 7pm-midnight; F-Sa 7pm-2am*

Located on popular Grant Avenue in the middle of North Beach, the Caffè is a quiet departure from the surrounding saloons, bars, and pool halls. The lighting is muted and the decor simple, with photographs and silhouettes of famous artists decorating the walls. The talent is usually local bands performing alternative jazz and blues on a stage positioned by the front window, which means customers view the musicians and street life at the same time. The small space ensures that the sights and sounds of the band are good from any seat in the house. The atmosphere is relaxed: any attire is acceptable, and the bar serves only wine, beer, coffee drinks, and a few desserts. This is a nice place for someone out alone, with a friend or two, or on a first date. In response to a recent surge in popularity, there is a $3 cover charge on the weekends, which includes a $1 discount at the bar (in other words, a $2 cover). Bands start around 8:30pm.

### GINO AND CARLO
*548 Green St. (Grant/Stockton), (415) 421-0896*
*Daily 6am-2am*

Its interior may have been refurbished and remodeled and its original owners may be long gone, but Gino and Carlo remains a North Beach institution, just like any place that's been around since 1942 would be. A classic neighborhood spot, it has green walls with paintings of Italian vistas, red-leather backed chairs, a traditional rock-and-roll jukebox, and a tiny but glistening wooden bar. There are also two pool tables in the back (the location of an annual 8-Ball Tournament whose winners are immortalized on the Wall of Fame plaque). The surprisingly diverse clientele includes the last stand of Italian old-timers, a flurry of rabid sports fans, and even a few counterculture types thrown in for good measure. The easy-going bartenders keep the drinks flowing seamlessly. On tap are six or so beers and Jaegermeister.

### GRANT AND GREEN
*1371 Grant Ave. (Green), (415) 693-9565*
*M-Th 4pm-2am; F-Su 1pm-2am*

Seven nights a week, this dark and dingy joint, coincidentally located on the corner of Grant and Green, presents live, bluesy rock—the loud, gritty kind—in a stripped-down format. The stage is actually on foot-high risers, and the audience stands wherever it pleases. The clientele matches the atmosphere of the place, with lots of leather-clad bikers imbibing at the bar, although some yuppie blues aficionados throw caution to the wind and step inside to listen. Good microbrews are on tap. If you happen to get lost, look for Grant's visage on the giant green $50-bill insignia on the exterior wall.

## Hawaii West

*729 Vallejo St. (Powell/Stockton), (415) 362-3220*
*Daily noon-2am*

The original North Beach tiki bar, Hawaii West has been serving drinks for almost four decades. It boasts a live-koi pond, a lighted fish tank, and a working waterfall complete with authentic dedication plaque. The bar is also packed with memorabilia collected over the years, from a stuffed Minnie Mouse to an empty hot-dog twirler to an assortment of tiki heads to a "no one's ugly after 2am" bumper sticker. Surfboards jut out

---

## *Fisherman's Wharf*

A certain part of town is always full of scary-looking people who just hang out all day. Locals know to avoid it. The Tenderloin? Hardly. It's Fisherman's Wharf, the epicenter of the City's tourist culture. Cheesy wax museums, overpriced "fudge shoppes," and countless locations to snap photos of family and friends against a fake Alcatraz backdrop fight for space in these teeming blocks. Still, amidst all the clatter there are a few bars of note that, if nothing else, provide amateur sociologists with the chance to study out-of-towners in their natural habitat.

**Buena Vista:** 2765 Hyde St. (Beach), (415) 474-5044. The Buena Vista likes to think of itself as the refined option on the Wharf, especially since it's located by the more elegant Aquatic Park and Ghirardelli Square. An old-time bar with mustard-colored walls, mosaic tiles, and dramatic picture-window views, this was where Irish coffee was invented back in 1952. (There's a plaque out front commemorating the event, so it must be true.) You can join the tweedy, middle-aged crowd for said drink or choose from a full bar selection. Come during the day for superb views of the Bay and to watch folks line up across the street for the cable cars. • M-F 9am-2am; Sa-Su 8am-2am

**Lou's Pier 47:** 300 Jefferson St. (Jones), (415) 675-0308. Lou's is considerably rowdier than nearby Tarantino's, owing to the fact that 17 bands—blues, rock, R&B, country—pass across its stage each week. The Bourbon Street-like ambience is furthered by what must be the world's longest happy hour: noon to 8pm on weekends (4 to 8pm on weeknights), a period during which folks pack the pink Formica bar and take up every seat at the closely arranged tables. There's a full snack bar, and the cover charge doesn't kick in until 8pm. Lou, the First Lady of Fisherman's Wharf, is often on hand if you'd like to chat. • Daily 4pm-2am (Restaurant open daily 6am-11pm)

**Tarantino's:** 206 Jefferson St. (Taylor), (415) 775-5600. This bar-restaurant, which dates back decades to when longshoremen still worked on these docks, has been locally owned since its inception. The walls of the large second-story room are covered with a sepia-toned photographic mural of the City in the old days. The wooden bar and a small group of cafeterialike seats are the only places to sit if you're drinking, but you'll be served by a friendly and gracious staff (whose conversations with one another sound straight out of a TV sitcom), and the slightly-higher-than-usual drink prices are offset by a view of the Golden Gate Bridge and Marin in the background. • Daily 11am-11pm

over the thatch-topped bar, which has two TVs usually turned to the sporting event du jour. Candid bar photos adorn the walls near the 75-cent pool table. Cigarette smoking is actually encouraged by the regulars, and the bartender may bum one from you as well. Rumor has it that the current owner occasionally whips up some fantastic food in the kitchen and serves the crowd, but this has yet to be substantiated by anyone with less than several scotches behind them. Be warned: this place operates on "Hawaiian time," so the doors sometimes don't open until 7pm.

### HI-BALL LOUNGE
*473 Broadway (Kearny/Montgomery), (415) 397-9464*
*Tu-Th 7pm-2am; F 5pm-2am; Sa 8pm-2am; Su 7pm-2am*

The key word here is *lounge*, as it reflects the '90s retro/cocktail revival trend among the city's young clubbers, a fad that shows no signs of passing anytime soon. The fashionable interior is one of red-velvet booths, circular candlelit tables, and dimmed lighting against darkly painted walls. The effect would look like a cliché, except that the Hi-Ball was one of the first places to jump on this particular bandwagon. As for the crowd, the preponderance of men in bowling shirts and women in baby-doll dresses drinking from Y-shaped glasses will tip anyone off to what sort of people hang out here. You can enjoy live jazz and swing music nightly, with dance lessons provided by the suave Johnny Swing on Sundays, Tuesdays, and Wednesdays. (Call 964-3654 for lesson information.)

### JAZZ AT PEARL'S
*256 Columbus Ave. (Broadway/Pacific), (415) 291-8255*
*M-Sa 8:30pm-2am*

Situated in the heart of the very busy nightlife scene of North Beach is a real "pearl" of a place—a popular venue for small jazz combos as well as some larger groups. Bay Area talent such as Bruce Forman and the well-known Pete Escovedo appear often, playing between walls covered with large, black-and-white photographs of jazz legends. There is no cover charge, but there is a stiffly-enforced, two-beverage minimum weeknights—two drinks per set (9pm and 11pm) weekends. Most patrons are in their mid-30s, with a few more-mature music lovers mixed in. The dress code permits casual attire, although most people are gussied up for a night out. Appetizers, burgers, pizza, and sandwiches are available for noshing in the well-lit, tableclothed rooms, front and back. Windows, which open to the street, draw many outside spectators, and the melodious sounds can be heard a block away.

### LA ROCCA'S CORNER
*957 Columbus Ave. (Chestnut/Taylor), (415) 674-1266*
*Daily 10am-2am*

This tiny, triangular-shaped drinking establishment dates back to 1922 and remains popular with neighborhood residents and tourists running the gauntlet between Fisherman's Wharf and North Beach. People stop by asking for directions (a tongue-in-cheek sign out front reads English Spoken Here) and end up having a drink at one of the simple wooden tables or sidling up to the welcoming bar. (The beers on tap—microbrews and

Guinness—irresistibly beckon.) Live entertainment here means a wandering guitar player with slicked-back white hair doing his best Hank Williams renditions. Singing along is encouraged.

## LI PO COCKTAIL LOUNGE
*916 Grant Ave. (Washington/Jackson), (415) 982-0072*
*Daily 2pm-2am*

The minute you step beneath the green-and-red neon sign and through the cavelike entrance to Li Po, you'll know you've found the coolest bar in Chinatown. The Buddhist shrine behind the bar is merely the most obvious evidence of that fact. Look further to discover the cheap red leather booths beneath cheesy beer posters of Asian models—including one in a darkly claustrophobic alcove. Notice the original Ms. Pac Man video game in the corner, looking as anachronistic as an Apple II. Hear the disco hits from another era that blare unironically from the jukebox. In other words, think *Barfly* starring Jackie Chan. If the bartender doesn't try to get you to join him and his cronies for a game of cards, he'll carefully pour you a mixed drink (such as a screwdriver made of five parts vodka and one part orange Gatorade). Most important, watch the stairs to the bathroom in the basement; they're black diamond if you're sober, double black diamond if you're not.

## LOST AND FOUND SALOON
*1353 Grant Ave. (Vallejo/Green), (415) 392-9126*
*M-F noon-2am; Sa-Su 6am-2am*

What is it about Grant Avenue anyway? Most neighborhoods need just one dive bar. Grant has three (The Saloon, Grant and Green, and this one) in a two-block stretch. The Lost and Found is actually the least disreputable of them all, but it still attracts the long-neck-beer-and-cigarette crowd in full force, and it's still the first place you'd go if you wished to hear all of *Exile on Main Street* on the jukebox. There are two rooms, the main barroom where the grizzled veteran drinkers, perched on old stools beneath faded football pennants, check in for lengthy stays, and the other room, a boxy space with a hull-shaped bar and orange lifesavers hanging from the walls. The latter hosts live blues, rock, and Pink Floyd-tribute bands six days a week on an Astroturf-covered stage with a whitewashed backdrop. (The schedule of bands is posted in the window on one of those month-at-a-glance desk calendars.) Anchor, Golden Gate, and Red Hook are all on tap. A cover charge is in force most nights.

## MR. BING'S
*201 Columbus Ave. (Pacific), (415) 362-1545*
*Daily 10:30am-2am*

Perhaps the swankest part of this low-to-the-ground drinking establishment is the outside sign above the corner entrance that elegantly proclaims Mr. Bing's in red curlicue script. The interior, on the other hand, is the Holy Grail to bar goers who delight in the art of slumming: a linoleum-topped, boomerang-shaped bar; three low-tech Hot Line video games that resemble ancient prototypes for Vegas slots; and a collection of decaying pool trophies. A satellite TV, a jukebox with surprisingly decent tunes from Sinatra to Presley to Madonna, and some local drunkards from neighboring Chinatown do their part to spice the place up. But this isn't the kind of bar you enter to see and be seen, and unless you're Nicolas Cage in *Leaving Las Vegas*, it's not the most romantic place in the world either. But given what it offers—a cheap drink, an available bar stool, and no hassles from the loner next to you—Mr. Bing's certainly delivers. Be nice to Bruce, a regular bartender who's been serving drinks for 10 of the 30 years the place has been around. (Buying him a shot of Crown Royal will endear him to you forever—or at least for an hour or so.) And don't miss the Aqua Net hair-spray dispenser in the ladies' room—a fabulous relic from the '50s.

## NORTH STAR CAFÉ

*1560 Powell St. (Green), (415) 397-0577*
*Daily 11am-2am*

This neighborhood spot has been around since 1882, and the folks playing pool and pinball likely have been patronizing it since its opening. Regulars are greeted by name and poured their usual beverages before they even make it to the bar. In fact, just the greetings take several minutes, as the early evening crew also all seem to know one another. (North Star may have proportionally a greater number of native San Franciscans than any other spot in town.) A solid sports-guy atmosphere—the kind of place where the TVs are tuned to two events at once so no one misses anything—this is where 49er football is passionately debated and extra pairs of Giants tickets are usually available from the person seated on the stool next to you. Late on Saturday nights, the crowd has been known to drown out the jukebox with its ear-splitting renditions of Rolling Stones' songs. On Sunday afternoons, bleary-eyed sports fans sip beers and munch pizza or cheese steaks from down the street. Drinks are inexpensive, but skip the wine and stick with tap brews or Budweiser. Paid parking is available next door; otherwise, a cab is recommended.

## O'REILLY'S IRISH BAR & RESTAURANT

*622 Green St. (Columbus/Powell), (415) 989-6222*
*Daily 11am-1:30am*

The Irish gift of gab is alive and well in O'Reilly's, a relative newcomer to the area. A mural of famous Irish writers lines the back wall of this pub of dark wood and stained glass. Nary a television is in sight, so regulars argue politics while taking turns buying rounds for one another. Regulars also take turns walking the owner's 185-pound Irish wolfhound, who guards the bathrooms or acts the erstwhile sentry at the door. Bartenders tend to call females "luv" as they draw a creamy Guinness or another of the 30 or so beers on tap. A separate dining room specializes in hearty pub fare with Irish flair. Most evenings the full menu is available at the bar as well. You can spot O'Reilly's by the green sidewalk and outdoor tables with giant white-and-green umbrellas. On a sunny weekend, locals gathered at these seats greet each other like old friends and argue like old enemies. It has become a destination spot on weekend evenings, where the charm is drowned by the crush of people. A better bet is to head down on a rainy weeknight, sip a pint, and enjoy the spirit of Ireland.

## PALLADIUM

*1031 Kearny St. (Pacific/Broadway), (415) 434-1308*
*Th, Su 9pm-4am, F-Sa 9pm-6am*

The Palladium is a longtime North Beach dance club that a) caters to a young crowd weaned on '80s and '90s Top 40 dance music and b) can often be heard by those having a drink next door at Tosca. Open on Thursdays, Fridays, Saturdays, and Sundays, the club welcomes folks 18 and over, which tends to keep the older, hipper club crowd elsewhere. The DJs are often on-air personalities from radio station Live 105. If this sounds like your cup of tea, look for two-for-one admission coupons in both the weekly and daily papers.

## PIER 23 CAFÉ

*Pier 23 (Embarcadero at Battery), (415) 362-5125*
*Daily 4:30pm-2am*

From the outside, this smallish cottage looks like it should be serving up some sort of fried fish product instead of being a serious—and seriously fun—drinking and dancing establishment. Live bands perform salsa, New Orleans R&B, reggae, and jazz, depending on the day of the week. (There's no music on Mondays.) The cover charge is usually very reasonable, given the waterfront location. What sort of crowd shows up depends on the music, but be prepared to dance or else cede your space on the floor, especially when salsa night packs the house; some of the regulars take this very seriously. Those taking a break from the music head for the triangular open-air patio in back, with plenty of plastic chairs for sittin' on the dock of the bay, a rare pleasure when there's no (or not much) fog or wind.

## THE PURPLE ONION

*140 Columbus Ave. (Jackson/Kearny), (415) 398-8415*
*F-Sa 9pm-2am*

A cellar room that was once a famous Beat hangout, the Purple Onion is now a rock club open only on Friday and Saturday nights. Since their promotional budget usually only covers a photocopied sheet of paper on a bulletin board at the entrance, it's best to stop by to see what all the fuss is about. Downstairs, you'll find garage, surf, and punk bands playing to a small, loyal audience sitting at brightly colored leather banquettes. The bar serves beer tapped from exposed kegs. Sure, it's low budget, but the minuscule cover charges and once-in-a-blue-moon celebrity appearances (like the unknown band who brought along Moe Tucker of the Velvet Underground to play drums) make this a can't-miss place for those seeking the authentic rock-and-roll experience.

## THE SALOON

*1232 Grant Ave. (Columbus/Vallejo), (415) 989-7666*
*Daily noon-2am*

The year is 1861. Back east, the Civil War has begun. In such momentous times, the opening of Wagner's Beer Hall on what was then DuPont Street probably did not register as a major event—just another place to get a beer in a small port town. Two major earthquakes, two world wars, and one ineffective Prohibition later, DuPont Street has become Grant Avenue and Wagner's Beer Hall is now the Saloon, the oldest operating bar in San Francisco. It looks like it, too: walking through the door on the corner of the alley is like stepping back in time to the days of the Barbary Coast; you almost expect to find a crowd of old salts engrossed in card games and a player piano tinkling away. All the old-time details are here: overhead fans, wooden stools, a bar with the original wood fittings, a stained glass window, faded murals on the walls, a dusty floor, and a few tiny tables at the back of the room. Bands set up in the back and play almost every night—even at 5 on a Monday afternoon, the sound of the blues wafts onto the narrow North Beach streets. Lots of old men and tourists seem to hang out here, a perfect match of historical figures and those searching for history. (The lumberjack-shirted regulars sit in the back of the room, while the tourists sit closer to the door, as though they might need to make a quick escape.) It's a bottled beer kind of place, and Sierra Nevada aside, microbrew aficionados would be advised to go elsewhere. Although the owners are hardly shy about capitalizing on their fame, the self-promotion is decidedly low-key, like the rest of the place. In a city that suffers from too many faux bars, this place is as real as it gets.

## SAN FRANCISCO BREWING COMPANY
*155 Columbus Ave. (Pacific), (415) 434-3344*
*M-F 11:30am-1:30am; Sa-Su noon-1:30am*

A bar has stood on this spot since at least 1907, when the Andromeda Saloon rose out of the ashes of the previous year's Great Quake and Fire. (Boxer Jack Dempsey was once the doorman here.) In its current incarnation, the gorgeous interior contains the original bar and wainscoting, both lacquered to a fine sheen, along with stained-glass windows, old-time ceiling fans, and a nice array of historical memorabilia. A side room offers extra table seating, with a picture-window panorama of the North Beach street scene. The beers are some of the best microbrews in the city, especially the Pony Express Ale and Gripman's Porter. Happy hour (4 to 6pm and midnight to 1am) includes half-pints for a dollar, perfect for imbibing at one of the sidewalk tables, although in nice weather these fill up quickly with office workers and tourists. A full menu is served—the burgers are excellent—and there's live music (mostly jazz; no cover) on Mondays, Wednesdays, Thursdays, and Saturdays.

## SAVOY TIVOLI
*1434 Grant Ave. (Green/Union), (415) 362-7023*
*Tu-Th 5pm-2am; F-Su 3pm-2am*

An indoor pool hall with two bars and a heat lamp–equipped, open-air patio lounge, the Savoy attracts a variety of people. Twentysomethings, thirtysomethings, and a few mature cocktailers mesh in surprising harmony. This is a great place to people watch, as the patio is situated smack in the middle of heavily traveled Grant Avenue between Green and Union. There is a full bar decked out in brass, and the beers range from plain domestic to exotic imports. Inside is a little smoky, especially near the bar (don't look at the natural smoke "designs" on the walls and ceilings), but the air on the patio is clear and refreshing. Good old American rock and roll plays in the background, yet the wrought-iron, marble-topped tables and chairs really give the place a European café feeling.

## SPEC'S 12 ADLER MUSEUM CAFÉ

*12 Saroyan Pl. (off Columbus btwn. Broadway/Pacific), (415) 421-4112*
*M-F 4:30pm-2am; Sa-Su 5pm-2am*

This jovial North Beach dive-in-an-alleyway attracts a diverse clientele of equal parts ancient regulars and curious visitors. The main attraction is not the range of drinks—only Budweiser on tap, a few bottled beers, and the rest is hard stuff—but rather the memorabilia that fills up all available wall, ceiling, and occasionally floor space. Collected from all over the world, whether at a trinket shop or by shrewd bartering with the locals, the knickknacks available on display include, among other things, a gold toilet plunger, a Pacific island license plate, a skull, and an unidentified garden implement. Mere words do not do justice to the glory of this bar; it's best to visit during late afternoon, when it is less crowded, so you can see it all more clearly.

## TOSCA CAFÉ

*242 Columbus Ave. (Broadway/Pacific), (415) 986-9651*
*Daily 5pm-1:45am*

Elegant without being pricy, refined without being stuffy, relaxed without being a dive, Tosca is the classiest bar in the city, at least when there's no room-shaking, rumbling bass coming from the Palladium disco next door. Matron Jeannette Etheredge's palace of good taste has dark walls, a high ceiling, faded floor tiles, giant red leather booths, Formica tables, a long wooden bar, and operatic arias playing in the background on the ancient jukebox. In this sepia-toned ambience, bottled beers like Anchor Steam are served, plus the usual array of cocktails as mixed by the professional bartenders—the house special is a potent coffee-free "cappuccino," and both the martinis and the cosmopolitans pack the requisite punch. The place gets quite crowded on weekends, drawing everyone from yuppies on a North Beach pub crawl to Swing Nation denizens decked out in vintage clothes. Come early; better yet, come early on weeknights, when there is no finer venue for hushed conversation. For what it's worth, actor Nicolas Cage has often been sighted here.

## VESUVIO CAFÉ

*255 Columbus Ave. (Broadway/Pacific), (415) 362-3370*
*Daily 6am-2am*

Once the infamous watering hole frequented by Jack Kerouac and his friends during the late '50s and early '60s (the famous City Lights Bookstore lies across Kerouac Alley from here), Vesuvio is now the hangout spot for '90s Beats and assorted literary wanna-Beats. Half the people in here at any given time will be dressed in black, smoking a cigarette, typing away on their laptop computer, or doing all three at once. It's not really the type of place you stop for a quick pint: the bar's low ceiling, dark corners, and cloistered, woodsy feel encourage long, drawn-out drinking sessions. Plus, it's virtually a museum of San Francisco history, with nearly every square inch of wall space covered with faded newspaper front pages from days gone by. Best to get a pitcher or two, head upstairs, grab a window seat, and while away the hours.

## WASHINGTON SQUARE BAR & GRILL
*1707 Powell St. (Columbus/Union), (415) 982-8123*
*Daily 11am-closing (varies between midnight and 2am)*

Primarily a restaurant, the Wash Bag (a nickname that is no reflection on the atmosphere or the food) is also a nice bar. It offers up nightly music with no cover charge or drinking minimum, and features small jazz combos pressed tightly against the wall. This place has character beyond it's obvious geographic advantage of facing the namesake park. The full bar, serving an extensive array of wines, bourbons, ports, and beers, is made of antique wood with polished brass rails. The backbar behind the pleasant bartenders is expertly carved and broken up with mirrors, including two propped at an angle that allows nearly the entire room to be seen from most bar seats. Tourists mix with the locals, a big-screen TV remains tuned to ESPN, and a hodgepodge of sports memorabilia covers the walls.

★

## Late Night Eats

### BASTA PASTA $$
*1268 Grant Ave. (Vallejo), (415) 434-2248*
*Daily 11:45am-12:45am*
Basta Pasta stays open until the wee hours, so rest your dancing feet while you down soggy pastas and pizza. End your meal with an Italian dessert or coffee with liqueur. Institutional-yet-comfortable atmosphere, swift service, and a downstairs bar that attracts a young clientele.

### BRANDY HO'S $
*217 Columbus Ave. (Pacific/Broadway), (415) 788-7527*
*Su-Th 11:30am-11pm; F-Sa 11:30am-midnight*
After you taste Brandy Ho's incendiary Hunan cooking, you'll be tempted to call the fire department. The young non-Chinese crowd comes for the larger-than-life flavors. The specialty is the flavorful house-smoked ham, chicken, and duck, which would do any Southerner proud.

### ENRICO'S $$
*504 Broadway (Kearny), (415) 982-6223*
*Su-Th 11:30am-midnight; F-Sa noon-midnight (bar open until 1:30am)*
A reborn North Beach landmark where diners can eat tasty California-Italian meals, listen to live music, or just graze on small dishes like garlic mashed potatoes or cockles and mussels. The outdoor patio—San Francisco's first sidewalk café—heated with lamps against chilly summer nights is a prime people-watching place.

### FRANKIE'S BOHEMIAN CAFÉ $
*443 Broadway (Kearny/Montgomery), (415) 788-7936*
*Daily 4pm-1am*
Frankie's is a great choice when the criteria is fun, good food, and handcrafted ales. Menu highlights include burgers, the Brambory, an unusual entrée or appetizer made from shredded potato and zucchini mixed into a pancake with various toppings, and the Jambalaya.

## GREAT EASTERN $$
*649 Jackson St. (Kearny/Grant), (415) 986-2500*
*Su-Th 11am-1am; F-Sa 11am-1am*

A Chinatown hot spot for Cantonese seafood. The neon board on the back wall lists the night's fresh catch, most of which are swimming in large tanks nearby. Seafood is clearly the highlight, although soups and chow mein dishes are also quite good. The brightly lit two-level restaurant sports upscale white-linen-black-lacquer decor with attentive service to match.

## HAPPY DONUTS ¢
*145 Columbus Ave. (Kearny), (415) 956-9189*
*Daily 24 hours*

The place to go if you're looking for a fresh-out-of-the-oven donut, cinnamon roll, or croissant. It's the safest place in town, too, given that there's probably at least one police officer there at any given moment. Open 24 hours.

## IL FORNAIO $$
*1265 Battery St. (Greenwich), (415) 986-0100*
*M-Th 7-10:30am, 11:30am-11pm; F 7-10:30am, 11:30am-midnight;*
*Sa 9am-midnight; Su 9am-11pm*

The San Francisco Il Fornaio boasts high-style Tuscan decor, a charming outdoor patio, and typically surly service. All of the pastas are excellent, especially the *tagliolini alla capresante*, thin flat pasta with scallops, shiitake mushrooms, and pesto.

## FOG CITY DINER $$$
*1300 Battery St. (Embarcadero/Greenwich), (415) 982-2000*
*Su-Th 11:30am-11pm; F-Sa 11:30am-midnight*

The slick interior of this San Francisco institution only marginally resembles a diner, with its black leatherette banquettes, gleaming chrome fixtures, and polished wood accents. The eclectic menu is full of tantalizing choices: cornsticks flecked with red pepper, grilled cheese-stuffed pasilla peppers, terrific chicken pot pie, and a diner chili dog. Portions are less than abundant so order a selection and share.

## JOHNNY ROCKETS $
*81 Jefferson St. (Powell/Mason), (415) 693-9120*
*Su-Th 7am-midnight; F-Sa 7am-2am*

A chain of diners suffused with nostalgic decor and bright fluorescent lighting. Serves up messy-but-tasty burgers, chili cheese fries and shakes. The jukebox blasts 50s tunes.

## LA BODEGA $$
*1337 Grant Ave. (Vallejo/Green), (415) 433-0439*
*Daily 5pm-1am*

Flavorful Spanish tapas, music, and flamenco dancers draw the faithful to the 42-year-old La Bodega. Fried calamari and mushrooms with garlic are two fine offerings.

## MARIO'S BOHEMIAN CIGAR STORE $
*556 Columbus Ave. (Union), (415) 362-0536*
*M-Sa 10am-midnight; Su 10am-11pm*

Wedged into the triangular space where Columbus meets Union, Mario's is not very welcoming from the outside, but take a seat at the bar (or wherever possible) and soak up the authentic Italian atmosphere. The focaccia sandwiches and cannelloni are authentic, and the beer selection is decent.

## MR. PIZZA MAN ¢/$
*759 Columbus Ave. (Greenwich), (415) 285-3337*
*Daily 10am-4am*

The mysterious Mr. Pizza Man must be good with a mound of dough because the crust on the pizza at this chain eatery is thick and excellent. If you're feeling gourmet, they offer a number of interesting topping options; the artichoke heart pizza is particularly good.

## Late Night Eats

### Mo's $
*1322 Grant Ave. (Vallejo/Green), (415) 788-3779*
*M-Th 11am-10:30pm; F 11am-11:30pm; Sa 9am-11:30pm; Su 9am-10:30pm*
Knowledgeable San Franciscans come to this modest eatery for one of the city's best burgers. A thick shake goes perfectly with the spicy fries—just don't tell your cardiologist. Bare-bones diner decor, complete with black-and-white tile and chrome-tube furniture.

### Moose's $$/$$$
*1652 Stockton St. (Union/Filbert), (415) 989-7800*
*M-Th 11:30am-11pm; F-Sa 11:30am-midnight; Su 9:30am-11pm*
It's unclear whether Moose's large front window was designed to allow diners to admire Washington Square or passersby to admire the see-and-be-seen crowd wheeling and dealing over pizza, pasta, and cocktails. The menu includes such Cal-Italian favorites as wood-fired gourmet pizzas, simple pastas, grilled salmon, and pork chops, but most patrons come for the lively energy, not the food.

### New Sun Hong Kong $/$$
*606 Broadway (Columbus), (415) 956-3338*
*Daily 8am-3am*
Open 19 hours a day, every day, New Sun Hong Kong truly has something for everyone. Seafood is favored at dinnertime, when live shrimp, fish, crab, and lobster can get pricy. Late nighters out enjoying North Beach will find New Sun Hong Kong a welcome site for an inexpensive plate of *chow fun* or a steaming bowl of soup.

### North Beach Pizza $
*1499 Grant Ave. (Union), (415) 433-2444*
*Su-Th 11am-1am; F-Sa 11am-1am*
*1310 Grant Ave. (Vallejo/Green), (415) 433-1818*
*M-Th 5-11pm; F-Sa 11am-1am; Su 11am-11pm*
The celebrated chain of San Francisco pizza parlors is loud and energized, with lots of families and large groups in attendance. Toppings are sometimes hidden between the gooey cheese and chewy crust. The menu includes other Italian favorites, but stick to the pizza. Service can be rushed when the place is packed and lines are long. The chain is very efficient and even has take-out only locations.

### North Beach Restaurant $$/$$$
*1512 Stockton St. (Green/Union), (415) 392-1700*
*Daily 11:30am-11:45pm*
This Tuscan restaurant was recently remodeled, and now sports bright marble floors, high ceilings, airy skylights, and colorful art on the walls; they've also added an oh-so-trendy cigar smoking room. The pasta portions are generous, and the fork-tender meats, especially the veal scaloppine with pine nuts and mushrooms, are in a class by themselves.

### Original Buffalo Wings $
*663 Union St. (Columbus/Powell), (415) 296-9907*
*Su-Th 11am-11pm; F-Sa 11am-2am*
They serve burgers, sandwiches, fries and onion rings, but their *raison d'etre* is clearly those meaty, messy wings dipped in mild, hot, or kamikaze sauce. Come with some friends, it's under twenty bucks for a bucket of fifty (!) wings. Don't miss the homemade, fresh-cut chips, either.

### Pasta Pomodoro $
*655 Union St. (Columbus/Powell), (415) 399-0300*
*M-Th 11am-11pm; F 11am-midnight; Sa noon-midnight; Su noon-11pm*
Large servings of pasta at incredibly cheap prices—it's a concept that has made this citywide Italian restaurant chain very popular

among those with big appetites and light pockets. Service is usually lightning quick yet still pleasant. Cash only.

### PIZZERIA UNO $
*2323 Powell St. (Bay), (415) 788-4055*
*M-F 11am-11pm; Sa 11am-11:30pm; Su 11:30am-11pm*
National chain famous for Chicago-style deep-dish pizza served in a bustling diner. Those who don't like the thick, flaky Chicago crust can opt for thin-crust pizzettas. The menu also includes pasta, salads, and burgers, but the big attraction is the pizza.

### ROSE PISTOLA $$$
*532 Columbus Ave. (Union/Green), (415) 399-0499*
*Su-Th 11:30am-midnight; F-Sa 11:30am-1am*
Located in the heart of North Beach, the restaurant sports a bustling open kitchen, sleek lighting, and lots of dark, polished wood. Based on the cuisine of Liguria, chef Reed Hearon's menu features warm, fresh focaccia, a warm salad of octopus, potato, and green beans, and outstanding meat entrées, including a roast suckling pig with polenta croutons. You can order perfectly fresh seafood cooked in a variety of styles.

### SILVER RESTAURANT $
*737 Washington St. (Kearny/Grant), (415) 826-0753*
*Daily 24 hours*
The Silver Restaurant offers inexpensive, decent Chinese classics around the clock and a waitstaff that somehow manages to be smiley despite the hordes of North Beach revelers that rush in after the bars close.

### TAIWAN $
*289 Columbus Ave. (Broadway), (415) 989-6789*
*Daily 11am-3:30pm, 5pm-midnight*
The Chinatown branch is a tiny hole-in-the-wall. Order any one of the dumplings (there are five kinds). They're among the very best in the city. You also can't miss when choosing from the dishes listed under Taiwan Specialties, such as wok-fried oysters with black beans or spareribs.

### YUET LEE $
*1300 Stockton St. (Broadway), (415) 982-6020*
*W-M 11am-3am*
This place has all the hallmarks of a dive—bright lights, Formica tables, and brusque service—but the Cantonese seafood is arguably unmatched for freshness and flavor. Try the clams in black bean sauce, the pepper-and-salt roast squid or prawns, and any other seafood items on the menu. Alas, the soup and noodle dishes are disappointing. Cash only.

# Financial District Embarcadero

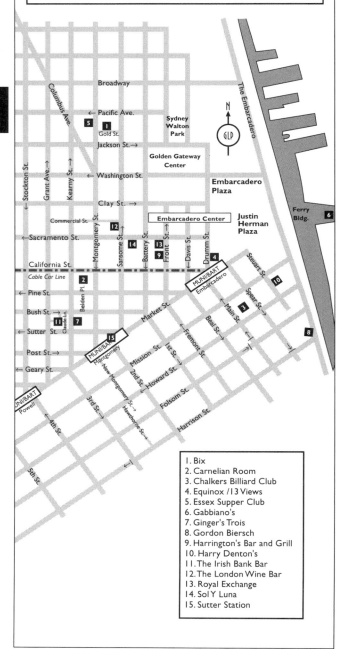

1. Bix
2. Carnelian Room
3. Chalkers Billiard Club
4. Equinox /13 Views
5. Essex Supper Club
6. Gabbiano's
7. Ginger's Trois
8. Gordon Biersch
9. Harrington's Bar and Grill
10. Harry Denton's
11. The Irish Bank Bar
12. The London Wine Bar
13. Royal Exchange
14. Sol Y Luna
15. Sutter Station

If the business of America is business, then what kind of business does one do after the business day is complete? The people known commonly as suits, and those employed by them, often choose to grab a drink in the Financial District after work before heading back to their homes in The Avenues, the East Bay, or Marin. Sometimes they stay quite a bit later. Bars in this part of town not connected with a hotel or restaurant are generally packed between five and eight and nearly empty or closed by nine, so make sure not to pull too much overtime at the office or you'll miss all the fun. For those who don't work around here, this area isn't much of a draw, unless a trust fund is burning a hole in your pocket and the view from the Carnelian Room that day is over 10 miles.

★

## BIX

*56 Gold St. (off Montgomery btwn. Pacific/Jackson), (415) 433-6300*
*M-Th 11:30am-1:30am; F 11:30am-2am; Sa 5:30pm-2am;*
*Su 5:30pm-1:30am*

You probably can't get any closer to the feel of a classic supper club than at the swank Bix, an Art Deco bilevel space done up in gunmetal gray and tucked surreptitiously into a Jackson Square alleyway. At the long mahogany bar, urns of chilled champagne and a silver bowl of iced martini glasses sit poised for the after-five crowd. In an atmosphere that one of the owners calls "too sophisticated to be happy hour," mixed drinks and luxury wines by the glass are served to tired workers. A pricy gourmet menu is available to those who choose to dine at one of the intimate tables lining the walls on both floors. If that level of opulence doesn't appeal to your palate or your pocketbook, you can raid bowls of nuts at the bar. During dinner hours, the live jazz begins. Mary Stallings, Merrill Hoover, John Goodman, Benny Miller, and Don Asher are the regulars. The patrons—Pacific Heights nouveau riche, well-heeled tourists, architects and designers who work nearby, the usual assortment of movers and shakers—range in age from 20 to 80. Just about everyone else in San Francisco winds up here at least once. Bix even sells its own souvenirs: embroidered dress shirts and silver cocktail shakers.

## CARNELIAN ROOM

*Bank of America Building, 52nd fl., 555 California St. (Kearny/Montgomery),*
*(415) 433-7500*
*Daily 3pm-10pm, cocktails 3pm-6pm*

Spectacular views of the city and the bay are the draw at this somewhat stuffy restaurant and lounge. Floor-to-ceiling picture windows meet at right angles and provide a dramatic, sweeping vista from bridge to bridge, plus Marin and the East Bay (come during Fleet Week, when the Blue Angels pilots blitz the surrounding skies, for an experience right out of a Schwarzenegger film). The cocktail lounge has the air of an exclusive social club from days of yore, done up in thick carpeting, leather padded chairs, and wood-paneled walls. You pay for the view, of course, and the service is particularly snooty here—there's a reception-ist's desk for visitors just past the gilded elegance of the elevator lobby, which should be a serious hint to either dress the part or booze it up at street level.

## CHALKERS BILLIARD CLUB
*Rincon Center, 101 Spear St. (Mission), (415) 512-0450*
*M-F 11:30am-2am; Sa 2pm-2am; Su 3pm-11pm*

Carpeted with ostentatiously fake Oriental rugs; replete with huge, ornate pillars; and jammed with rococo pool tables com-plete with huge, carved feet, Chalkers is the most upscale bil-liard hall you'll ever hope to see. The place resembles nothing more than a bordello—in fact, it might bring to mind Heidi Fleiss' dream pool hall. The equipment is well maintained, the bar serves a pretty good drink, and the elite and/or misan-thropic can hire out the glassed-in, semi-private rooms. Chalkers' convenient Financial District location attracts an after-work crowd, which thins out by 9 o'clock or so. Attention hus-tlers: due to the large number of corporate types here, the aver-age sucker percentage is much higher here than at other, more traditional pool halls. Rates vary according to the number of players and time of day.

## EQUINOX/13 VIEWS
*Hyatt Regency, 5 Embarcadero Center (Market/Drumm), (415) 788-1234*
*Daily 11am-1am*

Hotel bars are strange creatures. There's something odd about going into a place meant for tourists and business travelers just to have a drink that would cost far less money in your own neighborhood. Still, even a Hyatt has happy hour specials to cushion the blow. Besides, the views are nice, the seats are comfy, the soft echo from the piano is relaxing, and your local dive probably doesn't have an enormous atrium with glass eleva-tors. Those prone to vertigo will want to stay downstairs at the oddly monikered 13 Views, where two-dollar drink specials are available every weeknight from 4:30 to 7:30. There's plenty of seating, either on the soft leather chairs and sofas scattered around the lobby or at one of the tables in the angled window nooks overlooking Justin Herman Plaza. If you like imbibing at higher levels, head up to Equinox, the revolving restaurant and lounge with somewhat garish purple carpeting and tablecloths, on the top floor. Stay for at least half an hour and enjoy one complete revolution, taking in all of downtown before you take out your credit card to cover the bill. The extensive wine list fea-tures the ubiquitous Mondavi and some North Coast vineyards.

## ESSEX SUPPER CLUB
*847 Montgomery St. (Pacific/Jackson), (415) 397-5969*
*Tu-Sa 4:30pm-2am*

For a full evening of dinner, music, cigars, and snooker under one roof, head to the swanky Essex Supper Club. Enshrined in the former home of Ernie's, a formidable San Francisco land-mark, Essex boasts three levels of well-heeled imbibing in 1940s elegance. The main floor features the dining room (just past the heavy drapes) and a lively (and smoky) piano bar. Upstairs, guests sip cocktails and tap toes to live jazz and light R&B acts. Occasionally couples take a spin on the small dance floor. Below ground level is a medieval-feeling bar and humidor where patrons enjoy a postdinner cognac or scotch along with their cigars. Those looking for a turn at some British pool make their way to the small snooker room. Weekends tend to draw the Peninsula crowd, while Thursdays often find out-of-town businessmen soaking up the atmosphere. Dinner reservations are a must, and club memberships are available. A standard $15 cover is extracted from nondinner patrons Thursdays through Saturdays. When the urge to dress up and paint the town overtakes you, the Essex is the perfect address.

### GABBIANO'S
*1 Ferry Plaza (Embarcadero), (415) 391-8403*
*Daily 11am-9:30pm*

It's easy to miss Gabbiano's, since it's hidden behind the Ferry Building and overshadowed by the nearby hubbub of commuters heading back to Marin and the East Bay. Yet the view of the Bay Bridge and Treasure Island from this bar is unmatched, even if the skylit concrete interior has all the ambience of a BART station. If at all possible, avoid sitting indoors amid the potted trees and Christo-like, cream-colored umbrellas and get a spot in the outdoor garden instead. It's a great place to watch the sunset reflect off the bridge and forget the stress of daily life. There's a touristy restaurant upstairs for those too lazy to cross the Embarcadero to eat at Boulevard.

### GINGER'S TROIS
*246 Kearny St. (Sutter/Bush), (415) 989-0282*
*M-F 10am-10pm; Sa 2pm-10pm*

Talk about incongruous. In the shadows of the Financial District's skyscrapers squarely dedicated to commerce lies this tiny, clubby bar with a campy, Castro-esque sensibility. The walls are painted in a white clouds/blue skies/rainbows motif, there's a jukebox full of sappy country ballads and covers, a fully operational disco ball is suspended from the ceiling, and movie posters serve as paeans to the joint's namesake, Ginger Rogers. Not surprisingly, there's a strong gay presence here, although the occasional businessman will stop by to drown his worries about the future of capitalism in drink. Bottled beers and cocktails are dispensed by the chummy bartender, with free refills for sodas. So, where are Ginger's Un and Deux, anyway?

## GORDON BIERSCH

*2 Harrison St. (Embarcadero), (415) 243-8246*
*Daily 11:30am-1am*

This enormous branch of the successful brewpub chain occupies a prime spot in the beautifully restored Hills Brothers building, and never fails to pack them in. The magic ingredients? One: beer brewed on the premises—solid porters, hearty stouts, and mellow lagers. Two: an attractive, on-the-prowl clientele—young, loud, single suits and skirts who flock here after work for some serious mingling. Three: an all-around stylish ambience of industrial fittings, polished woods, and sleek lines. Those who want to chow down will find a menu of California cuisine that has a mixed reputation, but burgers are always a good wager, and the garlic fries are delicious. Expect wall-to-wall people around happy hour, especially on Friday nights.

## HARRINGTON'S BAR AND GRILL

*245 Front St. (California/Sacramento), (415) 392-7595*
*M-Th 9am-midnight; F 9am-2am; Sa 9am-midnight*

The darker, harder-drinking brother to its next-door neighbor, the Royal Exchange, this large Irish bar occupies two good-sized rooms and accommodates the after-work crowd of managers, temps, and ex-pats with plenty of vinyl booths and long tables. Among the beers on tap are Guinness, Sierra, and Bass; large pretzels with mustard are free during the afternoon rush.

## HARRY DENTON'S

*161 Steuart St. (Mission/Howard), (415) 882-1333*
*Daily 7:30am-2am*

There really *is* a Harry Denton, and on fortuitous occasions he may be found working the crowd of beautiful people in this popular nightspot in the shadow of the Bay Bridge. Behind the velvet-curtained entrance and the Pamela Anderson Lee look-alike hostess, you'll find the City's swells dancing the night away to a live band cranking out disco and Motown hits. By about midnight, the compact black-and-white deco-tile dance floor and traditional wooden bar are jammed with Financial District suits and Bebe-clad twentysomething females reminiscent of SaNdE in *L.A. Story.* Despite the sheer numbers, the presence of Harry Denton the man gives the place a surprisingly intimate feel: San Francisco's own Casablanca meets Generation X. If you just can't wear your beat-up Levis and Doc Martens one more night, slither into your sleekest black ensemble and slide on down to Harry's. He'll be waiting.

## THE IRISH BANK BAR & RESTAURANT

*10 Mark Ln. (off Grant Ave. btwn. Bush/Sutter), (415) 788-7152*
*Daily 11:30am-2am*

This spot is better known as the "Bar Formerly Known as the Bank of Ireland," thanks to a certain large, litigious, and, yes, humorless financial institution 6,000 miles away that forced the name change via court order. It would be difficult for anyone dropping by this cozy pub in a downtown alleyway to mistake it for a bank: there's Irish memorabilia, newspaper clippings, and photos hanging from every wall; low tables lit by warm orange lighting; and even a real confessional box (*sans* priest) with seating. The only deposits and withdrawals take place at the dark-stained wood bar (12 varied beers on tap), where the suits congregate after a long day of desk jockeying. A full menu is available throughout the day in the bright, airy back room.

## Comedy Clubs

What could be more fun than laughing the night away? The Bay Area, spawning ground for such major-league stars as Robin Williams and Whoopi Goldberg, boasts stand-up comedians worth an ovation. Although the scene has died down considerably since its heyday in the 1980s (thanks to overexpansion, diluted talent, and cable TV), and even though the legendary Hungry I club of the 1960s is now a strip joint, there are still opportunities to catch some very funny people in an intimate setting. Remember, however, that you must be 21 years old or older to enter most clubs. This doesn't mean that the humor is always risqué; it mainly means that a two-drink minimum is required of all who pass by the bouncer (based on the theory that liquor adds fuel to an audience's fire, especially on the oft-deadly open-mike nights). It isn't a hard-and-fast rule that everyone must consume something alcoholic, however; two diet sodas will do. Appetizers are often included.

Another rule of the comedy-club routine is the cover charge, although there are alternatives. During the week, for example, many establishments offer discounts or complimentary admissions. Discounted tickets are sometimes available for groups. To improve your chances of receiving free-admission offers, ask to be placed on the club's mailing list.

Make sure you're familiar with the scheduled comedian, or at least call ahead to ask about his or her sense of humor. There's nothing worse than expecting dry wit and getting raunchy tales that would make Richard Pryor blush. Many performers extend their routines into the audience, so you might not want to sit too near the stage. Arrive early enough to snag the seat of your choice.

**Bay Area Theatre Sports:** BATS hotline (415) 474-8935. While you won't find traditional stand-up comedy here, this avant-garde musical troupe performs an array of daring routines, including comedy acts. Call the hotline for a schedule of events.

**Cobb's Comedy Club:** in the Cannery, 2801 Leavenworth St. (Beach/Hyde), SF, (415) 928-4320. A San Francisco giant in the comedy arena, Cobb's will still let you in even if you're under 21 (provided your ID proves you're 18, and you're escorted by an adult). They also offer free validated parking, a real plus in busy Fisherman's Wharf.

**Comedy Sportz:** South Bay, Rancho Shopping Center, 3428 El Camino Real (Flora Vista), Santa Clara, (408) 985-LAFF/5233. The "Family Feud" of comedy clubs: watch improvisational comics compete for the best audience reaction.

**Punchline San Francisco:** 444 Battery St. (Washington/Clay), SF, (415) 397-7573. The Punchline is a major leaguer, usually with three comedians per night. Dinner is served, and the management boasts big-name marquees. Perhaps even Robin Williams will stop by to try out new material—stranger things have happened.

**Rooster T. Feathers:** South Bay, 157 W. El Camino Real (Murphy), Sunnyvale, (408) 736-0921. This is a medium-sized club with good visibility and layout, although the area next to the bar can get noisy. Typically two or three comedians perform each night, usually a local comedian followed by one or two well-known or national performers. There's a two-drink minimum. Reservations are required three to five days in advance, but you can sometimes get in at the last minute; call ahead for wait-list information. Open Thursday through Saturday.

## Late Night Eats

**BIX $$$**
*56 Gold St. (off Sansome or Montgomery btwn. Pacific/Jackson), (415) 433-6300*
*M-Th 11:30am-11pm; F 11:30am-midnight; Sa 5:30pm-midnight; Su 6pm-10pm*
The food is secondary to the scene at this moody supper club: the mostly retro food is good, but a Waldorf salad can only be so exciting. The potato leek pancakes with smoked salmon is a reliable favorite, as are the panfried chicken and grilled pork chop with mashed potatoes. (See bar listing.)

**PIZZERIA UNO $**
*2 Embarcadero Center (Davis at Clay), (415) 397-8667*
*Su-Th 10am-10pm; F-Sa 10am-11pm*
National chain famous for Chicago-style deep-dish pizza served in a bustling diner. Those who don't like the thick, flaky Chicago crust can opt for thin-crust pizzettas. The menu also includes pasta, salads, and burgers, but the big attraction is the pizza.

### THE LONDON WINE BAR
*415 Sansome St. (Sacramento/Clay), (415) 788-4811*
*M-F 11:30am-9pm (lunch 11:30am-2:30pm, hors d'oeuvres 2:30-9pm);*
*Saturdays by appointment*

San Francisco's first official wine bar, the London Wine Bar has been around since 1974, when happy hours were considered a healthy conclusion to the workday. The clubby interior, decorated with hundreds of bottles of fine wine, is comforting and solid, attracting a crowd of financial types who forge business deals in the capacious private booths. An extensive selection of wines by the glass is offered, as well as a menu featuring substantial appetizers and dinner items. It's a great place for company events as well as private parties.

### ROYAL EXCHANGE
*301 Sacramento St. (Front), (415) 956-1710*
*M-F 11am-10pm*

Aside from its seismically retrofitted brick-walled interior, what's most notable about the venerable Royal Exchange is the bar itself, a dark wood behemoth with awnings supported by giant posts, and stools that actually spin. Along the perimeter of the huge room are secluded wooden alcoves with booths, which are populated by yuppie lawyers holding clandestine business meetings during happy hour. This is a good place for the empty-stomach-and-full-wallet set, with a huge selection of pub grub ranging from salads to sandwiches. The forty beers on tap include McTarnahan Scottish Ale, plus many bottled selections. The St. Patrick's Day party here spills onto Front Street and draws thousands.

### SOL Y LUNA
*475 Sacramento St. (Battery/Sansome), (415) 296-8191*
*Daily 5pm-2am*

A lively Latin supper club sandwiched between two office buildings and done up in a sleek modernist/industrial decor, Sol y Luna is just getting going when the rest of the Financial District has packed up their briefcases and gone home for the night. On weekends, the crowd skews to the young and international, and the front patio becomes a crush of bodies. On Friday nights, house and Euro dance music blare from the speakers, and on Saturday nights there's a blowout flamenco show and salsa bands (reservations recommended). Live bands and DJs fill out the rest of the week's entertainment, with the occasional cigar night on Tuesday. Happy hour specials on both drinks (go for the pitcher of sangria) and Spanish tapas.

## SUTTER STATION

*25 Sutter St. (Market), (415) 434-4768*
*Daily 7am-2am*

For those who work long hours downtown, this serves as the neighborhood bar. Men in suits make up the crowd during lunch and happy hour, while tourists and hard-core alcoholics pick up the slack the rest of the time. (Weekend afternoons are especially grim.) A long, dark-stained wood bar anchors the large front room, a richly ornate space with a molded ceiling, mirrored wall paneling, and a giant cable car mural. Out back toward the Sutter Street entrance is the pool room, with two tables and a jukebox. Sports constantly emanate from the TVs lodged in the corners. Cappuccinos and a large selection of pub grub are also available, as well as large quantities of free popcorn.

★

# Union Square
# Tenderloin / Civic Center

California St.  *Cable Car Line*

Pine St.

Bush St.→

←Sutter St.

Post St.→

←Geary St.

O'Farrell St.→

←Ellis St.

Eddy St.→

←Turk St.

Golden Gate Ave.→

Redwood St.

McAllister St.|←

City Hall

Fulton St.
Main
Library

Grove St.

Davies
Symphony
Hall

←Hayes St.

Fell St.

Jones St.
Taylor St.
Mason St.
Powell St.
*Cable Car Line*
Stockton St.
*(Tunnel)*
Grant Ave.
Kearny St.
Belden Pl.
Montgomery St.
Claude Ln.

Campton Pl.

Union
Square   Maiden Lane

Civil Magnin St.

BART/MUNI
Powell

BART/MUNI
Civic Center

MUNI
Van Ness

Market St.
←3rd St.

4th St.

5th St.

6th St.

←7th St.

Mission St.

8th St.

Franklin St.→
Van Ness Ave.
Polk St.
Larkin St.→
Hyde St.
Leavenworth St.

10th St.
11th St.
12th St.

N
(GLP)

| | |
|---|---|
| 1. Backflip | 14. The Great American Music Hall |
| 2. Beer Cellar | 15. Harry Denton's Starlight Room |
| 3. Biscuits & Blues | 16. Lefty O'Doul's |
| 4. Blue Lamp | 17. The Red Room |
| 5. Bobby's Owl Tree | 18. The Redwood Room |
| 6. Cityscape | 19. 7-11 Club |
| 7. Club 181 | 20. Sherlock Holmes, Esq., Public House |
| 8. Club 36 | 21. Stars |
| 9. Deco | 22. The View Lounge |
| 10. Edinburgh Castle | 23. Warfield |
| 11. Fumé | |
| 12. Giraffe Video Lounge | |
| 13. Gold Dust Lounge | |

# ★ Union Square / Tenderloin Civic Center

It's a shame that locals mostly leave the downtown scene to tourists, because within a short walk of Union Square are some of the most breathtaking bars and clubs you could hope to find. They may not be as personal or intimate as the neighborhood dives locals frequent, but they make up for it with great views of the city (see the View Lounge or Harry's Starlight Room). Farther west, the Tenderloin is even more ignored, owing to its high crime and the general perception that it's in decay. It's true that you must be careful in this part of town at night, but the rewards for venturing along these not-so-mean streets are some great bars like Edinburgh Castle and beautiful clubs like the Great American Music Hall.

★

## BACKFLIP

*The Phoenix Hotel, 601 Eddy St. (Larkin), (415) 771-FLIP/3547*
*Tu-Su 5pm-2am*

If the crowds that flock here to see and be seen are any indication, Backflip, the City's hippest new restaurant-bar-hangout, is a more-than-worthy successor to Miss Pearl's Jam House, the nightspot that previously occupied this Phoenix Hotel space. It can't hurt that the '50s space-age-Jetsons interior is decorated within an inch of its life. Filled with a variety of synthetic materials bathed in blues, the room sports aquatic fountains, glittery padded booths and chaise lounges, sunken plastic chairs, numerous dark hideaways, wavy opaque glass and mirrored walls (make sure you don't bump into one), and a metallic bridge that separates the dining room from the doughnut-shaped bar. A cooler-than-thou bar staff dispenses regal cocktails—Cosmos, Greyhounds, and Belvedere Martinis (with a blue Italian liqueur)—along with a bunch of microbrews. Those who are underdressed here may feel sheepish, as the place is crawling with Beautiful People who all seem to know one another. Still, if you're on your way to or from a gig at the Great American Music Hall, this is a great new spot to stop for a drink.

## BEER CELLAR

*685 Sutter St. (Taylor), (415) 441-5678*
*Tu-F 5pm-2am; Sa 9pm-2am*

The Beer Cellar is a place for those whose memories of prom night have not yet faded. (The patrons are just learning how to have a good time as adults.) Legions from the City's far-flung neighborhoods stand in line here on weekends to gain entrance to "the Cellar." Most come in single-sex groups of four or five. The multicultural crowd is heavy on men, with a smattering of Europeans from nearby hotels and downtown hostels. The doormen are strict about IDs and the quasi-fascist dress code, which allows no athletic gear, tennis shoes, torn clothes, or baseball caps. The Beer Cellar itself is a small dance floor, with a mirrored disco ball, a chandelier or two, and a deejay spinning fusion, hip hop, and other crowd-pleasing fare. A couple of kinds of beer on tap. Cover charge $8 on Fridays and Saturdays, $5 other nights.

## BISCUITS & BLUES
*401 Mason St. (Geary), (415) 292-BLUE/2583*
*M-F 5pm-2am; Sa-Su 6pm-1am*

Formerly the Improv Comedy Club, Biscuit & Blues, located in the heavily touristed Union Square vortex, is a deservedly popular spot for live blues performances. Shows start nightly around 9pm, and the management promises "all seats unobstructed view." Local favorites include Nitecry, Tommy Castro, and the Paris Slim Blues Band, and Sunday nights showcase gospel music. The largely thirtysomething crowd demonstrates an obvious knowledge and appreciation of the blues. Weekends are busiest, so you may want to prepurchase tickets, or arrive early. Cover charges range from $5 to $10, with the Sunday evening tariff $15 including dinner. The menu of authentic Southern fare, from catfish to jambalaya, is served from 6pm to 11pm nightly. The lights are turned down very low during the shows, so bring your penlight in order to see what you are eating.

## BLUE LAMP
*561 Geary St. (Taylor/Jones), (415) 885-1464*
*Daily 11am-2am*

Like a shabby bag lady shuffling along Market Street, the Blue Lamp has seen better days. To paraphrase the current owner, it is a dive of the '70s that has survived to the '90s. Its deep red velvet walls have become somewhat threadbare, and so has the three-quarter pool table with the real blue felt, but the cozy copper fireplace gives a hint of what the old days were like here. The bar draws a youthful, live-and-let-live crowd liberally sprinkled with tourists from the nearby hotels, the main attraction being the nightly live music performed on the postage-stamp-sized stage at the back. In addition to the regular players, there are two open-mike nights a week: electric blues on Sundays and acoustic on Mondays. Music starts nightly at 10pm, Sundays at 9pm; until then, the jukebox fills the room with everything from the Allman Brothers to Sinatra. Newcastle Brown and Anchor Steam are among the twelve beers on tap, plus there's a full bar. It's a blessedly unpretentious hangout for those brave enough to take on the underrated Tenderloin scene.

## BOBBY'S OWL TREE
*601 Post St. (Taylor), (415) 776-9344*
*Daily 2pm-2am*

In the netherworld between Union Square's tourist sheen and the Tenderloin's squalor lies this ornithologist's dream of a bar. Owls, owls everywhere: paintings of them on the walls, stained-glass versions of them in the windows, and stuffed, real ones behind a glass case. As if that weren't surreal enough, there are low-slung tables with plush red Naugahyde seats, a women's room seemingly designed for midgets, a traffic light behind the bar (which the bartender occasionally switches from green to red if he feels you're too soused), and a clientele that runs from straitlaced businessmen to bewildered tourists to everyone in between. Bottled beer only, plus cocktails. Peggy Lee and Frank Sinatra are among the many great selections on the jukebox.

## CITYSCAPE
*San Francisco Hilton and Towers, Bldg. 1, 46th floor, 333 O'Farrell St.*
*(Mason/Taylor), (415) 923-5002*
*Daily 5pm-2am*

This restaurant and bar has a glass atrium high above the center of the room, which is done up in a somewhat outdated mauve-and-blue color scheme. Tall floor-to-ceiling windows with pink shades command sweeping city views, and jazz adds to the heady experience. Sleek-looking, with carpeted edges framing a marble dance floor. Beers will set you back almost five bucks; mixed drinks are even more.

## CLUB 181
*181 Eddy St. (Taylor), (415) 673-8181*
*F-Sa 9pm-3am*

The strangest juxtaposition in town: on one of the grimiest, sketchiest blocks in town lies this plushly decorated dinner club/dance spot with a tough dress code and the beautiful people who meet it. There are two different rooms: the groovily painted smaller one is for drinking and mingling, while the larger main room is where DJs spin dance tunes that range from '70s disco to '90s trip-hop and house. The club also brings in crowd-pleasing cover bands like the Cheeseballs and Jungle Bootie. A cover charge is in effect for all events except private parties (in which the club does an active business). Be wary of your surroundings when entering and leaving here, and if coming by car, it's a good idea to park farther up on Nob Hill.

## CLUB 36
*Grand Hyatt, 36th fl., 345 Stockton St. (Sutter/Post), (415) 398-1234*
*M-F 4pm-2am; Sa-Su 2pm-2am*

Lesser known than its fellow hotel bars dotting Union Square, Club 36 offers spectacular views if you can endure the nauseating Muzak on the elevator ride up. Its huge picture windows face north, overlooking Telegraph Hill and the bay. The decor is very 1980s, with a faux tan-leaf chandelier, brass planters, rounded brown leather chairs, and marble tables. Rarely crowded, the room attracts mostly older folks talking business; expect to hear the words *project* and *synergy* a lot if you drink here. Hosts both pianists and combos performing mellow, traditional jazz.

## DECO
*510 Larkin St. (Turk/Eddy), (415) 441-4007*
*M-Th 7pm-2am; F-Su 4pm-2am*

It may not be the most affluent area in town, but once you get past the entrance to Deco, the experience can be a treat. This has become one of the top spots in town for hip-hop, soul, and reggae dance music, with the dancing spread over two levels. A full bar in the front parallels a good-sized dance floor, while down on the basement level, there's a cozy nook featuring a DJ spinning softer grooves. The back room holds two pool tables, with a weekly tournament every Wednesday night. The crowd is mixed (boys and girls), although mostly male, which may explain why the new weekend policy of no cover charge for women before 11pm has been instituted. You'll find 12 beers on tap, and during happy hour, Wednesday to Sunday from 4pm to

7pm, well drinks are $2 and complimentary bar snacks are set out for the taking. A dress code (no sneakers, no caps, no sports gear) is enforced on weekends.

## EDINBURGH CASTLE
*950 Geary St. (Larkin/Polk), (415) 885-4074*
*Daily 5pm-2am*

Great Scot! The Edinburgh is not so much a castle as a veritable Viking beer hall, with a large bar and wooden booth area that sits under an enormous horseshoe balcony that overlooks everything. (They could have filmed the battle scenes for *Braveheart* here.) The crowd is young, hip, international, and literary. The latter trait is partially due to the many readings by Scottish authors that are held here, events that have included such luminaries as *Trainspotting* author Irvine Welsh. Pool tables and darts are available for sporting types, and there is a completely separate upstairs room that hosts rock and country bands in a casual, intimate space. For an authentic taste of the UK, order the mouthwatering fish-and-chips that are cooked across the street and delivered, wrapped in newspaper, to wherever your are standing or sitting. Twenty beers are on tap and, of course, some fine single-malt scotches are poured. Live music Wednesdays through Saturdays at 9:30pm.

## FUMÉ
*101 Cyril Magnin St. (Ellis), (415) 788-3863*
*Daily 3pm-1am*

Whether smoking clubs are just a passing fad or a harbinger of the new millennium, Fumé is here. The tiny interior of this recent arrival on the cigar lounge scene features a custom mahogany bar and many Asian touches: Ming-like vases, Japanese screens, a Thai sculpture, and a low ceiling inset with a checkerboard of wood and light panels. Catering to the traveling businessman, the bar is open from 3pm, and a healthy choice of unhealthy cigars and high-end cigarettes are for sale. The liquor selection is small, well chosen, and pricy, and the perfect glass is used for each beverage, right down to the numerous aperitifs. The solicitous bartenders refill water glasses, light cigarettes, banter with solo patrons, and discreetly refresh drinks for those deep in conversation. All this service comes with a price: the drink tab will set you back a bit. The clientele is friendly in that jovial, successful-boys'-club manner. Women smoking cigars are treated to a grin and asked if they do it often. A postwork, quiet alternative to the overcrowded downtown pubs (low murmuring instead of loud bravado).

## THE GIRAFFE VIDEO LOUNGE
*1131 Polk St. (Post/Sutter), (415) 474-1702*
*Daily 8am-2am*

In comparison to its lower Polk Street locale, this bar sparkles and glistens. Although there is generous space for dancing, shooting pool (only until the table is moved to accommodate the dancing), or just sitting at the bar (where you can watch the video screens hanging from either corner), you can't help but think you should explore further: the illusion of space, courtesy of the numerous wall mirrors, makes it seem like the bar goes on forever. Friendly bartenders and the relaxed atmosphere draw a mainly older gay male crowd, although women (real and faux) can be seen as well. Go for a drink and admire the lovely hardwood floors.

## GOLD DUST LOUNGE
*247 Powell St. (O'Farrell/Geary), (415) 397-1695*
*Daily 6am-2am*

One of the few places in the city to see live jazz (mostly Dixieland) seven nights a week, this bar has an unfair rap as a tourist trap, most likely due to the cheesy T-shirt and toy-cable-car shops all around it. Even if it *is* mostly out-of-towners lured here by the Herb Caen blurbs in the windows and the bright marquee, the Gold Dust, in business since 1933, is festive and comfortable, staffed by a very friendly set of bartenders in white shirts and funny ties who are perfectly willing to make a tomato beer (Bud and tomato juice) or pour a Nutty Monkey (banana and amaretto liqueur). There are high-backed wall seats for viewing the "interesting" ceiling murals or enjoying the music (from 8:30pm to 1:30am). This bar also features a framed collection of virtually every paper currency on earth, and by logical extension it's a pretty good place to practice whatever foreign language you may know.

## THE GREAT AMERICAN MUSIC HALL
*859 O'Farrell St. (Polk/Larkin), (415) 885-0750*
*Open for performances only*

There may not be a better place in the city to see live music than this gorgeous, ornate venue in a seedy block of the Tenderloin. A 19th century vaudeville hall restored to its former glory, the club has red velvet drapes, marble columns, a wrap-around horseshoe balcony, and a gold-leaf, molded ceiling. The size is just about perfect—not too large, not too small—and as long as you're not sitting behind one of those ground-floor columns, the sight lines are excellent. (Even "sold out" gigs here are slightly undersold, so claustrophobia is never a concern.) Best of all, the wooden floor and the high ceiling make the acoustics consistently superb, no matter what kind of music is being performed. It's no wonder a wide variety of national and international acts, from jazz to country to rock, do their damnedest to get booked in here on their swing through town. There's a full-service bar, too, with a wait staff that delivers drinks and food to the perimeter tables.

## HARRY DENTON'S STARLIGHT ROOM
*Sir Francis Drake Hotel, 21st fl., 450 Powell St. (Post/Sutter), (415) 395-8595*
*Daily 4:30pm-2am*

Much like the Top of the Mark up the hill, the Starlight Room harks back to an earlier gilded age when stylishness and elegance were a way of life. Walking into the opulent interior with its French doors, marble columns, silk drapes, burgundy velvet booths, plush carpeting, beveled mirrors, and crystal chandeliers, you easily sense the history of this place, even though it seems so fantastic as to be slightly unreal. Unlike most other hotel bars, this is really more a place for locals than for tourists, especially later in the evening, when a wide range of music sends everyone onto the dance floor. Wednesday night is the popular Indulgence dance party for the twentysomething crowd;

Thursday night is R&B; and Friday and Saturday the effervescent Starlight Orchestra always packs the house. Most well drinks are under three bucks during happy hour (Monday to Friday, 5pm to 7pm) and a very reasonable four bucks the rest of the time; beers range from three to five dollars. Excellent buffets are also available. Last but not least, and free of charge, there are the spectacular views to the east, south, and west (sunset here is spectacular). A romantic bar in the true sense of the word.

## LEFTY O'DOUL'S
*333 Geary St. (Powell/Mason), (415) 982-8900*
*Daily 10am-2am*

Lefty O'Doul's is the home of baseball-related memorabilia, specifically recalling the bar's namesake, who was the National League batting champion in 1929 and 1932. (The bar stool legs are made of baseball bats.) It's literally a hall of fame, a cavernous space almost big enough for a playing field, with a high ceiling and lots of dark corners making for a somewhat downbeat drinking atmosphere. (The smell of meat from the buffet in the middle of the front room lets everyone know this is more of a restaurant than a bar.) Those who persevere will find plenty of German and Australian tourists to talk with, an alcove piano bar to take refuge in, and plenty of TVs for watching sports. Sadly, Lefty's is scheduled to close at the end of 1997, a victim of skyrocketing Union Square rents, so be sure to get in those last, wistful drinks.

## THE RED ROOM
*827 Sutter St. (Jones/Leavenworth), (415) 346-7666*
*Daily 5pm-2am*

The entrance door is red. The rows of bottles stacked from floor to ceiling are red. The walls are red. The floors are red. The ceiling is red. The leather couches are red. The leather chairs are red. The backless bar stools are red. The Formica-topped, semi-circular bar is red. The giant plastic martini glass behind the bar is red. The straws are red. The bathrooms are red. Get the picture? This trendy watering hole is called the Red Room for a reason, and if that reason is not immediately apparent to you when you enter this Mecca of hip on the edge of Nob Hill, you need a few more drinks. The crowd is very young, smokes a lot, and likes their cocktails with a twist of background lounge music. The bartenders are friendly and amazingly good-natured about working in such an monochromatic environment. This up-to-the-minute bar gets more than its share of novelty-seeking crowds, so come early, stay late, and leave any color-blind friends at home.

## THE REDWOOD ROOM
*Clift Hotel, 495 Geary St. (Taylor), (415) 775-4700*
*Daily 11am-2am*

When you want to feel like a sophisticated adult, the Redwood Room, nestled in the ritzy Clift Hotel, is just the place. A true classic, the room features 22-foot aged-redwood walls, grandiose full-scale Gustav Klimt reproductions, original Art Deco chandeliers, and old-world elegance. A grand piano anchors center stage, and its softly played ivories fill the space with soothing melodies almost constantly (requests entertained). Drinks are pricy—this is the home of the (enormous) $8.50 sapphire martini. Bar service is knowledgeable and customer friendly. The appetizer menu ranges from steak tartare to smoked chicken quesadillas (perhaps to pair with the new Herradura tequila sampler?). The clientele, not surprisingly considering the location, is skewed toward business travelers in the early evening and the after-theater crowd later at night. Seating is almost always available at the long, brass-trimmed bar or at intimate tables. The perfect spot for a nightcap with someone you're hoping to impress.

## 7-11 CLUB
*711 Market St. (3rd St./4th St.), (415) 777-4455*
*M-F 10am-whenever; Sa-Su noon-whenever*
Down at the eastern end of Market Street, bars are few and far between. If not for the sign, it would be easy to pass right by this dimly lit joint without giving it a second thought. If you don't mind the occasional hard-core alcoholic for company plus a disproportionate number of smokers, the 7-11 is a pleasant respite from the hustle and bustle of the Financial District and Union Square. The tacky-yet-tasteful interior—glittery blue ceiling, red and gold striped wallpaper, walls of carved copper in the back, black lacquered bar—attracts a motley mix of drunks, tourists, and patrons in search of peace and quiet and a professional, unobtrusive bartender. Often the only audible sound is the drone of the TV. A few beers are available on tap, as well as bottled beers and various liquors.

## SHERLOCK HOLMES, ESQ., PUBLIC HOUSE
*Holiday Inn, 30th fl., 480 Sutter St. (Powell), (415) 398-8900*
*Su-Th 4pm-midnight; F-Sa 4pm-2am*
This unique cocktail lounge 30 floors above the city will appeal to those with an appreciation for the stranger things in life. It's anyone's guess why a major hotel chain would spend what looks like a lot of money on a bar/mini-museum dedicated to the famous British sleuth, complete with a painstaking recreation of 221-B Baker Street (in a back hallway opposite the loo). In fact, the decorative touches throughout the room, from the maroon velvet curtains to the backlit Victorian stained glass, almost distract from the vista outside, which encompasses everything from North Beach to Twin Peaks. As with all hotel bars, the ales and spirits are expensive, the food even more so; come during happy hour.

## STARS
*555 Golden Gate Ave. (Van Ness/Polk), (415) 861-7827*
*Daily 6pm-midnight*
This legendary Jeremiah Tower restaurant and bar is a San Francisco see-and-be-seen institution. The bar, set amidst the enormous main dining room, is *the* place to rub elbows with The City's social elite. On any given evening it's possible to spot politicos such as Willie Brown or visiting cinema luminaries. The atmosphere is lively and loud, and the drinks skew toward martinis and scotch. Curiously, few wines are offered by the glass. The smooth bartenders adroitly handle guests dining at the bar prior to dashing to the theater or opera. Facing every large leather barstool is a brass placard imprinted with the name of a VIP; in other words, you're literally sitting in someone's seat. Don't be surprised if the occasion arises when that name belongs to the

person standing next to you, eyeing your comfort. Complimentary breadsticks are the delicate perfect partners to the generously poured beverages. The preciously portioned food is pricy, while drinks are a bit more reasonable than you'd expect. The quintessential spot to hobnob with the glamorous.

## THE VIEW LOUNGE
*San Francisco Marriott, 39th fl., 55 4th St. (Market/Mission),*
*(415) 896-1600*
*Daily 11am-2am*

Some might say it's no coincidence that the San Francisco Marriott, a controversial architectural experiment with an exterior that has been likened to a jukebox, opened on the same October day in 1989 that the Loma Prieta earthquake rattled the City. That temblor shattered all the glass at the View Lounge, located on the 39th floor of the building, except for one martini glass and the crystal top of a Remy Martin bottle; both now sit proudly in a display case near the bar, symbols of triumph over adversity and questionable aesthetics. In calmer seismic times, this is a great place to have a beer, cocktail, port, or cognac at breathtaking prices while taking in the breathtaking views. Sunset is a great time to stop by, since the enormous fanlike windows on both the east and the west sides of the building afford panoramic vistas. Or head for one of the tables in the

---

### Late Night Eats

**BISCUITS AND BLUES $$**
*401 Mason St. (Geary), (415) 292-BLUE/2583*
*M-F 5pm-2am; Sa-Su 6pm-1am*
See bar listing.

**CAFÉ MASON $**
*320 Mason St. (Geary/O'Farrell), (415) 544-0320*
*Daily 24 hours*
Late night diner for the bleary-eyed scenesters looking to load up on meats and carbohydrates. Also attracts lots of tourists.

**THE EDINBURGH CASTLE $**
*950 Geary St. (Polk/Larkin), (415) 885-4074*
*Su-Th 5-11pm; F-Sa 5pm-1am*
Menu options are limited, consisting simply of fish and chips plus fried zucchini or onion rings as extra options; the food is from the Old Chelsea on Larkin Street, and your server actually runs over to pick it up. Still, those who eat here swear by the authenticity of the fish and chips (they're wrapped in newspaper), comparing them favorably to their British brethren.

**ESCAPE FROM N.Y. PIZZA ¢**
*7 Stockton St. (O'Farrell/Ellis), (415) 421-0700*
*M-Th 10:30am-10:30pm; F-Sa 10:30am-11:30pm; Su 11am-8pm*
Quick service pizzeria that serves up fairly faithful renditions of New York style pies—a thin, crisp crust, tangy tomato sauce, and a perfect layer of cheese.

**LORI'S DINER $**
*336 Mason St. (Geary/O'Farrell), (415) 392-8646*
*Daily 24 hours*
In the spirit of numerous downtown diners, Lori's brings the '50s to the '90s 24 hours a day with genuine nostalgic decor and decent, traditional diner fare.

remote corners of the floor, where each cluster of low-slung tables and green leather chairs has its own personal view. Local dance bands perform Thursday, Friday, and Saturday nights, with no cover charge.

## THE WARFIELD

*982 Market St. (5th St./6th St.), (415) 775-7722, general info; (415) 775-9949, directions; (415) 567-2060, office*
*Open for performances only*

One could easily mistake The Warfield for one of the Tenderloin strip joints that surround it, so (relatively) nondescript is its marquee. Step inside from the grime, however, and behold a beautiful old theater, one of the Bill Graham Presents venues of lore. The recently remodeled hall with old-style decor offers table seating with an oh-so-tiny mosh pit on the stage level and traditional theater seating (reserved) in the balcony. The Warfield has hosted everyone from Dylan to Dinosaur Jr., although in recent times it has done a heavy trade in the modern rock acts that are too big for the clubs, yet not quite ready to sell out the Coliseum. Folks with general-admission tickets should arrive very early to guarantee a good seat. The staffers are friendly but take their jobs seriously, moving along anyone who blocks walkways and fire exits. All-ages shows endure serious ID checks for drinks.

★

### MAX'S OPERA CAFÉ $/$$
*601 Van Ness Ave. (Golden Gate), (415) 771-7300 (take-out 771-7301)*
*M 11:30am-10pm; Tu-Th 11:30am-midnight; F-Sa 11:30am-1am;*
*Su 11:30am-11pm*
The kind of high camp that draws a crowd in Miami Beach. The brassy, boastful menu starts with New York-style chopped liver and corned beef sandwiches and then goes ballistic with sweet-and-sour duck and pasta galore. Best to take a doggie bag for the main course to save room for Sweet Max's larger-than-life desserts. The name refers to the singing wait staff. Decor is glitzy deli.

### SCALA'S BISTRO $$
*432 Powell St. (Sutter/Post), (415) 395-8555*
*M-Sa 7am-11:30pm; Su 8am-11:30pm*
This stylish dining room in the Sir Francis Drake hotel was meant to look like it's been around for years: chiaroscuro murals, burnished dark wood booths deep enough to hide in, and a bustle of white-shirted waiters. The innovative Californian-Italian menu is deliberately more contemporary, with modern combinations like seared ahi tuna salad, grilled mahi-mahi with preserved lemon and olive relish, and a variety of rustic pizzas.

### SHALIMAR RESTAURANT $
*532 Jones St. (Geary/O'Farrell), (415) 928-0333*
*Daily noon-3pm, 5pm-midnight*
It may have a beautiful name, but the restaurant is far from beautiful. Indeed, you may want to take out. And it's not fast; you may want to call in your order. So why bother? Because the food is cheap, simple, and delicious Indian and Pakistani fare.

### STARS $$$$
*555 Golden Gate Ave. (Van Ness/Polk), (415) 861-7827*
*Daily 6pm-midnight (hours vary with symphony and opera performances)*
See bar listing.

# Russian Hill / Nob Hill
# Polk Gulch / Van Ness

1. Beerness
2. Coconut Grove
3. Johnny Love's
4. Mick's Lounge
5. N'Touch
6. The QT Club
7. Rex Café
8. Royal Oak
9. Shanghai Kelly's
10. Tonga Room
11. Top of the Mark

Chestnut St.

N

GLP

Lombard St.

Greenwich St.

Leavenworth St.

Filbert St.

Jones St.

Taylor St.

Mason St.

Cable Car Line

Powell St.

Union St.

Macondray Ln.

Van Ness Ave.

Polk St.

Larkin St.

Hyde St.

Cable Car Line

Green St.

Coolbrith
Park

Vallejo St.

Broadway                    (Broadway Tunnel)

Pacific Ave.

← Jackson St.

Cable
Car
Barn ■

Washington St. →

Clay St. →

Cable Car Line

← Sacramento St.

Grace
Cathedral ■

California St.

Cable Car Line

← Pine St.

Bush St. →

Hyde St.

Leavenworth St. →

Jones St.

Taylor St.

Mason St.

Powell St.

# Russian Hill / Nob Hill Polk Gulch / Van Ness

Although a few bars and clubs are scattered along Van Ness and on Nob and Russian Hills proper—including Top of the Mark with its great views and the Tonga Room with its unbelievable kitsch—Polk Street, an interesting mix of residential and commercial space, is the nightlife center in this part of town. It has become somewhat analogous to the Cow Hollow-Union Street singles scene, as young professionals and folks who still wear their college sweatshirts crawl up and down Polk, stopping at each stylish-looking bar for a pint and a game of pool. (Of course, if they're at Johnny Love's, they just spend the whole evening there, or at least as long as it takes to find Mr. or Mrs. Right.) Visitors from other parts of town will do crawling of another kind if they drive: this is one of the hardest spots in the City (if not on planet Earth) to find a parking space. Head for a side street west of Van Ness or take public transportation.

★

## BEERNESS
*1624 California St. (Polk/Van Ness), (415) 474-6968*
*Daily 2pm-2am*

Beerness is a hodge-podge of a bar seemingly searching for an identity. The decor is artsy-meets-sports-bar: hand-painted swirl-and-stripe ceiling, exposed brick wall, concrete floor carpeted with peanut shells, and TVs muting a combination of MTV and ESPN. Couches surround a metal fireplace where quiet conversation is possible, while the back section boasts two pool tables, pinball, and Foosball. The upstairs currently hosts fiercely competitive Ping-Pong matches as a stopgap measure until the owners find DJs to spin records and give the space an aura of hippitude. All in all, the atmosphere reflects its off-neighborhood location: newly postcollege boys blow off steam at the gaming tables, Polk Street regulars sip quietly on barstools, and neo-Bohemians show portfolios and jewelry to the appreciative bartenders. This is a good spot for a pre- or postfilm drink since it's near the Lumiere, Galaxy, and Regency theaters. Seven beers (including a Beerness ale) and Jaegermeister are on tap. Happy hour from 2 to 8pm (all drinks 50 cents off).

## COCONUT GROVE
*1415 Van Ness Ave. (Bush/Pine), (415) 776-1616*
*Tu-Su 5:30pm-2am*

After a false start as a very expensive supper club with Vegas-like entertainment, Coconut Grove is trying again with lower prices (like no cover before 9pm) and younger bands. Happily, the speakeasy-meets-tropical decor remains from past lives: giant gold-leafed palm trees, wooden trim, floor-to-ceiling mirrors, and booths that look like they can hold a large family. Only the crowd has changed, as Nob Hill socialites have been replaced by yuppies and Cocktail Nation types. The musical offerings vary with the night of the week. Swing bands take the stage and pack the dance floor on Tuesday nights, rhythm and blues are on

Thursdays, and live gospel music and brunch are on the Sunday menu. The rest of the week, other live acts and DJs spinning music attempt to keep the place lively. Happy hour is Tuesdays through Thursdays, 5:30 to 8pm. Appetizers ($4) and a limited cocktail menu are available at all times, and if you're famished at night, a moderately priced full dinner menu is available. Call before you go: this has been a high turnover locale.

## JOHNNY LOVE'S
*1500 Broadway (Polk), (415) 931-8021*
*Daily 5pm-2am*

Early evening at Johnny Love's has the air of expectancy: awaiting the arrival of the infamous hordes of well-coiffed barhoppers, the live band, and Johnny himself. Infamous bartender Johnny Metheney, known for his uncanny ability to remember the name of every female that ever ordered a drink, opened this perennially popular spot several years ago, and the crowd continues to pour in. At least by legend if not by fact, this *is* the City's primary pickup joint for young urban professionals. The smooth, quick-handed bartenders revel in talking up the legend: last Monday's hip-hop night that resembled a weekend reverie, the Christmas party for the Raiderettes that featured bar-top dancing, the Saturday Johnny created a new drink and gave away free shots with every order all night long. The large space is divided by a central horseshoe bar, with leather banquettes for diners (traditional pub food with California flair), a band stage and dance area, and plenty of drinking room. When all those are full, lots of people simply end up dancing on tabletops. (It's that kind of place.) The crimson-and-forest-green walls are studded with European alcohol posters and photographs featuring Johnny and celebrities ranging from Steve Young to Weird Al Yankovich. A band plays 1970s music on Saturday nights. The line to get in usually runs halfway down the block. Unspoken dress code: Oxford shirts and Dockers for men, clingy dresses or miniskirts for women. The cover charge and waiting line varies according to the entertainment. A permanent party, all week long.

## MICK'S LOUNGE
*2513 Van Ness Ave. (Union/Filbert), (415) 928-0404*
*M-Th 6pm-2am; F-Sa 5pm-2am; Su 7pm-2am*

Mick's is a great place to lounge when checking out local and even international bands from Super Diamond to Modern English. The occasional DJ also stops by to spin progressive, house, and ambient music for the cutely-named Mix Lounge. The full bar has a huge selection of draught beers, cocktail service is readily available, and the requisite pool table stands upstairs. Mick's is packed with young Polk Gulch/Marina denizens from Thursdays through Saturdays. Come on a weeknight to watch the bands from a comfortable seat at a table.

## THE QT
*1312 Polk St. (Bush/Pine), (415) 885-1114*
*Daily noon-2am*

Live music is the draw here—the divas really get the crowd moving with tunes that run from old standards to Motown hits. The crowd consists of local Polk Street patrons—very mellow and congenial—and the bartenders range from semifriendly to down-right dull. Just get your drink, sit a spell, and wait to be entertained by the sultry songstresses. Between performances, a TV screen appears and bad '80s videos are off and running—or sometimes just *off*. Lotto, bingo, and pinball round out the attractions.

## REX CAFÉ
*2323 Polk St. (Green/Union), (415) 441-2244*
*Daily 5:30pm-2am*

In addition to being a busy restaurant, this airy, modernist neighborhood place enjoys a flourishing late-night bar scene, especially on weekends. A rectangular gazebo bar anchors the middle of the room, with a pool table in back and plenty of perimeter tables for the young and unattached, the predominant crowd here. There is also sidewalk seating, and the front windows slide open, so this place is particularly pleasant on a warm night. For those who like to anchor their beverage, Rex offers comfort snack food like polenta and garlic mashed potatoes. It's a fine place to start or finish a Polk Street pub crawl that takes in the other local watering holes such as Cresta, Mario's Bohemian Cigar Store, or the last of the 1970s fern bars, the Royal Oak.

## ROYAL OAK
*2201 Polk St. (Vallejo), (415) 928-2303*
*Daily 11am-2am*

Royal Oak, located on a section of Polk Street that boasts several upscale trattorias, a Real Foods, and a Peet's coffee, draws the same off–Marina District clientele as its neighbors. Dunhill-cigarette-red walls, Tiffany-style hanging lamps, and gilded beveled-glass mirrors set the scene of Victorian comfort. Hanging ivy and potted palms are reminiscent of fern bars of the 1970s. Brass-riveted leather chairs and velvet-upholstered couches are clustered to allow group conversation and enhance the feeling that you're on the set of *Friends*. Most nights the place is packed with stock-market types and other young Turks that all seem to know one another. There is an abundance of the latest hairstyles and career-on-the-rise fashions on both men and women. When a cellular phone rings, everyone reaches for their pockets, and the conversations generally include a shouted "just meet us here." The all-female crew serve with assurance and graciously deflect a myriad of nightly marriage proposals. A good selection of top-shelf tequila, scotch, bourbon, and vodka keeps glasses full.

## SHANGHAI KELLY'S
*2064 Polk St. (Broadway), (415) 771-3300*
*M-F 1pm-2am; Sa-Su noon-2am*

This tiny, basic neighborhood watering hole was named after a bartender from the gold rush days who got paid by ship captains to slip mickeys into the drinks of unsuspecting men. The poor drunks awoke the next day aboard a boat headed to sea, having been "shanghaied" to serve as crew members for months—sometimes even years (or at least that's how the legend goes). These days, there's little risk of encountering such a nasty turn of events here. The walls are covered with glowing newspaper reviews (Herb Caen penned his share of bons mots about the place) and feel-good photos of bar staff and clientele on wacky adventures. The friendly bartenders know so many people's names that nearly everyone who crosses the threshold feels like a regular. (The staff has discovered that their humble establishment was where some 35 married couples first met.) Three TVs broadcast sports, and the jukebox cranks out the Allman Brothers, Santana, and the Dead. Cheap drink specials add to the down-home ambience; try a Bart Simpson (vodka, Key Largo schnapps, o.j., and sweet and sour) for "a measly $2." But don't let the low price lead you to overindulge. That guy in the captain's hat at the end of the bar may have plans for you.

### TONGA ROOM

*Fairmont Hotel, 950 Mason St. (California/Sacramento), (415) 772-5278*
*Su-Th 5pm-midnight; F-Sa 5pm-1am*

Every once in a while it becomes necessary for those who love kitsch to make a pilgrimage to the Tonga Room. Sure, there are plenty of other cheesy Polynesian bars in the City serving up globular glasses of sickeningly sweet drinks with tiny umbrellas as decoration. This one, however, is the king, and not merely because of its regal location on Nob Hill. The space, more of a hall than a room, features table seating beneath thatched-hut roofs, fake bamboo trees, and an enormous center pool with a floating stage, on which the groovy house band performs night-ly. Best of all, every half hour there are simulated tropical storms, complete with lightning, thunder, and, yes, precipita-

## *Taxi!*

It's closing time at your hangout bar or club of choice, and either you've drunk too much to drive or you're far from home—or both. Time to step outside and hail a taxi, right? Maybe not.

Obtaining the services of a taxicab in San Francisco is a notori-ously difficult task even under the best of circumstances. There are simply not enough taxis on the streets to meet late-night demand, let alone any other time of the day. It's an intractable political prob-lem that various city ballot initiatives have failed to solve.

Your best bet is to call one of the cab companies listed below and ask them to pick you up. Be prepared to use the redial button and then wait 30 minutes or longer for the cab to arrive, depending on your location. Your luck may be better on weeknights than weekend nights or if you're calling from one of the City's busier nightlife areas (e.g., SoMa or North Beach) where coverage is heav-ier. As for simply hailing a cab out on the street, feel free to try, but know that you will need to possess extremely good karma and had better not be trying it out in the Avenues.

The alternatives, of course, are to wait for one of the MUNI Owl bus lines that run all night or simply to walk home. Anyone who has lived in San Francisco long enough knows that these two options are often one and the same thing.

**Taxi Companies**

**City Cab:** (415) 920-0700
**DeSoto Cab Co.:** (415) 673-1414
**Luxor Cab Co.:** (415) 282-4141
**Veteran's Cab:** (415) 552-1300
**Yellow Cab:** (415) 626-2345

tion. It must be seen to be believed. The band performs a dinner show after 8pm, but the prices for both food and drinks may be prohibitive for some. The penurious are advised to go during happy hour (5 to 7pm), when the Mai Tais and daiquiris are discounted and an all-you-can-eat buffet is only $5.

## TOP OF THE MARK
*Mark Hopkins Hotel, 19th fl., 1 Nob Hill (California/Mason),*
*(415) 616-6916*
*Su-Th 3pm-12:30am; F-Sa 3pm-1:30am*

Ever since it opened in 1939, atop the famed Mark Hopkins Hotel, the Top of the Mark has served as the quintessential place to take your out-of-town relatives or to have that big anniversary dinner. While the view remained as magnificent as ever, the atmosphere eventually began to feel a little, well, stodgy. Thus, the Mark remodeled, and turned from an outdated corporate-'70s look to the soon-to-be-outdated Pottery Barn-'90s look of blonde wood furnishings, beaded candle holders, and wrought-iron chandeliers. Still, it's an improvement, especially with the addition of a raised dance floor in the center of the room, where salsa and swing bands now perform starting at 8:30 nightly. (If you prefer the Mark of old, come early; it remains a piano bar from 4pm to 8pm). Best of all, there are still two rows of tables lining the perimeter of the room, from which you can ooh and aah over San Francisco to your heart's content.

★

## Late Night Eats

### CAFFE MONDA $$
*2032 Polk St. (Broadway/Pacific), (415) 923-9984*
*Su-Th 6pm-10:30pm; F-Sa 6pm-11:30pm*
Illuminated by dim lights and candles on the tables, Caffè Monda is the perfect place for a romantic evening. For starters, try the warm, garlic-marinated mushrooms in olive oil and garlic with a slight hint of balsamic vinegar. Entrees might include *linguini puttanesca* or penne with four cheeses and marinara sauce.

### COCONUT GROVE $$
*1415 Van Ness Ave. (Pine/Bush), (415) 776-1616*
*Daily 5:30pm-10pm*
See bar listing.

### MARIO'S BOHEMIAN CIGAR STORE $
*2209 Polk St. (Vallejo/Green), (415) 776-8226*
*M-Th 10am-midnight; F-Sa 10am-midnight; Su 10am-11pm*
Mario's larger branch on Polk Street has an expanded menu, more beer, and less charm. Still, the focaccia sandwiches and cannelloni are authentic.

### ZA PIZZA $
*2162 Polk St. (Broadway/Vallejo), (415) 563-8515*
*Su-Th 11:30am-10:30pm; F-Sa 11:30am-1am*
Za Pizza's Polk Street storefront—Little Za—serves takeout to passing pedestrians. The menu features some very palatable New York–style pizzas such as the potesto (potato and pesto) and the MOMA, a modernistic mix of onion, artichoke, basil, and oregano.

## Breweries

Ever since yuppies discovered the joy of microbrewed beer in the mid-1980s, it has become the drink of choice for many, and Northern California has been a national leader in providing its residents with quality suds from local breweries. Terms like *hops* and *barley*, previously reserved for exclusive use by midwestern farmers, have become conversational staples for a new breed, the beer *connoisseur*, for whom the sight of copper brewing tanks is pure heaven. In a throwback to the turn of the century, when every city had its own brewery, San Francisco and the Bay Area are now chock-full of microbreweries and brew pubs producing beers of various strengths, flavors, and consistencies. Microbrews are generally sold in bars and liquor stores, but most *microbreweries* also have tours and tasting rooms. By comparison, *brew pubs* manufacture smaller quantities of premium brews and usually sell it only in their own bar, pub, or restaurant.

The following list covers many area microbreweries and brew pubs, but look for an ever-growing number springing up like mushrooms after a rain (especially on the North Coast, where brewing beer seems to be replacing growing pot as the preferred way to earn a living). In fact, true microbrew fans will want to head up north to the beautiful coastal town of Arcata for the **BeBop and Brew** festival, held in an outdoor park every Mother's Day. It features live jazz and offers the chance to sample some of the best West Coast microbrews, all in the shade of the spectacular redwoods of the North Coast.

### Microbreweries

**Anchor Brewing Company:** Potrero Hill, 1705 Mariposa St. (DeHaro), SF, (415) 863-8350. The oldest microbrewery in the Bay Area, Anchor was started during the gold rush. Nearly bankrupt in the early 1970s, it was revived after its purchase by Fritz Maytag (heir to the appliance fortune), and today creates five different types of beer at its beautiful building on the slopes of Potrero Hill. Make a reservation for one of the free tours. They're great fun, and, yes, you can sample the product at the end, by which time you'll probably wish you worked here. Producing somewhere around 70,000 barrels of brew each year, Anchor has now far outgrown the "micro" in microbrewery.

**Anderson Valley Brewing Co.:** North Coast, 17700 Hwy 253, Boonville, (707) 895-2337. Try the beers at the bar, including the truly wonderful Boont Amber, and then make your money talk at the retail store. The brewery includes a restaurant with views of the golden hills of Anderson Valley. A new brewery has been built recently, and if you ask nicely, you'll probably get a tour.

**Anheuser-Busch:** East Bay, 3101 Busch Dr. (Abernathy), Fairfield, (707) 429-2000. Okay, it's the furthest thing from micro, but if you've always wondered how the most popular brewskis in the country are made, come here to taste beer the way it used to be, before the microbreweries started adding flavor. There are free 45-minute tours every hour from 9am to 4pm Tuesdays through Saturdays. Free tastings of the already-dirt-cheap Budweiser are included. As Alanis Morrisette would say, isn't it ironic?

**Mendocino Brewing Co.:** North Coast, 13351 S. Hwy 101, Hopland, (707) 744-1015. Home to the ever-popular Red Tail Ale, as well as such other ornithological derivatives as Black Hawk Stout and Peregrine Pale Ale. In addition to the brewery, you can visit the gift shop and an adjoining bar and restaurant—a laid-back, wisteria-draped beer garden. Brewery tours are by appointment only.

**Sierra Nevada:** Central Valley, 1075 E. 20th St., Chico, (916) 893-3520. This is hardly a microbrewery anymore, since production and distribution have grown wildly over the last few years. Beer connoisseurs are concerned about what a change in ownership will do to this famous ale maker. Stop by Tuesdays through Fridays at 2:30pm or Saturdays between noon and 3pm for a tour. A bar, restaurant, and gift shop are part of the operation.

**St. Stan's:** Central Valley, 821 L St. (9th St.), Modesto, (209) 524-4782. They have a gift shop, restaurant, and bar, and they offer free tours of the brewery at 2:30pm on Saturdays.

## Brew Pubs

**Barley and Hopps:** Peninsula, 201 South B St. (2nd Ave.), San Mateo, (650) 348-7808. The name Barley and Hopps makes it pretty clear that this is a brew pub. The beer is good, especially the India pale ale, and it complements the hearty menu: lots of smoky barbecue, gourmet deep-dish pizza, burgers, and the like. The house brews its own root beer, too, so save room for dessert and order up a float. • Tu-Sa noon-2am; Su-M 5pm-2am

**The Beach Chalet Brewery & Restaurant:** Sunset, 1000 Great Highway (Fulton/Lincoln), SF, (415) 386-8439. See bar listing.

**The Bison Brewery:** East Bay, 2598 Telegraph Ave. (Parker), Berkeley, (510) 841-7734. Probably the hippest of the local brew pubs, Bison attracts pierced and tattooed art-school bikers, slackers, and Deadheads. The striking space, with its high ceilings, giant brewing kettles, and upstairs balcony, is done in funky flea-market-meets-museum-of-modern-art decor. Servers are occasionally downright surly, but they're worth putting up with for the excellent homemade brews, which range from the typical (amber) to the bizarre (orange cardamom ale). Many evenings the Bison hosts live music. A small kitchen dishes up sandwiches, garlic bread, and pizza. • Daily 1pm-1am

**Black Diamond Brewing Co.:** East Bay, 2330 N. Main St. (Parkside), Walnut Creek, (510) 943-2330. One of the newer Bay Area brew pubs, sporting upscale shiny brewing tanks visible through the glass wall behind the bar. The menu features upscale comfort foods. • M 11am-10pm; Tu-Th 11am-midnight; F-Sa 11am-1a; Su noon-8pm

**Burlingame Station Brewing Company:** Peninsula, 333 California Dr. (Burlingame), Burlingame, (650) 344-6050. Located across from the Burlingame CalTrain station, this cavernous space teems with yuppies on the prowl, including lots of guys clearly let out of their sales routes early. House-made and local beers and typical pub grub provide sustenance while you try to find Mr. or Ms. Right among the many Wrongs sipping a pint of amber or stout before taking the train home. • M-Sa 11:30am-10pm (light menu until midnight); Su 11:30am-10pm

**Faultline Brewing Company:** South Bay, 1235 Oakmead Pkwy. (N. Lawrence Expwy./Arques), Sunnyvale, (408) 736-2739. This behemoth of a brew pub offers all the charm that a converted Rusty Scupper in an office park can muster. Fortunately, the target audience (Silicon Valley engineers-with-no-lives) doesn't seem very concerned about the lack of ambience. What they want is a nearby place to drop some of their excess cash on high-quality beer and delicious food, and Faultline certainly delivers. On weeknights between 6 and 10pm, this oasis is packed and you can easily wait an hour for a table. • M-Tu 11am-10pm; W-F 11am-11pm; Sa 5-10pm; Su 5-9pm

**Gordon Biersch:** SoMa, 2 Harrison St. (Embarcadero), SF, (415) 243-8246. See bar listing. Also with locations in Palo Alto and San Jose.

**Jupiter:** East Bay, 2181 Shattuck Ave. (Center/Allston), Berkeley, (510) 843-8277. Just down the street from its sibling pub, the venerable Triple Rock, Jupiter is a popular place for college students and townies alike to eat and drink with friends in an incredibly comfortable indoor (cozy pub) and outdoor (lovely courtyard) atmosphere. • Daily 11:30-1am

**Los Gatos Brewing Co.:** South Bay, 130 N. Santa Cruz Ave. (Grays), Los Gatos, (408) 395-9929. At this favorite haunt of beer drinkers and beach types alike, singles mingle over pints of the brewed-on-site ales, including Dunkle, Los Gatos lager, Nut Brown ale, and a rotating seasonal specialty. A long bar (salvaged from a St. Louis brothel) dominates one end of the soaring, barnlike space; another wall is occupied by a wood-burning pizza oven. The menu features designer pizzas, pastas, and grilled meats. • M-Th 11:30am-10pm; F-Sa 11:30am-midnight; Su 11:30am-10pm

**Marin Brewing Company:** Marin, 1809 Larkspur Landing Cir. (Sir Francis Drake), Larkspur, (415) 461-4677. Located in the Larkspur Landing Shopping Center across from the ferry terminal, this immensely successful brew pub offers high-quality microbrews and an eclectic menu ranging from wood-fired pizza to Asian salads to pub grub. It attracts a loud after-work crowd, and reservations are recommended if you want to bypass the bar on the way to your table. Attention fruit-beer lovers: the Blueberry Ale is worth its weight in gold. • Daily 11:30am-midnight

**Pacific Coast Brewing Co.:** East Bay, 906 Washington St. (9th St./10th St.), Oakland, (510) 836-2739. This downtown-Oakland brew pub occupies a beautifully restored historic brick building and sports a pleasant outdoor patio. In addition to house-made brews, they are notable for serving other microbrews. The food is an eclectic selection of pub grub: bangers, pasties, meat loaf, and nachos. • Su-Th 11:30am-11pm; F-Sa 11:30am-1am

**Pyramid Brewery & Ale House:** East Bay, 901 Gilman St. (7th St./8th St.), Berkeley, (510) 528-9880. Eat and drink in the shadow of gigantic brew tanks in this enormous testimonial to Seattle-based Pyramid Brewing Company. Choose from a $4.95 brew sampler and a thick espresso stout, among many others, and order up some of the reasonably priced pub grub. The brewery, housed in a former truck-body plant, is ideally located for outdoor enthusiasts who wish to make a pit stop between shopping at North Face and REI. • Su-Th 11:30am-10pm; F-Sa 11:30am-11pm

**San Francisco Brewing Company:** North Beach, 155 Columbus Ave. (Pacific), SF, (415) 434-3344. See bar listing.

**Stoddard's Brewhouse:** South Bay, 111 S. Murphy Ave. (Washington/Evelyn), Sunnyvale, (408) 733-7824. Opened by Bob Stoddard, former brew *meister* at the Tied House, the soaring two-story space houses a long, polished wooden bar, a wicker seating area, a downstairs dining room, and an upstairs aerie for quieter dining. Out back is a beer garden in case you're restless. The fresh-brewed ales are delicious. • M-Th 11:30am-2:30pm, 5:30-10pm; F 11:30am-2:30pm, 5-11pm; Sa noon-3pm, 5:30-10pm; Su 11am-2:30pm, 5-9pm.

**The Tied House:** Peninsula, 945 Villa St., Mountain View, (650) 965-BREW/2739 • South Bay, 65 N. San Pedro Square, San Jose, (408) 295-BREW/2739 • East Bay, 1051 Pacific Marina, Alameda, (510) 521-4321. The Mountain View Tied House is one of the area's original brew pubs. An always-crowded beer hall big enough to accommodate an entire fraternity with a big-screen TV, darts, shuffleboard, kegs to go—what more could a frat brother ask for? Eight delicious beers are served on tap, from Alpine Pearl pale to Ironwood dark. Order a sampler if you can't decide. The food here is secondary to the brews.

**Thirsty Bear:** SoMa, 661 Howard St. (New Montgomery/3rd St.), SF, (415) 974-0905. See bar listing.

**Triple Rock:** East Bay, 1920 Shattuck Ave. (Hearst), Berkeley, (510) 843-2739. The Berkeley institution that spawned Jupiter and 20 Tank. This is a favorite all-day student hangout and all-around great place. You can even pull in some sun on the tiny rooftop deck. • Daily 11:30am-midnight

**20 Tank Brewery:** SoMa, 316 11th St. (Folsom/Harrison), SF, (415) 255-9455. See bar listing.

# ★ Marina / Pacific Heights

Fairly or unfairly, the Marina and Pacific Heights are often derided by residents of other, more multicultural parts of San Francisco as being too something: too white, too yuppie, too mainstream. Likewise, conventional wisdom has it that no one else from San Francisco goes to the bars and clubs in these neighborhoods unless they live here, so bland and predictable is the pickup scene that swarms nightly around both Union and Chestnut streets. The fact of the matter is that while the Marina and Pacific Heights may be distinctly different from the rest of the City, they have as many laid-back, no-pressure bars as high-energy, unabashed meat markets. What they lack in dives they make up for in sophisticated, stylish spots that reflect the urban professionals who patronize them. And with so many great restaurants in this part of town, why pass up the chance for a postmeal nightcap if you're already in the area?

★

### ALTA PLAZA
*2301 Fillmore St. (Clay), (415) 922-1444*
*Daily 4pm-2am*

What two venerable institutions disappeared in the late '80s, only to return, better than ever, in the mid-90s? The answer: civility and Alta Plaza, the bar of choice for the Pacific Heights button-down gay set. And the two go hand in hand. Alta Plaza is the place to meet a man you can bring home to mother, especially if she's the old-fashioned sort who appreciates a gentleman who minds his manners. Polished wood and stenciled walls form the backdrop to an elegant bar, cleverly set in front of a mirror that makes checking out your neighbor easier. Happy hour runs from 4 to 7pm, and the crowd is very friendly, very male, and delighted to be reviving the phrase "smart cocktails." The music can be a bit loud (mitigating factors: it's jazz and often live), and you may have to get a grip on your finances (those smooth Red Hook drafts are four bucks each), but if you're looking for a civilized gay bar, Alta Plaza's the place to see. And be seen.

### BALBOA CAFÉ AND GRILL
*3199 Fillmore St. (Greenwich), (415) 921-3944*
*Daily 11:30am-1:30am*

This rectangular corner bar has been here since 1914, and it feels like a real saloon, with antique drop lighting, brass railings, and wood paneling. A big sofa sits in one corner and small tables line the windows; a more formal dining room is in back, with a menu that's overseen by the chef from the Plump Jack Café. Best of all, the beers are proudly displayed behind glass in lit refrigerators, making them seem like objects of worship. On Friday and Saturday nights, yuppies pack the place to overflowing, but the bar's elegance cannot be diminished by its location at the heart of the Triangle scene. On weeknights, Balboa becomes conducive to quiet, relaxed conversation.

# Marina
# Pacific Heights

**Marina Green**

Marina Blvd.

Jefferson St.

Beach St.

North Point St.

Cervantes Blvd.

**Fort Mason**

Bay St.

Broderick St.

Divisadero St.

Scott St.

Francisco St.

**Moscone Recreation Center**

Chestnut St.

Chestnut St.

**13** **10**

**14** **18**

Lombard St.
101
Lombard St.

**4**

Greenwich St.

**6**

Greenwich St.

**2** **15**

**7**

Filbert St.

Filbert St.

**11**

**17**

Union St.

**3** **5**

Union St.

N

GLD

Green St.

Green St.

Vallejo St.

Pierce St.

Steiner St.

Fillmore St.

Webster St.

Buchanan St.

Laguna St.

Octavia St.

Gough St.

Franklin St. →

Van Ness Ave.

101

Broadway

Pacific Ave.

Jackson St.

**Alta Plaza**

Washington St.

**1** Clay St

Broderick St.

Divisadero St.

Scott St.

Sacramento St.

**12**

California St.

**16**

**9**

← Pine St.

**8**

Bush St.,→

Sutter St.

1. Alta Plaza
2. Balboa Café and Grill
3. Blue Light
4. Blues
5. Bus Stop
6. City Tavern
7. Comet Club
8. Frankie's Bohemian
9. Harry's on Fillmore
10. Horseshoe Tavern
11. Left at Albuquerque
12. Lion Pub
13. Marina Lounge
14. Paragon Bar & Café
15. Pierce Street Annex
16. Rasselas
17. Union Street Ale House
18. Windows

## Blue Light Café
*1979 Union St. (Laguna/Buchanan), (415) 922-5510*
*M-Sa 4pm-2am; Su 11am-2am*

In Bram Stoker's *Dracula*, a blue light signifies ominous portents. Unbearable high-school English paper analogies aside, suffice it to say this bar is suitably named. Early on in the evening, it's a truly comfortable place to hang: televisions occupy both ends of the long bar, and you can order some pretty tasty food (well beyond the typical bar fare of soggy nachos and greasy buffalo wings). Your comrades at the bar are polite; the bartenders are attentive and engaging. (It's a good place to meet for a first date.) The bar isn't too crowded, you can actually speak without competing against loud music, and you can appear relatively hip in this Union Street locale. But then as late night closes in, the Blue Light changes. Obnoxious twentysomethings and gold-chained fortysomethings cram themselves into every square inch of the place. Many more spill out the front door just waiting to shove themselves into the madness. Cocktails spill from glasses, cigar smoke gets blown in your face, and shouting is the sole form of communication. Time to pay your bill and check your watch. You'll be back again, before the witching hour. After all, during daylight, even Dracula was just a laidback count sporting a pair of hip shades and looking for a cocktail.

## Blues
*2125 Lombard St. (Fillmore/Steiner), (415) 771-BLUE/2583*
*Sa-Th 8pm-2am; F 7pm-2am*

Although an unlikely setting for a cozy nightclub, Blues provides an inviting refuge from the Lombard Street clatter. Live acts play da blooz, R&B, and soul every night of the week. The cool atmosphere is in large part due to the decor: purple-velvet walls, white leather banquettes, a midnight blue linoleum bar, and an alcove shrine to Elvis complete with votive candles. A painting of questionable taste—a luxuriating woman with no clothes on—hangs above the bar, so some may wish to keep their eyes focused on the stage (and some may not). The crowd here is older and more mature than the usual Marina set, plus German and Japanese blues afficionados regularly stop by. Napa Red, Sierra Nevada, and the watery domestics are on tap. Special nights include Rockin' Rock-a-billy Thursdays, Grand Funk Fridays, and the acid-jazz-tinged Leopard Lounge on Sundays. Doors open at 8pm; cover charge after 9pm for the bands on Thursdays through Sundays.

## Bus Stop
*1901 Union St. (Laguna), (415) 567-6905*
*Daily 10am-2am*

The Bus Stop is, among other things, a good place to watch sports. Plenty of televisions are strategically placed at the bar and in the adjoining room, so there is hardly a bad seat in the house. Away from the bar, comfortable tables and chairs are in abundance. The bartenders and waiters are always there to serve you and, if nothing else, will never leave you wanting for pretzels. The place is not overwhelmed by Marina denizens, but instead is a welcome mix of folks in sweats and baseball caps. Although two pool tables command the back room, there's still space for those waiting for a table or wanting to watch a friendly

## Waterfront Bars

For a city that is surrounded by water on three sides, San Francisco has surprisingly few places to enjoy a drink while drinking in waterfront ambience, especially if you want to sit outdoors. Blame it on the city's practical nature: the piers were meant for working, and the weather—especially the famous fog—often sends people fleeing for cover. Nevertheless, the following San Francisco bars show the incredibly wide range of settings for enjoying that drink on the water; those beyond the city add even more variety.

### San Francisco

**Beach Chalet:** 1000 Great Highway (Fulton/Lincoln), (415) 386-8439. See Sunset bar listing.

**Buena Vista:** 2765 Hyde St. (Beach), (415) 474-5044. See Fisherman's Wharf sidebar.

**Gabbiano's:** Ferry Building, 1 Ferry Plaza (Embarcadero), (415) 391-8403. See Embarcadero bar listing.

**Jelly's:** 295 China Basin Way (off Mission Rock), (415) 495-3099. See SoMa bar listing.

**Mission Rock:** 817 China Basin Blvd. (Mariposa/3rd St.), (415) 621-5538. See SoMa bar listing.

**Pier 23:** Pier 23 (Embarcadero at Battery), (415) 362-5125. See North Beach bar listing.

**Tarantino's:** 206 Jefferson St. (Taylor), (415) 775-5600. See Fisherman's Wharf sidebar.

**The Ramp:** 855 China Basin Blvd. (Mariposa/3rd St.), (415) 621-2378. See SoMa bar listing.

### Outside San Francisco

**Guaymas:** Marin, 5 Main St. (Tiburon Blvd.), Tiburon, (415) 435-6300. Located in picturesque Tiburon, Guaymas is a little taste of Mexico on an American waterfront. The handmade tortillas and the margaritas are not to be missed. You can sit indoors or on the outdoor patio (heated in the winter) overlooking the water and enjoy a meal or just drinks. Guaymas is also a good stopover when you are returning on the ferry from nearby Angel Island. Keep in mind that the wait for a table can be long. • M-Th 11:30am-10pm; F-Sa 11:30am-11pm; Su 10:30am-10pm

**Miramar Beach Inn:** Peninsula Coast, 131 Mirada Rd. (Magellan), Miramar, (650) 726-9053. Right next to the ocean, this historic roadhouse dating back to Prohibition keeps the roar of the '20s alive. In fact, word has it that this is the place to party on the coast, especially if you're over 30. The rugged dining hall offers a good selection of seafood, steaks, and pasta dishes. • M-F 11:30am-3:30pm, 5pm-9pm; Sa 11am-3:30pm, 5-10pm; Su 10am-3:30pm, 5-10pm

**Moss Beach Distillery:** Peninsula Coast, Beach Way (off Hwy 1 at Ocean Blvd.), Moss Beach, (650) 728-5595. The sign on Highway 1 sums up the appeal of this Prohibition-era roadhouse: View, Food, Ghost. The restaurant boasts a large bar and deck area for viewing the Pacific sunset (blankets and heaters are provided). Young crowds mob the patio on sunny weekend afternoons, while live jazz plays inside. As you may have guessed, food isn't the main attraction. And yes, there is a ghost in residence—the "blue lady" even starred on an episode of *Unsolved Mysteries*. • M-Sa noon-8:30pm; Su 10am-2:30pm, 4:30pm-10pm

**Sam's Anchor Café:** Marin, 27 Main St. (Tiburon Blvd.), Tiburon, (415) 435-4527. Sam's is famous for the huge waterfront deck where the Corona beer crowd comes to hang out and scarf burgers, fries, and deep-fried seafood. Its location also makes it a popular place for yachters to dock for snacks. • M-F 11am-2am; Sa 10am-2am; Su 9:30am-2am (menu served until 10pm)

game to park it on a barstool, throw back a cold beer, and eat some snacks while catching Tiger Woods or Michael Jordan breaking yet another record. Standard sports-bar decor hangs from the walls: photos of athletes and posters of bikini-clad women. Clearly, this is a bar for people with simple needs.

## CITY TAVERN

*3200 Fillmore St. (Greenwich), (415) 567-0918*
*Daily 11am-2am*

City Tavern has been around for only a few years, but judging from the large group of well-dressed twenty- and thirtysome-things who surround the horseshoe bar three-deep on weekends, it appears to be a rousing success. (Stand here long enough and you're bound to hear some alcohol-fueled, ribald comments.) Overall the room has a classic '90s look, with lots of light wood, sleek wall sconces, and lamps hanging from the ceiling. There are booths for dining and a full California menu is served, although the real action is at the bar, as is to be expected at any Triangle institution. If for some odd reason you don't find the conversation lively, you can always fixate on the stack of glass shelves filled with expensive liquors and wonder just what would happen if an earthquake rumbled through.

## COMET CLUB

*3111 Fillmore St. (Filbert/Greenwich), (415) 567-5589*
*Tu-W 7pm-2am; Th-Su 5:30pm-2am*

This recently opened cocktail bar is a welcome alternative to the sometimes-predictable Marina bar scene. Run by the same folks who own North Beach's Hi-Ball Lounge, this dark and narrow room recalls its cousin. The large, glittery leather booths, red Formica tables, and always-rotating mirror ball attract a crowd of hipsters from other parts of town (who might otherwise never come this way) as well as intrigued neighborhood types checking out a space that used to be The Desert Moon (it gets really crowded around 11:30pm). There's a dance floor in back where

---

**Sand Dollar:** Marin, 3458 Shoreline Highway, Stinson Beach, (415) 868-0434. Not actually on the water, but it pairs perfectly with a day at Stinson Beach. The cozy bar inside is a local hangout—the gossip is juicier than the food—while the patio can be a gathering spot for postfraternal San Francisco singles. Sit in the sun, sip a beer, and slurp some local oysters while you admire tan lines. • M-Th 11:30am-3pm, 5:30pm-9pm; F-Sa 11:30am-3pm, 5:30pm-9:30pm; Su 11am-3pm, 5:30pm-9:30pm

**Skates on the Bay:** East Bay, 100 Seawall Dr. (University), Berkeley Marina, (510) 549-1900. Experience a breathtaking waterfront view at the expansive bar of this restaurant. The cozy, comfortable atmosphere is further warmed by a fireplace and open ovens, where fabulous focaccia is baked. • M-Th 11:15am-3pm, 5-10pm; F 11:15am-3pm, 5-10:30pm; Sa noon-10:30pm; Su 10:15am-10pm

**Stinson Beach Grill:** Marin, 3465 Shoreline Highway, Stinson Beach, (415) 868-2002. Just as with the Sand Dollar, this spot is not on the water. Burgers, seafood, Southwest dishes, and Italian cuisine are all served in a wood-frame house with a big deck, but most people come for the relaxing beach-hangout atmosphere following some time roasting in the sun or freezing in the fog. • M-Th 11:30am-9pm; F 11:30am-9:30pm; Sa-Su 11am-9:30pm

a DJ spins mellow bachelor-pad tracks Friday and Saturday nights. Golden Bear and Bass Ale are among the beers on tap, with $2.50 happy hour drinks until 8:30pm on Tuesdays and Wednesdays, and $2.50 martinis during happy hour on Fridays.

## FRANKIE'S BOHEMIAN CAFÉ
*1862 Divisadero St. (Bush/Pine), (415) 921-4725*
*Daily 4pm-1am*

From the outside, Frankie's appears to be a greasy spoon diner, what with the red clapboard frame, faded Coca Cola sign, and hand lettered posterboard proclaiming "You can come to work when you want, but when you come to the pub, be on time." In actuality, the darkly painted interior, where it is too dark for a restaurant yet too light for a bar, is a perfect place to go when both good eating and great drinking are on the agenda. Diners feast on a versatile menu featuring brambory (potato- and zucchini "pancake"), burgers, pasta, and salads. With ten beers on tap including IPA, Anchor Steam, Pyramid Hefeweizen, and Guinness (all served in pint and a half glasses for $4, $3 during happy hour daily from 4 to 7pm), it's easy to linger over your meal and your conversation. While Frankie's is often crowded, especially later in the evening, don't expect a lot of propositions or even sidelong glances from anyone; this is defintely a place where you arrive and depart with the same company. At closing time, with your beer in hand, travel two doors down to the co-owned Divisadero Alehouse for continued intimate enjoyment of great beer. A great place to go with a small group of friends, or on a second or third date. No liquor served.

## HARRY'S ON FILLMORE
*2020 Fillmore St. (California/Pine), (415) 921-1000*
*Su-M 3:30pm-1am; Tu-Sa 3:30pm-2am*

Going to Harry's on Fillmore is like going to a friend's party after most of the guests have pushed on to other events. In other words, something is missing. What's missing, of course, is Harry Denton himself. Opening this clubby hangout was Harry's first step in charming his way from behind the bar at the Balboa Café to the position of San Francisco's premier party *meister*. Three—at last count—eponymous bars and one financial blip (in Donald Trump's terminology) later, the gravelly voiced Harry is no longer involved in this bar. The new owners have kept the place virtually unchanged, including the name (which should be trademarked by now), the gorgeous mahogany bar, the baby grand piano, the live jazz, the fancy bar food, and the Fourth of July American flag theme. Nevertheless, when Harry left, he took the party with him, taking the crush at the bar and the raging lust, leaving a classy neighborhood hangout, perfect for an intimate gathering of friends.

## HORSESHOE TAVERN
*2024 Chestnut St. (Fillmore/Steiner), (415) 346-1430*
*Daily 10am-2am*

Located on trendy Chestnut Street, this bar looks like it's been here forever. Its trademark—the large black sign with the horsehead profile—is visible from blocks away. Once beyond the plain wooden door, it's clear a lot is going down here. Home to the young, urban, energetic sports afficionados—who come to shoot pool, play pinball, watch the games on the large TV at the head of the bar, and drink the great selection of imported and domestic drafts—this place really rocks on the weekends. The jukebox is loaded with '80s dance tunes, and its booming volume can be heard above the racking and breaking of balls at the two pool tables in the back room. The atmosphere is loud and vibrant, and a serious pick-up scene is part of the package. Sports are taken so seriously here that the outsized mirror behind the fully stocked bar has a chain of wooden plaques listing televised games. Like so many drinking holes in the City, the walls are covered with black-and-white photographs of historic local sports teams, and there are even some vintage shots of the Golden Gate Bridge under construction. There is never a cover charge.

## LEFT AT ALBUQUERQUE
*2140 Union St. (Fillmore/Webster), (415) 749-6700*
*Daily 11:30am-2am*

The owners of Palo Alto's Blue Chalk Café have struck pay dirt again with this southwestern-inspired bar and restaurant. The enormous, airy space features bold desert art and various shards of Americana (cactus paintings, neon Buick signs) chicken-wire racks of liquor bottles above the bar, and a bustling open kitchen in back. Speaking of bustling, the bar scene is wall-to-wall San Francisco singles, all in their bluest blue jeans, with talk of mountain bikes and stock options filling the air. It's actually one of the few remaining Marina bars that can still claim (at least on weekends) to have a line of people down the street eagerly waiting to get in on the fun. Margaritas are popular, as is just about every other tequila drink. The contemporary southwestern menu is flavorful, varied, and inexpensive, with several tapas-sized dishes.

## LION PUB
*2062 Divisadero St. (Sacramento), (415) 567-6565*
*Daily 3pm-2am*

The Lion Pub is the oldest existing gay bar in San Francisco that is not located in an identifiably gay neighborhood (such as Polk Gulch until the 1970s and the Castro ever since). First-time visitors may have trouble finding the place: there's no exterior sign (a throwback to an earlier, less-tolerant era), but the year-round Christmas lights—the tasteful kind—on the corner of Sacramento and Divisadero will guide you. Inside, the Lion is a gas: Corinthian caps on ersatz pillars, faux stone walls, a faux stone fireplace, even a faux fire. Although famous as a gay hangout, it's patronized by a mix of middle-class folks, including lots of downtown bankers and accountants unwinding from work. A continuously running MTV-esque disco tape keeps the party atmosphere intact. Liquor companies such as Tanqueray often hold promotions here, which can mean drinks are at least half-priced. Friday happy hour, when hors d'oeuvres are served, begins at 6pm.

## MARINA LOUNGE
*2138 Chestnut St. (Pierce/Steiner), (415) 922-1475*
*Daily 7:30am-2am*

At nightfall, this bar's vertical neon sign is visible from a block away, Tony Bennett's voice croons from the corner jukebox, and the young urban crowd gathers at the 16-seat mahogany bar along the right wall of the narrow room. Exposed brick walls, wall sconces, dark wainscoting, and atmospheric green-shaded banker's lamps give the Marina Lounge a low-key, comfortable elegance. The best seat in the house is the small, front-window table that opens onto Chestnut Street, making it perfect for people watching. Although no formal dance floor exists, couples often sway wherever they can find room, usually near the jukebox. At the back, a much-loved pool table and several video games keep many of the regulars occupied. A long church pew rests against one wall, a good perch for drinking a draft beer and relaxing while chalking a pool cue.

## PARAGON BAR AND CAFÉ
*3251 Scott St. (Chestnut/Lombard), (415) 922-2456*
*Daily 4pm-2am*

Before the recent remodeling, the Paragon fancied itself a hangout for frat boys and tanned Southern California surfer types who wanted to relive their pre-yuppie pasts. Now it has a more sophisticated feel, owing to the black-and-tan walls with sconces and moldings, the abstract artwork, the stone fireplace, and the hanging industrial light fixtures. The crowd has gotten older and more professional, but this is still the Marina, and the J. Crew/Gap/Banana Republic look predominates; no body piercings here. The revamped musical calendar leans towards the KFOG aesthetic, with lots of acoustic songwriters and retro rockers performing live Sunday through Wednesday, and a resident DJ spinning crowd-pleasing tunes the rest of the week. Food is served at the tables in the back of the room. Remains popular and packed on weekends.

## PIERCE ST. ANNEX
*3138 Fillmore St. (Filbert/Greenwich), (415) 567-1400*
*Daily noon-2am*

One very important resident of the legendary Triangle, the Fillmore-Greenwich intersection that's said to be the epicenter of the Marina singles scene, the Pierce St. Annex dutifully fulfills its part of the bargain. Judging by all the skimpy clothing and come-hither looks floating around this large room, people show up here to check one another out while loud dance music plays in the background. Two rectangular bars in the center are staffed by nimble bartenders who somehow have yet to lose their hearing. The beer selection is basic and the requisite sports events fill the TV screens. DJs spin tunes Wednesday through Saturday nights; there's live music Tuesday nights at 9pm and Sundays at 4pm. A strict dress code is in force after 8:30pm: no T-shirts, sweatshirts, et cetera. There's a cover charge for both live music and dancing.

## RASSELAS
*2801 California St. (Divisadero), (415) 567-5010*
*M-Th 5pm-1:30am; F-Sa 5pm-2am*

Rasselas is an Ethiopian restaurant with a club floor and bar adjacent to the dining room. On the entertainment side, comfortable couches with large, fluffy pillows stand along the windows, giving the space a homey feel. The middle of the room holds small cocktail tables and chairs, and there is a full bar at the rear. The club features outstanding smooth jazz and blues

## Late Night Eats

### AMICI'S EAST COAST PIZZERIA ¢
*2033 Union St. (Buchanan/Webster), (415) 885-4500*
*Daily 11am-midnight*
Amici's takes its cue from New York pizza parlors, offering thin-crusted pies baked in a wood-burning brick oven for extra crispness. Toppings are straightforward if not pioneering. Pastas and salads are pizza alternatives.

### BEPPLE'S PIES $
*2142 Chestnut St. (Steiner/Pierce), (415) 931-6226*
*1934 Union St. (Laguna/Buchanan), (415) 931-6225*
*Su-Th 8am-midnight; F-Sa 9am-2am*
Check out Bepple's sumptuous variety of pies both savory and sweet and you'll wonder if there isn't a little old Ma Bepple bustling around the back room in her ruffled apron. Ask what's fresh or you might find your selection a bit stale.

### BETELNUT $$/$$$
*2026 Union St. (Buchanan/Webster), (415) 929-8855*
*Su-Th 11:30am-11pm; F-Sa 11:30am-midnight*
This riotously popular place is an Asian snack palace and beer house. Grazing food, tidbits to accompany drinks, or a late-night snack: all can be had here. Chinese, Thai, Vietnamese, Japanese, and less frequently seen specialties from Malaysia and Singapore are all featured. Diners can sit at the sidewalk tables, in the lively bar, near the open kitchen, or in a spacious back room.

### CAFÉ DE PARIS ENTRECOTE $$$
*2032 Union St. (Buchanan/Webster), (415) 931-5006*
*Su-Th 11:30am-11pm; F-Sa 11am-midnight*
The house specialty at this rigorously French bistro is its namesake entrecôte, with a butter sauce kept hot in a warmer, but the à la carte menu also includes several options lighter than traditional French fare for those unwilling to commit to serious calories. Don't miss the *pomme frites*. Desserts are predictably extravagant.

### DENNY'S $
*1700 Post St. (Webster/Laguna), (415) 563-1400*
*Daily 24 hours*
Eating at Denny's can be a frustrating experience, as the question-ably awake hosts and hostesses are wont to keep you waiting a while despite the usual abundance of empty tables. If you do end up eventually hearing your name resonate over the unnecessary and rather eerie P.A. system, stick with difficult-to-destroy diner favorites like French fries and milkshakes—in other words, avoid anything with a photograph of its plastic replica on the menu.

### HARD ROCK CAFÉ $
*1699 Van Ness Ave. (Sacramento), (415) 885-1699*
*Su-Th 11:30am-11:30pm; F-Sa 11:30am-midnight*
Part of the chain of rock-and-roll tourist restaurants, this location does not disappoint, unless you are interested in conversation: very loud music plays to a huge and diverse crowd (tourists come from everywhere). The food is actually good and plentiful: huge burgers, salads, hot and spicy chili, and great shakes.

### INTERNATIONAL HOUSE OF PANCAKES $
*2299 Lombard St. (Pierce), (415) 921-4004*
*Daily 24 hours*
IHOP thrives here on motor hotel row; even in the wee hours the place is packed with a cast of characters whose quirky coolness com-pensates for the exorbitantly priced and sometimes downright unap-petizing menu choices. Any of the pancakes are a pretty safe bet.

## Late Night Eats

### JOHNNY ROCKETS $
*2201 Chestnut St. (Pierce), (415) 931-6258*
*Su-Th 11am-midnight; F-Sa 11am-3am*
A chain of diners suffused with nostalgic decor and bright fluorescent lighting. Serves up messy-but-tasty burgers, chili cheese fries and shakes. The jukebox blasts 50s tunes.

### LEFT AT ALBUQUERQUE $
*2140 Union St. (Fillmore/Webster), (415) 749-6700*
*Daily 11:30am-11pm (bar open till 1:30am)*
See bar listing.

### LIVERPOOL LIL'S $$
*2942 Lyon St. (Lombard/Greenwich), (415) 921-6664*
*M-Sa 11am-1am; Su 11am-1am (lighter menu after midnight M-Sa; after 11pm Su)*
A traditional British public house, Liverpool Lil's is cozy and comfortable. Its menu selection is broad and satisfying: in the bar area, there are Thai kabobs, baked Brie, or baby pizzas, among other finger foods; and in the restaurant, daily specials range from pasta to fish dishes. At any time of day, you can order the hearty Lil's burger, topped with cheese, mushrooms, and onions—definitely one of the best burgers in town.

### MEL'S DRIVE-IN $
*2165 Lombard St. (Fillmore/Steiner), (415) 921-3039*
*Su-Th 6am-2am; F-Sa 24 hours (from F 6am through M 2am)*
Mel's is part of the movement to recapture the glory of the '50s, with coin-op jukeboxes at every table and a menu with favorites like meat loaf sandwiches and bread pudding. A popular late-night hangout, especially with teens, Mel's is perfect for a milk shake after the movies and is a fun place to go with a group. Be sure to save room for dessert. No credit cards.

### PASTA POMODORO $
*2027 Chestnut St. (Fillmore/Steiner), (415) 474-3400*
*M-Sa 11am-11pm; Su noon-11pm*
Large servings of pasta at incredibly cheap prices—it's a concept that has made this citywide Italian restaurant chain very popular among those with big appetites and light pockets. Service is usually lightning quick yet still pleasant. Cash only.

### PIZZERIA UNO $
*2200 Lombard St. (Steiner), (415) 563-3144*
*M-Th 11am-11pm; F-Sa 11am-1am; Su noon-11pm*
National chain famous for Chicago-style deep-dish pizza served in a bustling diner. Those who don't like the thick, flaky Chicago crust can opt for thin-crust pizzettas. The menu also includes pasta, salads, and burgers, but the big attraction is the pizza.

### ¡WA-HA-KA! ¢
*1980 Union St. (Buchanan/Laguna), (415) 775-4145*
*M-W 11:30am-10pm; Th 11:30am-10pm; F 11:30am-midnight;*
*Sa 11am-midnight; Su 11am-11pm*
This taqueria exudes youthful energy, drawing hungry nighttime revelers from the surrounding bars. Bright, industrial decor sports warehouse-high ceilings, rough concrete walls and floor, mismatched wooden tables and chairs, and Mexican billboard murals. Their unique addition to the fresh-Mex scene is pretty good fish tacos. No credit cards.

shows starting nightly at 8pm, and there is a two-drink mini-mum. (There is no cover charge, however.) The ethnically diverse crowd runs older than most nightspots, but it is in line with this part of town. Most are couples, gay and straight, and a large number of them are interracial—rather unusual for Pacific Heights. Restaurant seating opens up to bar patrons after dinner service, but it is advisable to arrive by 8pm if you want a seat during the early sets. Take note: although smoking is permitted, very few people are.

## UNION STREET ALE HOUSE
*1980 Union St. (Laguna/Buchanan), (415) 921-0300*
*M-F 3:30pm-2am; Sa-Su 10:30am-2am*

A basement-level pickup joint once described as Ground Zero for Lust, the Ale House is not quite as popular as it used to be before the nightlife scene began to shift away from the Marina. But it still draws the fresh-out-of-college kids who are nostalgic for its campus-bar-like ambience of bright lighting, wood floors, and low ceilings. The center of the action is the wraparound bar from which an excellent selection of drafts, from Golden Bear to Pintail PSB, are served. A couple of pool tables and dart-boards are tucked at the back, along with a wide-screen TV locked in to ESPN. REM and Pearl Jam are usually blasting from the stereo system, but if you listen closely enough, you'll be sure to hear the three words that are repeated here all night like a mantra: What's your name? Come during happy hour (Monday through Friday, 3:30 to 6:30pm) for half-priced appetizers.

## WINDOWS
*3259 Pierce St. (Lombard/Chestnut), (415) 567-4466*
*Daily 10am-2am*

Windows advertises itself as a place serving Beverages for Adults. As it happens, everything about it is geared toward the 30-and-over crowd (women wearing knit sweaters, men wearing slacks), the ones who are settled down and only go out for a drink to escape the rugrats for a few hours. Likewise, the design of the bar is probably intended to make this clientele feel at home: a narrow room painted nautical blue, it sports spotless carpeting and tables straight out of a Pottery Barn cata-log. Golf is the predominant theme, with real clubs mounted over the bar and hundreds of golf balls encased on the walls. Bruce Springsteen and the Beatles are typical of the jukebox options. There's even a bookshelf full of murder mysteries near the bathroom. Great mixed drinks with a limited bottled-beer selection. As the evening progresses, Windows becomes slightly more singles oriented.

★

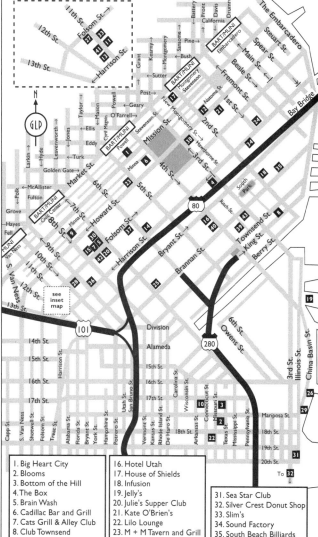

# SoMa (South of Market) Potrero Hill / China Basin

1. Big Heart City
2. Blooms
3. Bottom of the Hill
4. The Box
5. Brain Wash
6. Cadillac Bar and Grill
7. Cats Grill & Alley Club
8. Club Townsend
   Club Universe
   Pleasuredome
9. CoCo Club
10. Connecticut Yankee
11. DNA Lounge
12. Eddie Rickenbacker's
13. Eleven
14. The End-Up
15. Hole in the Wall

16. Hotel Utah
17. House of Shields
18. Infusion
19. Jelly's
20. Julie's Supper Club
21. Kate O'Brien's
22. Lilo Lounge
23. M + M Tavern and Grill
24. Maritime Bar & Grill
    Maritime Hall
25. Mars Café
26. Mission Rock Resort
27. Paradise Lounge
    Transmission Theater
28. Powerhouse
29. The Ramp
30. Rawhide II

31. Sea Star Club
32. Silver Crest Donut Shop
33. Slim's
34. Sound Factory
35. South Beach Billiards
36. The Stud
37. 1015 Folsom
38. The Thirsty Bear
39. 330 Ritch Street
40. Trocadero
41. Twenty Tank Brewery
42. Up & Down Club
43. Zeke's Diamond Bar
    and Grill

# SoMa / Potrero Hill China Basin

The Mission may have cooler bars, but SoMa has the coolest nightclubs in town. After all, it's an area full of very long and very wide blocks, with scads of warehouse space that's been reincarnated as multilevel techno-disco emporiums. In addition, owing to the influence of the cyber neighbors in Multimedia Gulch, SoMa is where the cutting edge of high-tech culture finds its expression in nightclub music and design. Like that accelerated culture, the local club scene seems to change every week, a slave to the whimsy of the clubbing set. It's a good idea to call ahead before making the trek to a nightspot in the middle of nowhere that might no longer be what you're looking for.

All this exciting spirit occasionally manifests itself in attitude: long lines, stringent dress codes, and diluted, overpriced drinks. To avoid that, try the edges of SoMa, especially away from the 11th Street scene. Both Potrero Hill and the bars around 2nd and Mission, for example, are far more laid-back. The industrial China Basin area offers a waterfront experience and a mix of weekend madness as epitomized by the Ramp, and workaday longshoreman hangouts such as Sea Star. No matter where you head in SoMa, be careful walking the long, deserted streets between venues.

★

## BIG HEART CITY
*836 Mission St. (4th St./5th St.), (415) 777-0666*
*Hours vary*

It doesn't seem quite right to call this a nightclub, despite the two-story-high neon sign depicting a cocktail glass hanging over Mission Street. By day and early evening, Big Heart City is a Thai restaurant, Bangkok Lounge. After nine in the evening, the restaurant in front becomes the bar area, and a curtain is pulled back to reveal a giant, open, studiolike space in the rear, with bare wood floors, steel columns, a railed balcony, and a makeshift stage. Both the local party bands that play here and the DJs who spin records on Friday and Saturday nights have the burden of overcoming this deficit in ambience, and management is still trying to figure out how to draw a crowd to the northern end of SoMa. Call or check listings before making the trek.

## BOTTOM OF THE HILL
*1233 17th St. (Texas), (415) 621-4455*
*Open for performances only*

This small rock club at the far reaches of Potrero Hill attracts punters with its intelligent and prescient bookings. This is the best place to see local bands practice their craft and up-and-coming national acts before they move on to bigger venues. Also, it's usually the first place to see heavily hyped Britpop acts on their virgin U.S. tours. With its tiny raised stage and low ceilings, the intimate space turns even sold-out shows into intimate affairs, and the quirky cartoonish wall decor skews perspectives even before the drinking starts. There's a set of pool tables in the back room a few feet from the stage and an outdoor patio for catching a breath of fresh air. The kitchen serves very good burger-and-fries combos, along with other grub, and is now open until 11pm on gig nights. The rockin' all-you-can-eat barbecue on Sunday afternoons is legendary. Plenty of microbrews on tap.

## THE BOX
*715 Harrison St. (3rd St./4th St.), (415) 206-1652*
*Th 9pm-2:30am*
The Thursday night home of funk and house, this diverse dance space is divided into two parts. In front by the entrance-way is what could be called the funk room, a small floor with a balcony overlook—for those with a superiority complex—where '70s and '80s favorites drift from the speakers. Farther into the building is the house music area, the forum for cutting-edge dance tunes, complete with a lively light system, Box dancers, and a stage for those interested in attention. If the DJ plays a song that you really love, stick around, you will probably get to hear it again.

## BRAIN WASH
*1122 Folsom St. (7th St./8th St.), (415) 861-FOOD/3663, 431-WASH/9274*
*Daily 8am-1am*
With risks come rewards: someone decided to take a chance on opening a café-Laundromat on the less-traveled edge of SoMa, leaving the rest of us to say, "Of course! Music and fabric soften-er—why didn't I think of that?" In its execution, Brain Wash simply combines both a cyber-hip café and a surfeit of washers and dryers in an industrial-design setting and attracts the sort of young, artsy crowd you'd expect. Live shows are always free, with acoustic artists on Wednesday nights and avant-jazz bands on weekends. DJs spin ambient beats on Thursday nights (Phonomat) and acid jazz on Saturday nights (Spin Cycle—get it?). Budweiser goes for $1 and premium pints run $2.50 during selected shows. Don't drink so much that you leave behind the clothes you brought here to wash.

## CADILLAC BAR AND GRILL
*325 Minna St. (off 5th St. btwn. Mission/Howard), (415) 543-8226*
*M-Th 11am-11pm; F 11am-midnight; Sa noon-midnight; Su noon-10pm*
There are times when cool and detached and ironic just don't cut it. When the loud, J. Crew-wearing, rugby-playing guy or bridge-and-tunnel, big-hair girl in all of us wants to cut loose, it's time to head for the Cadillac, where the margaritas flow liberally, the tortilla chips are free and plentiful, and the acoustics are designed so that even people standing three inches apart can't hear one another over the blaring music. The Cadillac, a Tex-Mex themed hall so large that it was clearly built before SoMa rents skyrocketed, attracts a boisterous, heavy-drinking crowd at happy hour and later on weekend nights. So what if the hipsters living in the Mission find it too Walnut Creek by half? It still beats Chevy's.

## CLUB TOWNSEND
*177 Townsend St. (2nd St./3rd St.), (415) 974-1156*
*Sa 9:30pm-7am; Su 9pm-6am*
The largest gay dance space in town, Club Townsend hosts two of the biggest SoMa weekend parties for the queer scene. (See Gay Nights sidebar for more information.) In addition, Club

Townsend holds rotating dance parties, appealing to all sexual orientations, throughout the week.

## THE COCO CLUB
*139 8th St. (entrance on Minna btwn. Mission/Howard), (415) 626-2337*
*Tu-Su 7pm-2am*

Live music and other performances are regular offerings at this cool little joint for women tucked away on one of the City's many quaint alleyways. After you enter the double doors out front, head downstairs to a cellar: it has the decor of a bar from the late '60s, complete with seashell light fixtures and deep red curtains. In addition to the acoustic singers and R&B bands who stop by for gigs, women DJs spin funky tracks nightly for an appreciative audience. Although mainly a lesbian bar, all are, and feel, welcomed. There is a cover charge for both live music and dancing.

## CONNECTICUT YANKEE
*100 Connecticut St. (17th St.), (415) 552-4440*
*Daily 11am-2am*

Don't be fooled by the name: this Potrero Hill bar/restaurant is strictly about Boston sports. It's also a friendly neighborhood gathering place and, during football season, a haven for rabid Niners fans. However, on certain afternoons (such as when the Patriots, Red Sox, Celtics, Bruins, or UMass college basketball are on), the place gets taken over by beefy, red-faced New Englanders who talk funny, drink a lot, and scream at the TV. (Pandemonium can ensue: when the Sox lost four straight to Cleveland in the 1995 playoffs, the bar's residential neighbors complained about the noise and the spectacle of inebriated men weeping openly and group-hugging in the middle of 17th Street.) The bartenders and wait staff are very friendly, and if no one else is watching TV, the manager will gladly point the satellite dish in any direction you desire. There's even a heated patio out back to while away those sunny-but-windy afternoons. During Sunday brunch the bar serves superb Bloody Marys, the real reason most of the neighborhood crowd is here. There are plenty of good "bee-ahs" to choose from, too.

## DNA LOUNGE
*375 11th St. (Harrison/Folsom), (415) 626-1409*
*Hours depend on events; doors open at 9pm, shows start at 10pm*

How you feel about SoMa—whether you love it or hate it—depends a lot on how you feel about the 11th Street Scene, the nightclub ghetto between Folsom and Harrison that, on weekends at least, is a cacophony of nubile girls and studly boys who only know the word *party* as a verb. The DNA, a blacklit warehouse space that features a large stage, a horseshoe bar, and a recently remodeled perimeter balcony, is the epitome of that scene. Nakedly catering to the East Bay bridge-and-tunnel crowd with '70s cover bands like Grooveline (the erstwhile Friday-night house band), the management occasionally remembers the club's roots as an industrial hangout and invites edgy rock groups in for a show. The cover charge on weekends runs about $10, and drinks aren't cheap either. Rest assured, however, that all the A-list folks end up here one time or another, from the Artist Formerly Known as Prince to the Former Mayor again known as Frank Jordan.

## EDDIE RICKENBACKER'S
*133 2nd St. (Mission/Howard), (415) 543-3498*
*Daily 11am-2am*

Spacious, with wood-paneled walls and marble tops—the very definition of ornate—Rickenbacker's looks like the type of place Al Capone and his cronies would have hung out in if it had been in Chicago. But it's in San Francisco, so there are oddly endearing decorative touches like custom motorcycles hanging from the ceiling and a model train that regularly takes a trip around the perimeter of the room, far above the madding crowd of Financial District suits and SoMa cyberkids. Anchor, Bass, and Sierra are among the beers on tap. Happy hour here is an embarrassment of riches: a generous, varied collection of appetizers is brought to each table free of charge. If you hang around long enough you can almost make a meal out of it. Rest assured, though, that full meals are also available.

## ELEVEN
*374 11th St. (Folsom/Harrison), (415) 431-3337*
*M-Sa 5:30pm-2am*

Across the street from Slim's and the DNA Lounge, this classy restaurant and bar is at the heart of the SoMa nightclub scene. Once through the white, glass-paned double doors, you'll be surprised by Eleven's spaciousness. The interior is open to the roof, with large papier-mâché gold stars suspended from the rafters. The Tuscan villa decor has warm gold-and-green sponge-painted walls, while wrought-iron banisters and accents give it a crisp, urban feel. The fully stocked bar offers a respectable selection—inscribed in wax crayon on the back mirror—of wines by the glass. There's also a good selection of draft beers, including Gordon Biersch, Sam Adams, and Guinness. The upstairs stage overlooks the bar, and the nightly live music ranges from jazz to rockabilly folk. This place—and its hip, flashy crowd—really jams, but be forewarned: the music is loud, and when the space hits its 200-person capacity, it's all you can do to hear your companions. There is a cover charge of $5 on weekends for nondiners.

## ENDUP
*401 6th St. (Harrison), (415) 357-0827*
*Hours vary with events*

A publication circulating through the local area for the past few years is entitled, *I Found God at the Endup*. True to its name, after a long nights' clubbing, when there is no place left to go, this is your place to Endup. Open almost all the time during the weekend, with different parties seemingly every few hours, including the infamous Saturday-night G Spot and Sunday Tea Dance—call their phone line for details. Huge space with an outdoor patio.

## HOLE IN THE WALL
*289 8th St. (Howard/Folsom), (415) 431-4695*
*Tu-Th noon-2am; F-M 6am-2am*

A passerby glancing inside this bar, better known to its regulars as Hole in the A**, would be hard-pressed to conclude it was anything but the dwelling of hard-core, leather-chewin', tobacco-spittin' male homosexuals expressing their raunchiest thoughts to one another both verbally and physically. Pool tables and pinball machines are available for the patrons' playing pleasures, but this crowd seems more interested in other ways to pass the time. No wonder the pool table is covered by hairy bottoms, and the pinball machine is merely used as good back support for all that bumpin' and grindin'. Go clad in leather and get free beverages! Wear clothes and get free gropes on the behind! The bartenders are rough, the music rougher, and the very back of the room is the roughest of all. Go but hold on!

### Hotel Utah Saloon
*500 4th St. (Bryant), (415) 421-8308*
*M-F 11:30am-2am; Sa-Su 6pm-2am*

This old-fashioned bilevel bar still carries a hint of Wild West decor. But these days there's no hint of a cowboy, or a hotel, or Utah anywhere. Instead, you've got just bartenders behind a massive mahogany bar serving up good microbrewed pints, along with such delicious pub fare as vegetarian chili, chips, and spicy salsa. The small, creaky stage, which perfectly fits the intimacy of the place, hosts a wide variety of live acts—rock, pop, punk, country bands, and acoustic singer-songwriters. The cover charge is almost never more than $5, and open-mike Mondays, when the local talent often surpasses signed acts, are free. Use the quarters you save for the Buzz Ball machine, which dispenses chocolate-covered espresso beans.

### House of Shields
*39 New Montgomery St. (Market/Mission), (415) 392-7732*
*Daily 11am-10pm*

The beautifully refurbished House of Shields, established in 1908 and once called "a place for career drinkers" by an old *Chronicle* columnist, is a traditional saloon that is guaranteed to bring on a wave of nostalgia for a bygone time. Featuring a massive Brunswick bar (the oldest in the city) as its centerpiece, with a high molded ceiling, lacquered wooden booths, and deer and bulls heads mounted on walls decked with graceful columns, the clubby setting is a magnet for Financial District types. There is more intimate balcony seating in the back, and pub food is served in the afternoons. Due to its downtown location and popularity among local workers, the bar gets packed around 6 and winds down before 9, so get here early to imbibe, but don't expect any happy hour specials. Feel fortunate just to be here, and worry some other time about the extra you're spending on drinks.

### Infusion
*555 2nd St. (Bryant/Brannan), (415) 543-2282*
*M-F 11:30am-10:30pm; Th-Sa 11:30am-2am*

Down the block from the Capp Street art gallery and across the street from South Park, the heart of Multimedia Gulch, Infusion attracts a diverse crowd of artists, executives, hipsters, and young professionals. By early evening, this place is three deep at the bar, packed with a crowd that's both friendly and casual. The long bar down the left side of the room serves the house specialty, Skyy vodka infused with a variety of flavors. The infused hype is undeniably big, but ordering a Bombay Sapphire martini is highly recommended. Infusion serves decent Euro-bistro meals at lunch and dinner, so one of the best ways to experience the scene fully is to gather seven or eight of your friends in the large round booth at the end of the room and order plates of fried calamari, garlic fries, and buffalo wings along with a round of Guinness. If you're here Thursday through Saturday starting '9:30, you can catch eclectic live music, from jazz to blues to acoustic rock. No cover charge.

## JELLY'S

*295 China Basin St. (off Mission Rock), (415) 495-3099*
*Club hours vary; lunch M-F 11:30am-2:30pm; Sa-Su 10am-3pm*

Jelly's, a diamond-in-the-rough club on the outskirts of the city at Pier 50, offers a great view of the city skyline, an outdoor patio overlooking the water, and a loud, pumping, dance-oriented ambience. It's primarily a party-for-rental hot spot, so the events change weekly, but the Sunday salsa jam can be counted on for a serious swing, and on the last Friday of every month the TamTam Queen rocks the house with African soukous, samba, soca, reggae, salsa, and merengue. If you catch wind that SpinCycle Productions is throwing one of their legendary party jams, don't miss it. The crowd changes depending upon the party but tends to be multicultural, open, and friendly. No matter what the night, there's always good music, great margaritas, and a good wine and beer selection.

## JULIE'S SUPPER CLUB

*1123 Folsom St. (7th St./8th St.), (415) 861-0707*
*Daily 5pm-2am*

Julie Ring's landmark restaurant was not only one of the first SoMa hot spots, but also the center of the supper club revival phenomenon. Years later, this remains a popular place with those who were here when the scene started, as well as with recently legal-to-drink East Bay and South Bay clubbers. The decor and the atmosphere of the bar and main dining space is Jetsons–Space Age meets '50s diner, with a back room done up in an aquatic motif. Weekdays attract the typical SoMa types looking for a quick drink before heading to the latest digital/art/poetry happening. A small corner sound stage hosts live music on weekends (mostly jazz and swing), when the place starts to jump and revelers begin to make room for dancing. Unless you're just drinking, reservations are recommended for Fridays and Saturdays. As there is nothing like Julie's in most other parts of the country, this is a great place to take your less-sophisticated out-of-town friends. Trendy, sure, but Julie's Supper Club started the trend.

## KATE O'BRIEN'S

*579 Howard St. (1st St./2nd St.), (415) 882-7240*
*Daily 10am-2am*

Sometimes it seems like every last neighborhood in the city has at least one Irish bar, and Kate O'Brien's is "north" SoMa's entry. This classic smoky Irish pub has brick-and-green wainscotted walls adorned with mirrors and black-and-white photographs and high ceilings covered with Irish rock posters (those with keen eyes can spot one featuring owner-partner Colette). Old-country memorabilia mixed with Americana (think washtubs with escaping Barbie Dolls) lies around the imported bar. The mostly Irish bartenders serve drafts to groups of young Irishmen buying one another rounds of Guinness, throwing in a bit of Celtic sarcasm with each order, and to the mingling multimedia types endemic to the neighborhood. Open from lunch until late night, Kate's dishes up hearty pub food, including outstanding fish-and-chips, bangers and eggs, and black-and-white-pudding thin-crust pizza. Come for Sunday brunch when there's a traditional Irish breakfast, a free glass of mimosa, and the sounds of a live blues band. Upstairs is available for private parties, plus the increasingly popular Club Ri Ra (DJs and dancing) moves into the space on most weekends. Fridays are usually mobbed, while Sunday evenings have been taken up with impromptu bagpipe performances.

## LILO LOUNGE
*1469 18th St. (Connecticut), (415) 643-5678*
*Daily 5pm-2am*

Lilo is the spot to go when you want to take an island vacation without leaving the comforts of the City. Choose from an excellent selection of alcohol, admire the furniture design, and sit among a *très* cool crowd, all while soaking up the funky tropical atmosphere. Piña coladas advertise themselves as "the best in town," and while they are tasty, it is advisable to order an additional shot of rum on the side. Good Mai Tais and superlative Blue Hawaiians are just a few of the specialty drinks. Dine from the excellent Thai food available at the adjoining restaurant; the full menu is served in the bar. Unfortunately, service is needlessly clumsy: drinks and food must be ordered from different staffs and are paid separately as well, even when you use a credit card. The mixed-metaphor decor still suggests the former Indian restaurant, with various elements of the tropics. The clientele swathed primarily in black, however, is a reminder that this ain't the South Pacific.

## M + M TAVERN
*198 5th St. (Howard), (415) 541-9069*
*Daily 11am-midnight*

If you're interested in finding out tomorrow's headlines, this is the place. A hangout of the late, great Herb Caen, this watering hole still attracts an ink-stained crowd of *Examiner* and *Chronicle* staffers who toil at the other end of the block. You can instantly tell from the newspapers mounted on the walls and beneath the glass tabletops that this place caters to reporters, although in its earlier days it was more of a dive. Management remodeled the space a few years back, setting off grumbling among the regulars, who compared it to wallpapering the Sistine Chapel. The new interior features a blond wood bar, painted yellow walls, and stool-high rectangular tables. To match the new decor, the bar crowd is mostly smartly dressed professionals.

## MARITIME HALL
*450 Harrison St. (1st St.), (415) 974-0634*
*Open for performances only*
## MARITIME BAR & GRILL
*375 1st St. (Harrison), (415) 974-0634*
*Daily 10am-6pm, evening hours depend on events*

Just like the name promises, the Maritime Hall is a big room and the only place in town to bring in slightly more eclectic artists than the white rock bands booked by the Warfield and the Fillmore. For example, many of reggae's biggest names (Eek-a-Mouse, Burning Spear, and the like) have wowed the crowds here. The Maritime has also brought in electronic-jazz artist Jean-Luc Ponty, country legend Willie Nelson, and even the reborn ELO! One downside to this otherwise welcome alternative is that the staff can be somewhat disorganized, possibly because they are largely volunteer. The Bar and Grill, a cramped basement level space around the corner on First Street, is where the popular Labyrinth and So What dance nights (Fridays and Saturdays, respectively) have now moved. One dollar beers are served up there during happy hour (8 to 9pm). The Grill is open until 8pm on show nights.

## MARS CAFÉ
*798 Brannan St. (7th St.), (415) 621-6277*
*M-F 4pm-2am; Sa 5pm-2am*

You can spot Mars Café by its completely red exterior anchored by large metal doors—a spot of color in an otherwise drab gray sea of warehouses. Opened by a former bartender from Julie's Supper Club, the Mars crowd has the feel of a techno-hip gathering. Bartenders serve with the panache of party hosts. The small main space has cozy, bright leather booths and comfortable bar stools. There is a perfect selection of top-shelf alcohol and a nice array of local beers on tap. Appetizer and dinner menus are served quickly, with awesome French fries being the must-have choice. Late nights sometimes feature a DJ, and although there is little room for dancing, the with-it crowd enthusiastically responds. The hectic, festive atmosphere seems to convince everyone to have that one extra drink and abandon the idea of intimate conversation. In fact, the noise encourages very loud talking, which makes for terrific eavesdropping for anyone in the multimedia industry.

## MISSION ROCK RESORT
*817 China Basin St. (Mariposa/3rd St.), (415) 621-5538*
*Hours vary, generally 7am-sunset*

Don't let the name get your blue blood pumping too fast: "resort" should be taken here as a figure of speech, since this well-weathered, multidecked waterfront dive is the clear antithesis of the word's stereotype. Dock workers, Mission residents, black leather, and Tevas all lounge here together on what-it's-cool-kick-back-and-enjoy afternoons. The downstairs bar blends into the open short-order cook grill (serving up cheap burger food on plastic plates), so customers tend to gather up their choices and then wander outside with their fries and beers, plunking themselves on one of a variety of mismatched chairs on the main or upper deck. Pinball machines and a not-usually-working mechanical pony round out the self-entertainment. On a sunny weekend, facing the industrial waterfront while seated under a faded umbrella and listening to the live Latin band, you feel as casual as you could in your own backyard. Pigeons stroll the railings, occasionally hopping on your table to investigate the beer pitchers and plastic tumblers. In addition to monitoring the birds, keep alert for great gusts of wind and dancing between the tables. Drink quality and availability vary by the day, and wait service is only possible if you can actually find a waiter.

In fact, the staff embodies the come-as-you-are atmosphere. Open until the sun sets, approximately.

## PARADISE LOUNGE
## TRANSMISSION THEATER
*1501 Folsom St. (11th St.), (415) 861-6906*
*Daily 3pm-2am; doors open for shows at 9pm, bands start about 9:30pm*

The Paradise is more like a house than a lounge, what with its numerous "spaces" separated by walls: the bar, the multiple performance stages, and the dark drinking corners. Six nights a week, a young, with-it crowd shows up to check out hip local bands and esoteric national acts, from grungy rock to country twang (although the emphasis is certainly on the former). Right next door, connected by a short hallway, is an additional warehouse-sized room called Transmission Theater. With its sprawling wooden floor, the Transmission looks like it should be hosting a square dance, but the art videos on large screens hanging from two of the walls betray the experimental, eclectic nature of the acts that play/perform here. Don't miss the craziness that ensues when Incredibly Strange Wrestling makes its occasional stop. The upper-loft area faces 11th Street, and is a good place to relax. During happy hour, which runs from 3 to 8pm, well drinks are $3.25, beers are $3; look for the occasional special offering $2 domestic beers.

## THE POWERHOUSE
*1347 Folsom St. (9th St./10th St.), (415) 552-8689*
*Daily 10pm-2am*

Known to be "diva free," The Powerhouse, open from just 10pm to 2am, certainly lives up to that reputation: nothing but hardcore, rough-looking guys for days. A cozy space with a dark upper-level dance floor and a mirrored wall for those who'd rather watch themselves feel the beat—and watch it happen. Most of the music played is of the alternative-'80s variety. Pinball and videos offer additional entertainment.

## THE RAMP
*855 China Basin St. (Mariposa/3rd St.), (415) 621-2378*
*Hours vary, late on Fridays*

When the sun has come up and the nightlife has yet to wind down, The Ramp is hangover paradise: a kaleidoscope of umbrellas shade wooden waterfront tables, the smell of jumbo omelets and burgers fills the air, and bustling waiters quickly serve spicy Bloody Marys and screwdrivers. Open late spring through early fall, the bar fills quickly with every conceivable type of urban dweller looking to soak up some sun in a congenial atmosphere. A thatched bandstand with strings of multicolored tiki-head lights awaits the afternoon live R&B or salsa combo. Once the band kicks into gear, the atmosphere is pure outdoor block party. Women in impossibly high mules intricately grind around their partners, making the men look like salsa masters. The rhythmically challenged, emboldened by sun and beer, join the dance party, creating moves that gain applause for their pure enthusiasm. The indoor bar gets slammed, and late afternoons regularly include a wait for tables. Recommendation: arrive early, claim your spot, put on some sunscreen, and settle in for a day-long party.

## Gay Dance Nights

### LITTERBOX (AT CATS GRILL AND ALLEY CLUB)
*1190 Folsom St. (7th St./8th St.), (415) 431-3332*
*F 10pm-3am, $6 cover*

Here's a place that seems to have (so far, anyway) avoided the death spiral that too many of the City's gay and lesbian bars have experienced. That's probably due to the variety of people continually making their way into the place. It's also credit to the DJ who's funkin' it up one minute, then flipping to that grunge thing the next. (What a way to keep everybody happy!) But let's talk about the crowd: once the main venue of the sisters, Litterbox is now the playpen of the males, as is often the case with bars in this town that are initially frequented by women. Regardless of which gender is more numerous, people are here to let loose. Dance on the bar, dance on the platform next to the DJ booth, or dance on the large stage with the enthusiastic booty shakers—but for goodness sake, *dance*! Be sure also to check out the small platform, complete with exotic go-go dancers, next to the entrance to the bar, while the area behind the stage is chock-full of groovin' clientele. A lounging space is available down the corridor, and there are various bars throughout, including one for coffee and espresso. The food menu consists of burgers and fries and various other fast foods.

### FAG FRIDAYS (AT THE ENDUP)
*401 6th St. (Harrison), (415) 487-6277*
*F 10pm-2am, $6 cover*

If you want the big club atmosphere in a small space, then this place may be the answer—at least for some folks. Granted, there's that club that rhymes with unitard, complete with all the attitude and beefcake you could stand, but this particular space is a bit more relaxed and neighborly. The crowd ranges from club, skater, and grunge boys to older men and sugar daddies, from the very attractive to the very average looking. There's also the rhythmless nation of beefy boys that do what they call go-go dancing on the stages by the bar. Although the DJs can be uncreative and the music mundane, just lick those tabs and down that booze (like your fellow club goers seem to be doing) and *voilà*! Enchantment! The drugged and the outdoor enthusiasts alike will appreciate the enclosed patio complete with trees, a faux Niagara Falls, and a raised deck.

### TRANNYSHACK (AT THE STUD)
*399 9th St. (Harrison), (415) 252-STUD/7883*
*Tu 9pm-2am, $5 cover*

You never know what to expect when you explore the further reaches of transvestitism, which makes Trannyshack worth a visit. The highlights of the evening are the performances by the resident trannies: these guys-gals (or gals-guys) lip-synch to every song under the sun, and pull it off well. The place gets quickly packed with a crowd that's extremely festive. Just beware of the wandering faux divas, looking for fun anywhere they can get it! If you're not the kind to get into this sort of thing, and were dragged (pardon the pun) here by a friend, the front of the bar provides refuge in the form of a pool table and pinball machines. Still, we guarantee that the unenthused will be pulled away from that pool cue for a glance at the goings-on in the other room. After the main event, the DJ spins all sorts of ditties, ranging from industrial to funky. Come in drag and get a discount on both admission *and* drinks.

### ANTHEM (AT 1015 FOLSOM)
*1015 Folsom St. (6th St./7th St), (415) 431-1200, events; (415) 431-0700, office*
*Th 11pm-6am, $7 cover; free before 11:30 with flyer*

This large space has been through some serious changes over the last few years, and it's still experiencing a bit of a metamorphosis. After entering the club, the first room is vaguely themed—the early,

early '80s funky rhythm-and-blues room, perhaps? The DJ *wants* to entertain but just can't quite hit the proverbial nail on the head. Maybe he should take a few lessons from the DJ in the other, larger room. Now *there* is a hardcore spin—and mix—master. The music is extremely clubby, with some funk thrown in (these grooves can be tribal). This larger room sports a big main stage, tiny dance platforms, an enormous round lighting system suspended from the ceiling, and an extravagant sound system. It's all rather impressive. There's also a downstairs space complete with a DJ spinning funky grooves, plus an upstairs room with a balcony that's open on occasion. For your convenience, an ATM machine on the premises dispenses cash (a way to keep the crowd juiced up, perhaps?), but be prepared for a $2 service charge to use it. And lastly, let us not forget the clientele: one cup bridge and tunnel, two tablespoons SF, and a dash of club kid-dom!

### Junk (at The Stud)
*399 9th St. (Harrison), (415) 252-STUD/7883*
*Every 4th Sa, $5 cover*

It's refreshing to know that there is at least one place in the City that hip lesbians can call their own—at least for now—where a bouncerette and a doorWOman are on the staff. This night attracts women from ruffian bald gals to voluptuous divas, with the obligatory gay boys delighted by the lack of testosterone and abundance of good fun. The DJ plays heavy metal, mega-funk, and more, so please go to the dance floor to see the many folks groovin'. What a great time one finds here, plus the folks are nice and cool to boot.

### Club Universe
### Pleasuredome
### Club Q
### (at Club Townsend)
*177 Townsend St. (2nd St./3rd St.), (415) 974-6020 events, (415) 974-1156 office*
*First F of month 9pm-whenever, $7 cover; Sa 9:30pm-7am, $10; Su 9pm-6am, $10*

One of the largest dance spaces in town, Club Townsend hosts two of the biggest weekend parties in SoMa for the queer scene. Club Universe is the Saturday party, running 9:30pm-7am. Once a diverse haven of joy for gay, bisexual, and straight-clubbing San Franciscans, the atmosphere has been transformed into the strictly gay male genre, complete with snobbery and shirtless beef boys. Any time a space has the nickname Club Unitard, watch out! More attractive aspects include intense lighting and music and the fact that there's practically a different theme every week, clearly a plus when trying to attract clubbers with a nanosecond attention span. Try and catch a big-name performer here sometime; it can be rather festive. Pleasuredome takes the floor on Sundays. Pleasuredome's front dance bar caters to the "boy"-ish crowd with house music and smart drinks. Traveling through the black-Lycra time tunnel leads to the back dance bar, which sports a spinning, mirrored ball and moustaches. (Need we say more?) In addition, on the first Friday of every month, the space becomes Club Q, the infamous women's dance party featuring lesbians who can dance, flirt, take your breath away, and break your heart all at once. The cover charge is steep (usually around $10), so it pays to pick up some free passes—good only before 10 or 11pm—available around the Castro by day. The same passes are occasionally published in the gay papers, so start clipping those coupons. (Savvy clubbers slip in and out before 11pm to get their hands stamped and then return at a more fashionable hour.)

## RAWHIDE II

*280 7th St. (Howard/Folsom), (415) 621-1197*
*M-Th 4pm-2am; F-Su noon-2am*

The Rawhide is a unique experience: country-western dancing for gays and lesbians in one of the friendliest venues in any city. Formal dancing is the mode, mostly two-step with a dose of line dancing, plus the occasional waltz to spice things up. Pair after pair of cowboys spin 'round, while lesbian couples promenade in the sweetheart pose. If seeing a packed and fanatically loyal crowd dancing the two-step to plaintive country music doesn't melt your (cheatin') heart, nothing will. The club also offers two-step lessons gratis in the hours before the bar gets heavily populated (usually around 7pm). Showing up for a lesson is well worth it, and then be sure to stick around for the fun. Wear your cowboy boots (or at least leather-soled shoes) and be prepared to dance, because the Rawhide is about the only place in this or any other universe where total strangers will mosey right on up and ask to escort you out on the floor. The answer had better be yes. A $5 cover on weekend nights gets you in the door and includes a drink token.

## SEA STAR CLUB

*2289 3rd St. (20th St.), (415) 552-9144*
*M-F 5pm-whenever customers leave; Sa-Su hours depend on customers*

In the old days, bars on this side of town were filled with sailors and dockers. Today, their business still relies on seasonal ship dockings, so most nights they remain empty. The Sea Star Club is typical of such dives. A true mom-and-pop operation, the owners-bartenders delight in greeting patrons. They serve bottled beers only, and make a mean, cheap mixed drink. "Mom" also dishes up inexpensive pot stickers with awesomely fiery hot sauce. There is a long bar down the narrow room and no tables. The back area features 75-cent pool, usually with no waiting for a game. An eclectic jukebox plays a smattering of funkadelic, pop, and country. The men's bathroom has a freestanding ashtray, in homage to the days before those pesky secondhand smoke studies. In the ultimate case of strange bedfellows, regulars from the nearby piers mix with neighborhood software developers from the local warehouse-lofts-turned-office-space. However you earn a living, this is a good group hangout for a kick-back-and-have-a-cold-one type of evening.

## SILVER CREST DONUT SHOP, RESTAURANT & BAR

*340 Bayshore Blvd. (Oakdale/Cortland), (415) 826-0753*
*Open 24 hours*

A neon sign on the front of this no-nonsense spot glows We Never Close, so it's an unfortunate irony that the neon martini glass above it has shorted out. As you pass by the restaurant booths and doughnut displays on your way to the back bar, you might imagine the Silver Crest as the inspiration for Edward Hopper's "Nighthawks at the Diner." Beer choices are limited to bottled Coors and Budweiser. A pool table dominates half the room, and the decor is strictly wood panel/linoleum/beer-poster babes. The road-weary regulars seem to sink in their stools. The generous bartender pulls additional duties as the doughnut pusher out front and greasy-spoon hash slinger in back. He's even been known to pour an occasional complimentary Ouzo shot. The perfect antidote for the jaded bar scenester, the Silver Crest is unlike any other in San Francisco. If Tom Waits munched jelly-filleds with his beer and cigarettes, this would be his haunt.

## SLIM'S
*333 11th St. (Folsom/Harrison), (415) 522-0333*
*Open for performances only*

A big-time venue for live music, Slim's (part-owned by singer Boz Scaggs) is a large, airy space that hosts a wide variety of performances, mostly rock but also blues, country, and mainstream hip-hop and ska. When a nationally known act comes here it's usually SRO on the expansive floor, which means those stuck behind one of the numerous support columns are SOL. A larger problem is that the space is completely lacking in intimacy. The high ceiling muddles the sound, which makes the already-distracted crowd even less attentive, which often makes for an unsatisfying concert experience. It also doesn't help matters that drinks are ridiculously overpriced, and the staff can be very curt and businesslike. To escape the scene, head for the non-smoking balcony. Even with a two-drink minimum "penalty" for sitting there, it's a good place to see the gig and eat the greasy bar food.

## THE SOUND FACTORY
*525 Harrison St. (1st St./2nd St.), (415) 243-9646*
*Th 10pm-2am; F 9:30pm-6am; Sa 9:30pm-4am*

The Sound Factory, right near the entrance to the Bay Bridge, is a massive dance warehouse divided into several rooms each color coded by theme. The music varies depending on the night and the event, but the spectrum runs from near-Top 40 mainstream (for the bridge-and-tunnel crowd) to the rave-influenced house-jungle-ambient beats (for the psychedelic-shirts-and-baggy-pants crowd). All the rooms have a bar so thirst will never be an issue. They also have a thankfully efficient and reliable coat-check room—important because you'll work up a sweat dancing and freeze when you go outside in the chilly late-night air. Call ahead to check for special events or to find out which DJ will be appearing.

## SOUTH BEACH BILLIARDS
*270 Brannan St. (1st St./2nd St.), (415) 495-5939*
*M-F noon-2am; Sa-Su 2pm-2am*

Now *this* is the cool, understated atmosphere you'd expect from a South Park pool hall patronized by the denizens of Multimedia Gulch. The huge, functional space is decorated with rotating artwork from Bay Area artists and is packed full of pool tables for hire by the hour, as well as a bocce court for the internationally inclined seeking a change of pace. The bar has a wonderful selection of refreshments and snacks and a standard selection of beer, wine, mixed drinks, plus Weidmann's pear cider, that fermented beverage that packs a punch. Come early with your cronies if you plan to play—happy hour is prime time for prime table choices. The clientele is a focused crowd—intent on their game and their group of friends, not much for mixing and matching. But for a game of pool, it's cool.

## THE STUD
*399 9th St. (Harrison), (415) 252-STUD/7883*
*Daily 5pm-2am*

A veritable old-timer as far as clubs go, the Stud provides music for all types of crowds, seven days a week. There are a few pinball machines and pool tables in the front room, with a full bar running along one wall and a narrow counter with stools along the other. Small strings of white lights glow overhead, and there's even a model train circling the room near the ceiling. This is not a place to sit and mingle, as all socializing is done on the dance floor with music provided by a DJ. Monday night, so jam-packed you think it's Friday, is heavy funk and soul. There's no cover charge, and it's hot enough that a T-shirt on top is more than enough. The crowd is primarily black and hispanic gay men, with a few whites and straights mixed in. Tuesday is Tranny Shack—transvestite and transsexual night. Come in your best pumps and don't forget your mink. (Now all you drag kings, don't feel excluded; bring a date.) Drinks are discounted for those "dressed" and make-up counts! Wednesday is equally crowded for Oldies night (i.e., '70s), with a $1 admission for students and military personnel (show ID). This is primarily a collegiate crowd, and beers are $1.50 all night. Thursday is Vibe, and Friday is Club Confession—funk, industrial, soul, disco, and no attitude. Finally, Saturday is Lowrider night until 3am. A mix of queer boy and girl ruffians with some other folks dance to trip-hop/industrial. Check out the fun-and-freaky apple-red light on the south wall, and please be patient with the new-to-their-profession bartenders.

## THE THIRSTY BEAR
*661 Howard St. (New Montgomery/3rd St.), (415) 974-0905*
*M-Th 11:30am-11pm; F-Su 11:30am-1am*

Yet another microbrewery aimed at young, up-and-coming, after-work drinkers from the Financial District. All that saves the Bear from "been there, done that" status is the Spanish twist to the menu and a couple of pretty decent brews. Don't look for Spain in the decor or atmosphere: with the exception of the long, beautiful burled-maple bar, the place is self-consciously sterile and overly spacious. Bar seating includes high stools clustered around small tables from which you can order anything on the restaurant menu. The tapas are unusual and tasty, but small for the price; try the *kokotchas* (fish cheeks) or a plate of *fruta* with a home-brewed barley wine for a sweet finish. As for beer, the bartender recommends the ESB, the Lorca Ruby is interesting, the stout very acceptable, and the ales mostly unremarkable. Fridays and Saturdays are amateur drinker nights; try Thursdays for a more sophisticated crew.

## 330 RITCH STREET
*330 Ritch St. (off Townsend btwn. 3rd St./4th St.), (415) 541-9574*
*W-Su 5pm-2am*

Although the main room is small, with a tiny dance floor and an even tinier bar, 330 Ritch is always tightly packed. A good night may draw hundreds of folks for a hot, sweaty, see-and-be-seen affair. Chrome tables and maroon-painted wooden folding chairs ring the dance floor and give a chic, urban look to the interior's exposed brick and hewn beams. Do it up right here: go during happy hour (Wednesdays to Saturdays 6 to 8pm, Fridays 5 to 8pm) and order two-for-one Cosmopolitans; the Aussie bartender is happy to put two in one glass if you're drinking with a friend who prefers wine. The bar has live music and DJs Wednesdays through Saturdays, with a different scene each night until 2am. Wednesday is Swing Night, with free dance lessons and that big band sound beginning at 8:30pm. Thursday is Popscene, with Britpop and indie music and its mod followers. Friday is TGIF, with all-out disco funk and DJs spinning the classics of the '70s and '80s. On Saturday, 330 Ritch returns to its steamy roots with Tu Pueblo, the club's original salsa and Latin jazz evening. Free salsa lessons begin at 8:30pm. The cover charge varies but expect a $5 minimum (it's free before 10pm).

### TROCADERO

*520 4th St. (Bryant/Brannan), (415) 495-6620*
*Hours depend on nightly events*

Sure, the Trocadero is enormous, with a main dancing area the size of an airplane hangar and an upper level bigger than some other clubs. And yeah, Neil Young did drop by here once for an unannounced gig. And, okay, in the fly-by-night world of dance clubs, the longevity of this place, once one of the City's premier gay nightspots, is impressive. But what truly distinguishes the Trocadero is the Wednesday night mainstay known as Bondage-a-Go-Go. Advertised as San Francisco's Longest Running Fetish Party, it features amateur S&M—chips, dips, chains, and whips—and draws a wildly diverse crowd of participants and observers, although you'll be surprised which side some of the people fall on. (That woman from the suburbs who arrives wearing a business suit may be a dominatrix by the end of the evening.) During the comparatively tame rest of the week, alternative and techno dance beats are *de rigueur*, and industrial-goth bands often play live.

### TWENTY TANK BREWERY

*316 11th St. (Harrison/Folsom), (415) 255-9455*
*Su-Th 11:30am-1am; F-Sa 11:30am-1:30am*

You'd think this huge bilevel beer hall had been around forever, what with its sawdust-covered floors and pressed-tin ceiling, but actually the Twenty Tank is a relative newcomer created by the folks behind Berkeley's Triple Rock and Jupiter. It's a good place to use as a jumping-off point for an evening at such nearby clubs as Slim's or the DNA Lounge. Slightly hipper than your average brew pub, it's popular with young flannel-clad single types, who like to sit at one of the large round tables with a group of friends, a couple of pitchers, and a bunch of appetizers. Select from six different microbrews, such as Kinnikinick Ale or the new, cleverly titled Holstein Heifer-weizen (sure to redefine the term *cow tipping*). If you're restless, you can play shuffleboard, watch sports on TV, or check out the brewing equipment that sits behind glass walls. The food—nachos, sandwiches, chili—is good and you get plenty of it. This is an excellent place to scope out the hip SoMa scene, especially during prime-time drinking hours when San Francisco's biker barflies come out to play.

## Late Night Eats

### ALL STAR DONUTS ¢/$
*399 5th St. (Harrison), (415) 882-0889*
*Daily 24 hours*
This little shack near a freeway off-ramp serves donuts, burgers, and teriyaki to neighborhood scenesters and crackheads alike.

### CHAT HOUSE $
*139 8th St. (at Minna, btwn. Mission and Howard), (415) 751-6204*
*M-Tu 8am-9pm; W-F 8am-1am; Sa 10am-1am; Su 10:30am-midnight*
Upstairs from the CoCo Club, this pretty café bedecked with bright wall murals offers small, casual meals and tasty coffee to keep you going on a lengthy SoMa frolic.

### ELEVEN RISTORANTE & BAR $$
*374 11th St. (Folsom/Harrison), (415) 431-3337*
*Tu-Su 11am-midnight*
See bar listing.

### 42 DEGREES $$$
*235 16th St. (at Illinois off 3rd St.), (415) 777-5558*
*M-Tu 11:30am-3pm; W-Sa 11:30am-3pm, 6:30-11pm*
James Moffat has turned the former Caffè Esprit into a sleek dinner spot serving California comfort food along with jazz music until midnight. Generously portioned dinners might include roasted lamb chops heaped on celery root mashed potatoes or grilled salmon with white beans and chanterelle mushrooms. Grazers can pick from tapas-sized chalkboard specials such as herb-roasted potatoes with aioli or a charcuterie plate.

### HAMBURGER MARY'S $
*1582 Folsom St. (12th St.), (415) 626-1985*
*M-Th 11:30am-1:15am; F 11:30am-1:15am; Sa 10am-1:15am; Su 10am-12:15am*
This SoMa institution is perfect for a quick meal before hitting the clubs. Not surprisingly, burgers (choose from beef or tofu) are the house specialty. You can also get breakfast all day long. The atmosphere is cluttered junk collector, the patrons are fascinating to watch, and the home fries are deliciously spicy.

### HAPPY DONUTS ¢
*761 3rd St. (Townsend/King), (415) 543-1407*
*Daily 24 hours*
The place to go if you're looking for a fresh-out-of-the-oven donut, cinnamon roll, or croissant. It's the safest place in town, too, given that there's probably at least one police officer there at any given moment.

### HAWTHORNE LANE $$$$
*22 Hawthorne St. (Howard/Folsom), (415) 777-9779*
*Bar Area: M-F 2:30pm-midnight; Sa-Su 5:30pm-midnight*
The location is highly unlikely for one of the city's most celebrated eateries: on a SoMa alley. An enormous bar area with long hours and table seating makes it easy to sample starters or order from the dining room menu. The food expands upon the East-West California cuisine the chefs developed at Postrio, from foie gras to grilled beef to halibut with cellophane noodles.

### INFUSION $$
*555 2nd St. (Bryant/Brannan), (415) 543-2282*
*Daily 11:30am-2am (late night menu till 1am on weekends)*
Infusion gets its name from a gimmick of sorts—the jars of Skyy vodka infused with different flavors, available for consumption, of course. The menu features comfort-food staples like mashed potatoes and roasted chicken, but stylized (like the vodka martinis).

### JAMES & JAMES RIBS 'N' THANGS $
*5130 3rd St. (Shafter), (415) 671-0269*
*Su-Th 8am-pm; F-Sa 8am-2am*
The sumptuous barbecue aroma that emanates from this bastion of soul food speaks for itself. Antiques and an open kitchen allow you to enjoy standard favorites like cornbread and pork ribs done perfectly in a comfy and attractive environment.

### LULU $$
*816 Folsom St. (4th St./5th St.), (415) 495-5775*
*M-Th 7-11am, 11:30am-10:30pm; F 7-11am, 11:30am-11:30pm;*
*Sa-Su 9-11am, 11:30am-11:30pm*
This grand café has captured the fancy of San Francisco's epicureans with its intriguing Mediterranean menu. The large, open dining room, done up in muted shades of blue and gray, encourages people watching. The food deserves your full attention, though, especially side dishes like olive-oil mashed potatoes and grilled asparagus with shaved Parmesan and lemon. Main dishes are equally alluring, in particular anything off the grill.

### MAX'S DINER $
*311 3rd St. (Folsom), (415) 546-MAXS/6297*
*M-Th 11am-10pm; F-Sa 11am-midnight; Su 11am-10pm*
The kind of high camp that draws a crowd in Miami Beach. The brassy, boastful menu starts with New York-style chopped liver and corned beef sandwiches and then goes ballistic with sweet-and-sour duck and pasta galore. Best to take a doggie bag for the main course to save room for Sweet Max's larger-than-life desserts. Decor is glitzy '50s diner.

### PALOMINO $$
*345 Spear St. (Harrison/Folsom), (415) 512-7400*
*M-Th 11:30am-2:30pm, 5-10pm; F 11:30am-2:30pm, 5-11pm;*
*Sa 5-11pm; Su 5-10pm (light menu served in the bar M-Th until 11pm,*
*F-Sa until midnight)*
This is a place where all the senses are stimulated: colorful Matisse reproductions and tantalizing smells from the wood-burning hearth greet you at the door; the people are friendly and the California-Mediterranean food is pretty good; and in true San Francisco style, the bay view from the slick dining room is breathtaking!

### SILVER CREST DONUT SHOP & DINER ¢/$
*340 Bayshore (Oakdale), (415) 826-0753*
*Daily 24 hours*
See bar listing.

### 20 TANK BREWERY ¢
*316 11th St. (Harrison/Folsom), (415) 255-9455*
*Su-Th 11:30am-midnight; F-Sa 11:30am-12:30am*
See bar listing.

### ¡WA-HA-KA! ¢
*1489 Folsom St. (11th St.), (415) 861-1410*
*M-W 11:30am-10pm; Th 11:30am-11pm; F-Sa 11:30am-midnight; Su 5-10pm*
This chain of taquerias exudes youthful energy, drawing hungry nighttime revelers from the surrounding bars. Bright, industrial decor sports warehouse-high ceilings, rough concrete walls and floor, mismatched wooden tables and chairs, and Mexican billboard murals. Their unique addition to the fresh-Mex scene is pretty good fish tacos. This location has the best food by far. No credit cards.

## UP & DOWN CLUB
*1151 Folsom St. (7th St./8th St.), (415) 626-2388*
*M, Th-Sa 8pm-2am*

Two separate bars under one swell name, this has been a land-mark spot for the new generation of jazz artists in the City during the 1990s—whatever one might think of the scene. The down-stairs offers a sleek bar charmed by golden walls, candlelight, and a small stage showcasing various combos six nights a week. Upstairs is more of a "gimme a beer, Mac!" joint, with sticky-in-the-heat vinyl booths and a DJ pumping loud music—generally soul, hip-hop, funk, and acid jazz—for a too-small-by-half dance floor. The attractive patrons may be a reflection of and tribute to one of the club's owners, supermodel Christy Turlington, who is known to drop in on occasion. Hey, at least it's not Cindy Crawford or Naomi Campbell just putting their names on the Fashion Café. A dinner menu is available downstairs, and upstairs or downstairs can be rented for private parties.

## ZEKE'S DIAMOND BAR AND GRILL
*600 3rd St. (Brannan), (415) 342-5311*
*M-F 11:30am-2am; Sa-Su 10:30am-2am*
*(opens at 9am for early Niners kickoffs)*

In a few years, when the Giants are finally playing baseball at China Basin and finally drawing five-digit crowds on a consistent basis, you probably won't be able to get in the door of this long-time sports bar on game days. That should be reason enough for you to spend at least part of these interim years occupying space at Zeke's. Sit at one of the bar stools or padded red booths, sip a brewski, munch on one of the hearty pub-grub offerings—quesadillas, burgers, beer-boiled Wisconsin bratwurst—and take a close look at the quirky collection of ties hanging from behind the bar. Is it any wonder that, years ago, Hunter S. Thompson was a regular? This place also has multiple TV screens, a pool table, and a motley collection of old-timers and cybergeeks.

★

To paraphrase Chico Escuela, the Latino ballplayer on the old *Saturday Night Live,* the 1990s have been very, very good to the Mission. It has gone from a downscale neighborhood of empty storefronts to one of the hippest areas in town. Indeed, an unmistakable energy ripples through here that is hard to find anywhere else in the city. It's driven in large part by the artistic- and multimedia-oriented members of that dreaded demographic, Generation X, who moved here because rents were cheap. Their presence (and disposable income) has allowed a whole series of bars and clubs to thrive, especially in the two-block radius around Valencia and 16th streets.

The flip side is that the Mission can come across as insufferably smug if you're not in the right mood. On the wrong night, everyone seems too cool for their own good—even the folks from other, less-hip parts of town who are here slumming for the evening. Still, many superb bars and clubs line these streets, all within walking distance of one another. You could spend a month's worth of nights in this 'hood and not get bored. Plus, the bars on Cortland Avenue in Bernal Heights offer a nearby, mellow respite from the crowds on Valencia.

★

### THE ALBION

*3139 16th St. (Valencia/Guerrero), (415) 552-8558*
*M-Sa 2pm-2am; Su 1pm-2am*

The Albion is dark and inviting, a small oasis on the edge of the general craziness of the Devil's Triangle (the area surrounding the 16th and Mission BART station). It's famous all over town for the neon sign above the bar, which proclaims "Service for the sick." The regulars are an unpredictable mix of bohemians, street folk, and neighborhood drunks. The draws are three pool tables and three pinball machines, happy-hour drink specials, hors d'oeuvres on Fridays (straight from Costco, along the lines of cocktail weenies and mini-quiches), and a lot of beer and cider on tap. It's your basic full-service friendly neighborhood bar much like the nearby 500 Club (as well it should be: both are owned by the same person). The main difference between the two is that while the 500 Club throws out any street people who wander in, the Albion will let them stay if they have money and don't cadge drinks. In fact, it's not uncommon to see the homeless guy you gave a dollar to on your way in sipping an icy Pabst Blue Ribbon at the bar later on—courtesy of you!

### ARABIAN NIGHTS

*811 Valencia St. (19th St./20th St.), (415) 821-9747*
*Tu-Th 6pm-11pm; F-Sa 6pm-midnight*

It's a restaurant! It's a bar! It's a museum of Arabian carpets, mural scenes, and exquisite decorations! Arabian Nights is all three at once, so when the live Middle Eastern music is blasting (which it does on Thursday, Friday, and Saturday nights), the staff belly dancer is doing her thing, and the place is packed with

# Mission
# Bernal Heights

N

GLP

Market St.

Duboce St.

36

101

14th St.

Alameda St.

15th St.

16th St.

19 11 20

BART 16th St.

16th St.

1 10 30 17

23

12

Albion

3 6

28

17th St.

17th St.

18

34

Guerrero St.

15

Mariposa St.

Valencia St.

Mission St.

Capp St.

18th St.

18th St.

31

2

26

19th St.

19th St.

Mission Dolores Park

7

4

13

21

16

20th St.

21st St.

Dolores St.

Fair Oaks St.

San Jose Ave.

South Van Ness Ave.

Shotwell St.

Folsom St.

Treat St.

Harrison St.

Alabama St.

Florida St.

Bryant St.

York St.

Hampshire St.

Potrero Ave.

5 24

22

22nd St

25

27

23rd St.

24th St.

BART 24th St.

Bartlett St.

25th St.

9

26th St

33

César Chavez / Army St.

27th St.

14

Precita Ave.

Duncan St.

28th St.

Coso Ave.

Valley St.

29th St.

32

Bernal Heights Park

Day St.

30th St.

Bocana

Wood

Andover

8

29

35

Cortland St.

8. Charlie's Club
9. Clooney's Pub
10. Dalva
11. Doctor Bombay's
12. Double Play
13. Dylan's
14. El Rio
15. Elbo Room
16. Elysium Café
17. Esta Noche
18. 500 Club
19. Jack's Elixir
20. Kilowatt
21. La Rondalla
22. Latin American Club
23. Liquid
24. Lone Palm
25. The Make-Out Room
26. McCarthy's
27. Radio Valencia
28. Rite-Spot Café
29. Skip's Tavern
30. Skylark
31. The Slow Club
32. 3300 Club
33. Tip Top Inn
34. Uptown
35. Wild Side West
36. Zeitgeist

1. The Albion
2. Arabian Nights
3. Blondie's Bar and No Grill
4. Bruno's
5. Café Babar
6. Casanova Cocktail Lounge
7. Chameleon

revelers, don't expect to be able to carry on much of a conversation, let alone a quiet one. If that isn't a problem, park yourself on one of the floor cushions and settle down for an evening of atmospheric overload, courtesy of this L-shaped room's stylish, jaw-dropping riches. Several beers are on tap, the long bar is fully stocked, and there's even a chance for couples to dance on occasion. Topping it all off, the food is superlative—delicious baba ghannoush, sumptuous rack of lamb with herbs, and excellent shish kebab. A light menu is offered during happy hour from 3pm to 8pm, served by the efficient and friendly staff.

## BLONDIE'S BAR AND NO GRILL
*540 Valencia St. (16th St./17th St.), (415) 864-2419*
*Daily 2pm-2am*

Blondie's is cool and spacious, with high ceilings, black and white tiles, French doors in front, and an enormous, highly polished bar complete with an enormous, highly polished espresso machine. A nice pool table stands at the back, and another table is tucked into a too-small alcove in the rear wall. Blondie's also has the coolest juke in the Mission for those who think jazz is where it's at. All in all, Blondie's is a really nice place to have a drink. Many other people feel this way, as the place is usually full, excepting afternoons and early evenings. There's live music with no cover (blues, jazz, and the like) on Saturday nights, and the space is always packed. Sunday nights, starting at 9pm, Blondie's charges $3 admission and becomes the popular Club Red, a dance club for women. All in all, the funky, relaxed atmosphere always makes you feel hipper the moment you walk in.

## BRUNO'S
*2389 Mission St. (19th St./20th St.), (415) 550-7455*
*Daily 6pm-2am*

Bruno's has been a Mission mainstay for ages, but since its renovation in 1995, the demographic profile has skewed to younger and hipper. Maybe that's because the place now looks like a cross between a 1960s bachelor pad and a suburban steakhouse. One-half of the place, with gorgeous rounded vinyl booths, is, in fact, a well-regarded restaurant. The other half is made up of a long bar with white Naugahyde stools and a colorfully lit lounge. There's live music six nights a week, featuring avant-jazz and various experimental combos of note (don't miss the Clubfoot Orchestra). Not surprisingly, it fills up on weekends, and if you're planning to make an evening of it (dinner and a show), reservations for the meal are absolutely essential.

## CAFÉ BABAR
*994 Guerrero St. (22nd St.), (415) 282-6789*
*Daily 5pm-2am*

The cool and stylish Café Babar is a major destination for young Mission residents. The relaxing corner bar consists of three distinct spaces: a large room painted forest green and done up in a vintage-moderne motif; an intimate, candlelit back room with slatted wooden benches; and a tiny bar space, which sports a cream-colored overhang that the pharmaceutically inclined may temporarily mistake for a large mushroom. The drink menu is limited, but at least the choices are good:

wines, ciders, sodas, and plenty of fruity or otherwise esoteric microbrews. A pool table and a photo booth supply amusement. On weekends, various DJs spin funk and acid jazz to add to the urbane mood. Babar makes a good start or finish to a 22nd Street Bohemian bar crawl.

## CASANOVA COCKTAIL LOUNGE
527 Valencia St. (16th St./17th St.), (415) 863-9328
Hours unavailable at presstime

The Casanova certainly reflects the diversity of its neighborhood. The interior is black (black bar, black walls, black stools) with Day of the Dead touches (skeleton headlights around the bar, Mexican dolls and emblems). One wall is graffito-covered corrugated metal, another is sculpted plaster. Religious candles provide mood lighting. The music choices are just as eclectic, ranging from live acid jazz to the current Tuesday night menu of country western with some blues thrown in. A black-and-white television above the bar continuously plays old films with the sound turned off. Mixed drinks served in large tumblers are a bargain at $3. There are seven beers on tap, all available by the pitcher. This is a cash-only joint, but the liquor store on the next corner will work your ATM card for a fee of 10 percent on the withdrawal. *Note:* The Casanova has recently changed ownership, and the new management has plans to re-emphasize the innovative music program from a few years ago, when the house was known for breaking in bands that went on to become fixtures in the club scene. As of August 1997, it is closed for remodeling. Watch this spot. It may well become the Next Big Thing.

## CHAMELEON
853 Valencia St. (19th St./20th St.), (415) 821-1891
Daily 11am-2am

The Chameleon feels like an older sibling of the Armadillo: bigger, hipper, wiser, and more laid-back. It has the same grunge motif but with nice added touches like the amazing collection of black-velvet art adorning the walls, an espresso machine, lots and lots of beer on tap, and a stage. Yes, they have music five nights a week, with a cover charge that's never over four bucks. And the music—garage rock with an emphasis on the first of those two words—is about what you would expect for that price in this neighborhood. Those familiar with the wacky, hand-lettered band flyers that adorn every telephone pole and mailbox in the Mission will know most of them advertise gigs here. The very best part of the Chameleon is the rec room, which is down a flight of stairs. It has an old couch, an ancient stereo with equally ancient records, and a rickety Ping-Pong table. It's the perfect place to slip away to while the band is playing and flip through the records until your turn at some serious beer pong comes up.

## CHARLIE'S CLUB
309 Cortland Ave. (Bocana), (415) 206-9367
Daily 10am-2am

The runt of the Bernal Heights litter of bars, this small pub with a tacky stone facade will appeal to enthusiasts of that anachronistic medium known as the vinyl record. Charlie's boasts a faded yellow ceiling covered with hundreds of 1970s album covers and walls cluttered with Beatles and Lou Reed memorabilia. (Charlie, the owner, is a major Lou Reed fan, and his jukebox is full of Reed, the Stooges, and their ilk.) The only other distractions are the pool table and baseball/pinball machines that swallow up most of the available floor space. Bar food is offered in the form of burritos and pizza. Monday is open mike night, and on quiet Saturday nights the bartender often has time to shoot a round of pool with the customers in between serving drinks.

## CLOONEY'S PUB
*1401 Valencia St. (25th St.), (415) 826-4988*
*Daily 8am-2am*

Back in the days when San Francisco ports were booming centers of commerce, the Mission District was studded with bars that opened at six in the morning to cater to third-shift customers. One by one, these bars gave up the practice, though many still have out-of-date signs promoting their early hours. It's good to know that some places still carry the flag: for instance, Clooney's, which opens at 8 in the morning daily. A spacious and dark bar, most of the available light is provided by neon signs advertising various permutations of Bud and Miller. Many Naugahydes gave their lives so this place could exist. And there's lots and lots of smoke. The clientele, a motley collection of stubborn old souls who have refused to leave despite the neighborhood's changing demographics, are stolidly attempting to kill themselves with Royal Gate vodka and king-size Kools. (It seems to be working, but very slowly; sundry bohemian youngsters are still in the minority here.) The old-timers are always good for a cigarette if you need to bum one, and during holidays (including the Super Bowl), the various grannies who inhabit the joint bring their crockpots, set them up on the bar, and put on the feedbag. So if you want ham for Easter but don't want to see your folks, Clooney's is the place.

## DALVA
*3121 16th St. (Valencia/Guerrero), (415) 252-7740*
*M-Th 4pm-2am; F 2pm-2am; Sa-Su 4pm-2am*

Dalva, a self-described "cocktails/jukebox/hideout" bar, is proof of two axioms: 1) Timing is everything, and 2) Location, location, location. Debuting a couple of years back, just as the 16th Street renaissance was approaching its apex, Dalva's darkly cool atmosphere—narrow room, high ceiling, subdued lighting, walls painted in Mediterranean hues—has been drawing steady crowds since opening day. It's a perfect place to have a drink, whether before dinner (there should be a crossing guard controlling the traffic between here and Ti Couz across the street), or after a movie at the Roxie Cinema next door. Many people, of course, make an evening of it right here, since there's a myriad of drink choices: microbrews on tap, bush malt, Belgian ales, fine wines, and sweet Sangria, among others. Owing to the crowds and the acoustics of the room, it gets pretty noisy at night, when seating at the long bar or the high tables is hard to come by. (There is also a small, secluded back room with tables—usually occupied, alas—which looks like a clandestine meeting spot for the French Resistance.) If you come by very late, however, the crowd sometimes clears out. Anglophiles will appreciate the jukebox.

## DOCTOR BOMBAY'S
*3192 16th St. (Guerrero), (415) 431-5255*
*Daily 2:30pm-2am*

Pity Doctor Bombay's, which probably would be the hippest bar around in most other cities. Here in San Francisco, it's not even the coolest bar on the *block*. For that reason, it's slightly less crowded than the other 16th Street establishments, even during weekend nights. What Doc Bombay's does have over its neighbors is bottled Jagerméister (if you view that as a plus), a $2.75 pint during happy hour (with all the usual microbrewed suspects available), and an infamous six-dollar drink called "Pixie Piss." The usual Mission bohemian boys and girls hang out here when the Albion or the 500 Club is SRO. Try to grab a space at one of the wooden booths across from the bar, which sit beneath Spanish roofing and walls covered with hieroglyphics and Egyptian iconography. A pool table and pinball machine can be found in back, and a way-cool jukebox is up front.

## DOUBLE PLAY
*2401 16th St. (Bryant), (415) 621-9859*
*M-F 7am-8pm*

For baseball fans who also enjoy a drink or six, the Double Play is living history. Forty years ago, when there was no Candlestick—er, 3Com—Park, the Giants played in Seals Stadium, catercorner from the Double Play. And for many years prior to the Giants' arrival, the Seals, of San Francisco's Pacific Coast League, made their home here. (A bit of history: Joe DiMaggio, the Yankee Clipper, played for the Seals, and was managed by none other than Casey Stengel. No Dario Lotagiani, they.) Not surprisingly, the interior of the Double Play is dedicated to Seals and Giants greats, past and present, with a liberal sprinkling of other San Francisco notables. These days, it functions more as a restaurant that closes by eight in the evening and on weekends, except for private parties. So be sure to stop by some afternoon, order a draft, raise your glass to the ghost of Lefty O'Doul, and try to imagine what it must have been like when Seals Stadium was across the street instead of the present inhabitant, Sammy's Pet World.

## DYLAN'S
*2301 Folsom St. (19th St.), (415) 641-1416*
*Daily 3:30pm-2am*

Dylan's is the dream of its owner, Alan "Titch" Jones, turned into the stuff of reality. The pleasantly appointed pub is also a mini museum devoted to telling the story of Wales, where Titch was born. The walls are covered with everything from flyers promoting long-ago bantamweight championship fights (they grow their champs small in the old country) to a gigantic Welsh flag (dragon rampant) to album covers from Welsh pop stars (Tom Jones, Shirley Bassey, Spencer Davis) to loads of stuff about the pub's namesake, and everyone's favorite Welshman, Dylan Thomas. Titch's vision has turned out agreeably egalitarian: he gives his pub over to a weekly jazz jam session, various and sundry neighborhood bands, art exhibits, and both amateur theater (a wonderful, boozy "Child's Christmas in Wales") and professional theater (a local actor portrays Dylan Thomas every Sunday). There's even the odd Sunday cookout. All this, and a Ping-Pong table, too. Dylan's neighbors can count themselves lucky indeed.

## EL RIO

*3158 Mission St. (Cesar Chavez/Valencia), (415) 282-3325*
*M 3pm-midnight; Tu-Su 3pm-2am*

Located in the netherworld between Bernal Heights and the Mission, this casual hangout, home to a diverse crowd, advertises itself as "your dive." Friendly servers and old-timers aside, the bar space itself is nothing special. The real drawing card here is the expansive outdoor patio—one of the best in the City—filled with tropical plants and strings of colored lights. On a warm night, it's a great place to sit and have a drink or listen to the great musical offerings: rock and salsa bands play Wednesdays, Fridays, and Saturdays. El Rio's famous margaritas are only $2 on Tuesday night's Margaritaville, while an occasional oyster special draws crowds on Friday nights. There are games, too, from a pool table (with tan felt) to indoor shuffleboard.

## ELBO ROOM

*647 Valencia St. (17th St./18th St.), (415) 552-7788*
*Daily 5pm-2am*

One of the finest-looking nightspots in town, with a wavy Formica topped bar, wooden arches, and candles to enhance the mood lighting. The long bar spans the length of the room downstairs, with cocktail tables set behind a hip-high wall, dividing the traffic from those sitting down. Beers on tap include Red Hook and Guinness. Liquor, like the heavenly Laphroaoig Scotch, is also abundant. Two pool tables anchor the back of this level. Upstairs, Elbo Room hosts bands playing everything from ambient jazz to rap/funk for a modest cover charge (usually no more than $5). An additional bar, pool table, and pinball machines occupy the back area, but the remainder of the room is solely for body gyrations. The ethnically diverse crowd, straight out of a Benetton ad, is twentysomething on average and heavy on the scenesters. If you're a hep cat, you can hang here comfortably. This lively outpost gets packed, so dress casual (jeans, T-shirts, skimpy dresses) and lightly. Tuesdays are for samba, Wednesdays feature jazz, and Fridays and Saturdays bring the funk. DJs spin funk and soul Monday and Thursday nights, with special live bands turning up occasionally as well, often to premiere their new CDs.

## ELYSIUM CAFÉ

*2438 Mission St. (20th St./21st St.), (415) 282-0337*
*Daily 5pm-2am*

Look for the blue lights wound around a tree for the entrance to the Mission's hottest new addition. The sophisticated decor is warm, inviting, and will keep the eye wandering. Overstuffed couches, armchairs, low coffee tables, and even a koi pond make for such comfort that the only thing missing seems to be hookah pipes. As the mixed crowd converse over long-stem cocktails and good Italian wines, ultrasmooth DJs enhance the mood, creating experimental soundscapes (everything from old-school jazz to Latin American standards). A full bar and kitchen complement the scene, and the Hell Damnation spareribs and haystack shoe-string potatoes are highly recommended.

## Beer: Pick Your Poison

Most people couldn't tell you anything about the beer in front of them other than its name (and the later in the evening you ask, the less likely they can even do that!), but there are a number of reasons why some beers are called lager, some called ale, and why some are darker or more bitter or have more alcohol. Read on to learn the correct names of that magical elixir you are so used to calling brewski, beevo, or, Heaven forbid, Natty Light.

Making beer is an age-old practice. Although the variations are numerous and complex, the basic process is very straightforward. Malt and toast some grains (traditionally barley, although rice and corn are used as cheap filler in many American beers, and wheat creates a beer of its own); add water and heat to create a mush (called wort); add yeast, which converts the sugars into alcohol and carbon dioxide; add some hops—a vine that imparts a bitter flavor—let it sit, and *voilà*, you've got beer. Each ingredient affects the flavor: the type of grain, how darkly it is roasted, the type of hops, even the type of yeast.

**Lager** or **Beer:** To brewers, the term beer refers to a specific type of brew, a lager. Lager means "to store" or "to cellar" in German, and 90 percent of the beer consumed in America is of this style. Production is characterized by fermentation at cold temperatures with a yeast that sinks to the bottom of the tank and a period of storage (the lagering) before bottling. Lager characteristics include pale color, light body, and mellow taste, which can be attributed to the lesser amount of hops introduced during the brewing process. Watery domestic examples include Bud, Miller, and Coors, but lagers don't have to be flavorless: international counterparts include Heineken, Becks, and Pilsener Urquell, considered the finest beer in the world by many afficionados. (Budweiser's name, although not its taste, is actually licensed from a similar Czech beer.)

**Ale:** Ales are fermented at higher temperatures (approximately room temperature) with a yeast that floats. Typically, more hops are added in the brewing of ales. Ales generally have a stronger taste and a higher alcohol content than lagers. Making ales requires less sophisticated equipment than lagers—less temperature control required—and no extended storage, so they are especially popular with home brewers and microbreweries. Examples such as Bass Ale, Sierra Nevada Pale Ale, and Pete's Wicked Ale are typically amber colored—actually the result of using darker-roasted barley, not the process—and complex in taste. According to their tour narrators, Anchor Steam Beer is unique because it is brewed using lager yeast but at room temperature, a technique dating from the frontier days when ice was scarce.

**Porter:** A very British beer, porters such as Anchor Porter are made using dark roasted barley and top fermenting yeast. Less hops is added to porter so it is smooth and rich without being bitter. It is hard to find imported porter, but for a close equivalent, try a dark ale.

**Stout:** Every serious beer drinker is familiar with Guinness Stout. Whether you're acquainted with it by renown or experience—it is definitely an acquired taste, especially for us Yanks—stout can be recognized by its very dark brown color, dense texture, creamy head, and pleasantly bitter flavor (like a good cup of Peet's coffee). Like porter, stout is colored and flavored by dark roasted barley. Since Stouts aren't very popular in the U.S., few breweries make them—Sierra Nevada is one—and most make them too sweet. There are other stouts, but there is only one Guinness.

**Weizen:** Another acquired taste, this sublime, predominantly Germanic beer is made using wheat instead of barley. Hefe-weizen is a type of wheat beer in which a small amount of yeast is added to the beer just before it is bottled, producing a small amount of sediment at the bottom of the bottle—and a lot of foam when you pour it. Done the German way, using a wild strain of yeast—similar to the yeast used in the Belgian Trappist ales—weizen beers have a rich, bread-like flavor, perfectly complemented by a slice of lemon in the glass. Most American weizen beers use bland yeast and are nothing like their German brethren, tasting sour and/or watery. The most readily available German examples are made by Paulaner and Spaten, although interesting varieties are made by Aktien and Schneider (notable for its dark version).

## 500 CLUB

*500 Guerrero St. (17th St.), (415) 861-2500*
*M-F 2pm-2am; Sa-Su noon-2am*

What gives the 500 Club its undeniable *je ne sais quoi?* Perhaps it's the giant neon martini sign out front, which has beckoned thirsty travelers since martinis were hip the first time. It could be the eternally blazing faux-fieldstone fireplace, the inviting round booths that line the far wall, or the homey knotty-pine paneling. Maybe it's the alcoholic afternoon clientele, always found either huddled en masse at the far end of the bar or playing slap-and-tickle to the '50s numbers on the jukebox. Maybe it's the foul-tempered U.K.-expat bartender, inordinately fond of Kahlúa and orange juice, whose impenetrable accent became even more so when he finally got his (extremely) rotten teeth pulled. Very possibly it's the ever-present Arnold (his favorite drink is red wine and Coke—no lie!), who can be found either scrounging change out front or ferociously hustling unsuspecting hipsters on one of the two threadbare pool tables. Whatever "it" may be, you won't find it on weekend nights, when the place is packed full of twentysomethings smoking cigars and getting their piercings caught on one another's clothing.

## JACK'S ELIXIR

*3200 16th St. (Guerrero), (415) 552-1633*
*Daily 2pm-2am*

The name Jack's graces a number of bars in the City, but this one is especially popular with beer lovers, who can choose from some five dozen different brews on tap and many others bottled. In business since 1932, there are just stools and window tables for decor, a checkerboard linoleum floor, and a young Mission crowd. Pints are generally $3.25. Bloody Mary Sunday has the self-described Best in the Mission version of that drink for $4.50, but beer is really the *raison d'être* of this corner bar.

## KILOWATT

*3160 16th St. (Valencia/Guerrero), (415) 861-2595*
*M-F 4pm-2am; Sa-Su 1pm-2am*

Kilowatt has become a rock Mecca since it opened a few years ago on the ashes of the Firehouse. Walk right in and you'll see where the old name came from: the room is narrow but the ceiling is high, the floors are varnished wood, and there's even a spiral staircase where the fire pole used to be. (One half-expects to see a Dalmatian guarding the door.) A cool-enough drinking establishment in its own right, music-wise the club is a college-radio programmer's dream, with lots of local bands filling the place on weeknights (no cover) and many willfully obscure national acts playing on weekends. Pints are generally under $4 ($2.50 during happy hour, 4-7pm weekdays, 1-7pm weekends), pitchers are $8 at happy hour, and even earplugs are under a buck. In the absence of live music, darts and a 50-cent pool table provide the entertainment. A cheap place to hang out and listen to great music.

## LA RONDALLA
*901 Valencia St. (20th St.), (415) 647-7474*
*Daily 11:30am-3am*

Hate your digestive tract? Well then, go to La Rondalla, get real drunk, eat some of the kitchen's food, and pour two or three pitchers of margaritas down your throat. This venerable bar has been allowing unsuspecting drunks and tourists to do some low-level late-night poisoning for many many years now. You can tell the place has been around for a while because of the over-whelming aroma of stale beer, stale grease, and stale cigarettes that emanates from the interior. Still, it's a fun room, decked out in red-leather upholstery, Christmas lights, fake wooden paneling, and streamers, with a separate dining area where they corral the spillover from the bar. When the wandering minstrels of the Mission—the dressed-up fellas with the bass, the guitar, and the accordion who wander from taqueria to bar, singing and playing for money—stop here on weekends as part of their appointed rounds, the scene turns into a veritable fiesta of mari-achi. La Rondalla is open until 3am, and sometimes the place is *jamming* as that time approaches. It's worth pondering where all those people are coming from, however, because nobody could have ever gone to La Rondalla twice. In fact, it's a point of neighborhood honor to boast of surviving a boozy, barely remembered visit here and then, forever after when you walk by, to remain safely across the street, lest the door open and you catch a fulsome whiff.

## LATIN AMERICAN CLUB
*3286 22nd St. (Valencia/Mission), (415) 647-2732*
*Su-Th 6pm-2am; F 5pm-2am; Sa 4pm-2am*

Despite a name that conjures up images of crusty old men sit-ting around in polyester pants, drinking cheap beer, and talking about the old country, this dark, somewhat disreputable-looking spot caters to low-key hipsters who smoke, play pool, drink decent beer, and who don't wash their hair before going out for a night on the town. The decor is nothing more than a simple wooden bar, '50s Formica-topped tables and chairs, two charm-ingly dingy booths in the front windows, and a pool table that you almost trip over when you walk in the door (turn around to view the giant neon-red "Sin" sign, visible only to those sitting inside). Behind the bar are stuffed birds, a deer head wearing a Happy New Year tiara, and a pigtailed bartender in an old house dress and combat boots—a good sample of this arty scene. Hit-or-miss art from a local upstart graces the walls. Red Man, an eccentric local who is always covered in red makeup and answers to the name Prince Charming, wanders the room. At the end of the night remember to stifle any alcohol-induced urges to laugh really loud or call across the street to your friends. The sign on the door will remind you that the neigh-bors are "trying to f**king sleep!"

## Liquid
*2925 16th St. (South Van Ness/Capp), (415) 431-8889*
*Daily 7pm-2am*

The 16th Street scene is so healthy that it has begun creeping eastward to Potrero Hill. As it happens, Liquid resembles a SoMa dance space more than its Mission brethren, with an industrial interior of sheet metal and pipe fittings. The tight quarters don't leave much room for the gorgeous, fresh-faced club crowd who pack the place on Thursdays through Saturdays, but good vibrations flow from the dance floor nonetheless. The DJs play the latest in trip-hop and jungle beats, along with plenty of funk and acid jazz. A nice selection of beers is on tap, and a full bar (complete with goldfish) holds whatever suits your fancy. If back-seat necking is your thing, you will feel at home on any of the club's bench-back seats that were once inside classic American roadsters. Beers and well drinks are $2 during happy hour. DJs start at 10pm, at which point expect to wait in a long line to get in.

## Lone Palm
*3394 22nd St. (Guerrero), (415) 648-0109*
*Su-M 7pm-2am; Tu-Sa 6pm-2am*

The Lone Palm was keeping the neon-lights-and-cocktail-glass faith on 22nd Street long before some of its fashionable neighboring bars came into being. It's one of those cool nightspots with the kind of backlit, dim glow that makes everyone appear slimmer and more attractive. (Actually, the sleek, well-dressed people that come in here start out quite slim and attractive.) Many small tables, bathed in white cloths and candles, are crammed into what little space is available. There's music during the weekends, mostly acoustic stuff but also some blues, plus the piano stylings of Sam Peoples, who occasionally brings along his trumpet-playing friend. Lone Palm is always full then (as opposed to early weeknights, when it's quiet and inexplicably eerie, straight out of *Twin Peaks*), but if you can somehow jam yourself in, wend your way to the bar and ask for a martini. The bartender will make a big show about misting your glass with vermouth sprayed from an old perfume atomizer, which counts for major style points. If you ask for a Cosmopolitan, be prepared to hear everything from snickering to outright verbal abuse.

## The Make-Out Room
*3225 22nd St. (Mission/Valencia), (415) 647-2888*
*Daily 6pm-2am*

Half a block off of the perpetually up-and-coming Valencia corridor, The Make-Out Room is the ultimate in the current gentrification-with-an-edge wave. It's a place where the savvy bartenders have deemed tiny cocktail straws a superfluous drink garnish and raise an eyebrow at the uninitiated who ask for one. The regulars are generally drawn from the neighborhood genetic pool: goateed and/or pierced, cigarette smoking, and fluent in conversational multimediaese. The decor is a combination of utilitarian, minimalist, concrete-meets-lush, baroque, and garage sale. The back area has plenty of cocktail tables, while the front bar is lined with booths. Kudos to whoever dreamed up the idea of antlers placed sporadically along the walls. Bathrooms are small, but festooned with cheerfully bright paint. On occasion, The Make-Out Room is also a venue for live music, turning over

## My Favorite Club

### EL RIO
### by Tom Ammiano

I remember when El Rio opened 20 years ago. People said it wouldn't last. Malcolm, the owner, has never been afraid to take risks, offering music, comedy, and bands throughout the year. I remember doing comedy on Wednesday nights out on their beautiful patio. They have made an oasis in the middle of a city block.

The mix of people, gay, straight, and of color, has always made El Rio a unique place. It readily will host a political fundraiser or a pool tournament. Unscrupulous competitors have tried to sabotage the bar, but cannot defeat the place it has carved out for itself in the community. And Malcom: you go, girl.

*Tom Ammiano is a member of the San Francisco Board of Supervisors.*

the stage to ultra-alternative acts that hail from as far away as New Zealand. Comfortably active on weeknights, this place is packed on weekends. Bring a date, but be forewarned that he or she may be distracted by the attractive "scenery."

### MCCARTHY'S
*2327 Mission St. (19th St./20th St.), (415) 648-0504*
*Daily 6am-midnight*

McCarthy's is the last of the old-time bars in what was once the city's Irish enclave. The white walls, long, horseshoe-shaped countertop, and painfully bright overhead fluorescent lights make it feel like a cross between a VA hospital and Woolworth's. It used to be a restaurant, too: notice the old menus on the wall advertising a steak dinner for $1.60. (Indeed, Tom McGovern, the crusty bartender who's worked here for nearly six decades, growls, "I worked that kitchen 32 years, and when I left they couldn't get someone who lasted 32 days!") Still, the amiable clientele of older Irish and Latinos appreciates the fact that pints here are cheaper than at the much hipper Bruno's next door, and a makeshift blues band plays once in a while to keep things interesting.

### RADIO VALENCIA
*1199 Valencia St. (23rd St.), (415) 826-1199*
*M-Tu 5pm-midnight; W-Su noon-midnight*

Radio Valencia is really more of a café-restaurant than a bar (and the healthy, homemade fare here is truly excellent), but it does become a club of sorts from Friday through Sunday nights. That's when the enlightened and sophisticated folks who run the place showcase a spectrum of live music—acoustic, bluegrass, and jazz improv—to entertain a suitably bohemian crowd of artists, writers, and Mission scenesters. Friday and Sunday nights are free, and the Saturday night jazz (shows at 7:30pm and 9pm) can be enjoyed for a nominal $3 cover charge. You can grab a seat at the tiny bar that serves a dozen beers on tap, or find an open table in this midsized storefront room. Check out the musical instruments suspended from the ceiling, the horse tapestries mounted on one wall, and the vinyl records (remember those?) stuck on the other. If you're wondering why the linoleum floor is fire-engine red, find someone here willing to tell you the now-legendary story behind it.

## RITE-SPOT CAFÉ
*2099 Folsom St. (17th St.), (415) 552-6066*
*M-Th 4pm-2am; F 2pm-2am; Sa-Su 8pm-2am*

The Rite-Spot, with its old dineresque Rite Spot, Wrong Time sign above the inside doorway, is the epitome of cool—so cool, in fact, it's beyond trendy. A muted hipster San Francisco crowd without the usual attitude sips cocktails around the bar or at the café-style tables. Discussion on the revolving display of works by local artisans punctuates most conversations. It is not unusual for one of the regulars to wander over to the upright piano and play show tunes over the jukebox music. A dinner menu is served until 10pm. Head here early in the evening for quiet conversation before the more upbeat, friendly scene late at night. It's also the place to go on a weekend night if you and a friend want to (1) find a parking spot, (2) score a place to sit, and (3) meet someone interesting. Tip: the policy here is cash only, and the nearest ATM is several desolate blocks away.

## SKIP'S TAVERN
*453 Cortland Ave. (Andover), (415) 282-3456*
*Daily 10am-2am*

Like a lot of drinking spots on the less-explored edges of the city, Skip's is a real neighborhood dive, the type of place where the *Cheers* cliché about everybody knowing your name is true. The crowd tends to be older and working-class, and since lots of native San Franciscans have been coming here forever, it's a great place to get a feel for the rhythms of the city. The bartenders serve their friends from the middle of a giant oval bar in the center of the room, a well-worn space with fake wood-paneled walls, the requisite pool table, and a *Baywatch* pinball machine. There's salsa, R&B, and rock music Friday and Saturday nights, and an open-mike jam of epic proportions on Sunday afternoons. Malo Santana, brother of Carlos, sometimes drops by to join in on the fun.

## SKYLARK
*3089 16th St. (Valencia), (415) 621-9294*
*M-F 4pm-2am; Sa-Su 7pm-2am*

Whatever the saturation point is for bars at the intersection of 16th and Valencia, it hasn't been reached yet. Skylark opened in December of '96 and within months, it was already (in the words of one bartender) "wound up" on weekends. It is certainly a pretty space: think of a wider, brighter Dalva, with a red bar, enormous gold glitter banquettes, and a high yellow ceiling that sports a beautiful mural. It attracts a similar crowd to Dalva's, too, one that's looking to kick back anonymously and at the same time be seen. A DJ comes along on weekends to keep everyone in a good mood. The rest of the time, a largely retro-'70s jukebox spits out Carole King and friends. Golden Bear, Red Tail, and Newcastle Brown Ale are among the wide selection of beers on tap.

## THE SLOW CLUB
*2501 Mariposa St. (Hampshire), (415) 241-9390*
*Tu 11am-11pm; W-Sa 11am-midnight*

Don't be fooled by your first glance into what looks like an intimate and subdued restaurant. The bar at the back, with its glass shelves and underlit, glowing bottles, merits your wading your way to it. How the decor and atmosphere manage to be chic and cozy, minimalist and kitsch all at the same time is a bit of a mystery. After a couple of the best Cosmopolitans in the city, however, it all begins to make sense. Michael the bartender, a character from beyond where coolness lies, warns that Thursday and Friday nights are ruled by the twentysomething Marina crowd, but Tuesday's excellent and varied selection of tapas attracts a more diverse group. (Happy hours here are usually full of staff from the nearby *Bay Guardian* and KQED, talking shop—consider this a warning.) It's a great place to bring a first date, but be prepared to drop some cash, then sit back, relax, and enjoy the Slow.

### 3300 CLUB
*3300 Mission St. (29th St.), (415) 826-6886*
*Daily 6am-midnight*

Those familiar with Edward Hopper's paintings may feel like they've entered one when they step inside this dark, sepia-toned, Americana-drenched corner bar, a mainstay at this location for over half a century. The booths are brown leather, the tables are linoleum, the checkered floor is dusty, and the Venetian blinds are usually at half-mast. The jukebox plays trad jazz at barely perceptible volume, and the wall posters encourage patrons to buy War Bonds. Solitary figures, generally older, sit at the bar reading a book or staring into their drinks. (There are *no* microbrews, and only bottled beer is available.) The grizzled, enigmatic bartender probably has lots of stories to tell but goes about his job quietly. All in all, it's the perfect place in which to start or end an evening of drinking—just don't linger here all night, unless you're carrying the Samaritan's hotline number in your wallet.

### THE TIP TOP INN
*3001 Mission St. (26th St.), (415) 824-6486*
*Daily noon-2am*

The outside of the Tip Top Inn looks like your typical outer-Mission dive. But don't let the exterior put you off. Inside, this place caters to savvy cocktailers who know where the hot spots are, but instead choose to go off the proverbial beaten path. Top-shelf tequila, scotch, and vodka are prominently displayed, the bartenders can whip up any drink on the planet, the beer on tap is well chosen, and the CD jukebox features a wide selection of quality sounds. (There are live rock bands a couple of nights a week as well.) The decor is a parody of Mission icons: an enormous dried-flower arrangement hangs in the center of the bar, crucifixes appear everywhere, a few velvet paintings and images of the Virgin Mary and various saints dot the walls. The mirror behind the bar is painted with pitchforks and a scrawled announcement of Sunday Services, which appear to be Ana's Hair of the Dog Bloodys (served from noon to 8pm) and John's James Dean Double Header (don't ask). Prices are reasonable, even by Mission standards. Tap beer is $2.50 a pint, and pool games are 50 cents. Rumor has it that regulars are not anxious to share the Tip Top, so keep this one under your hat.

## THE UPTOWN
*200 Capp St. (17th St.), (415) 861-8231*
*M-Tu 4pm-2am; W-Su 2pm-2am*

The Uptown is a Mission legend. This corner bar is the quintessential neighborhood crash pad, with sagging couches that form a "living room," an upright piano, and great gossipy bathroom graffiti. A centrally located horseshoe bar dominates, separating the game room (featuring pool and pinball) from the roomy booths and table area (where you're free to munch on brought-from-home food). Music is supplied by an eclectic jukebox, although someone recently removed Meatloaf's "Paradise by the Dashboard Lights," which put an end to the infamous impromptu sing-alongs. The regulars range from professional barflies to postwork beer boys to pool sharks to neighborhood dwellers looking to escape the ultrahip Valencia Street scene. The Uptown certainly doesn't qualify as a pickup joint, but patrons are generally friendly and most claim to be available. A great place for groups looking for a spot as comfortable as their living rooms but with a better-stocked bar.

## THE WILD SIDE WEST
*424 Cortland Ave. (Wood/Andover), (415) 647-3099*
*Daily 1pm-2am*

If the Wild Side were located at Valencia and 16th instead of on the less-traveled byway of Cortland Avenue, there would probably be a line of hipsters outside, waiting to get in. Instead, this cheerful bohemian saloon attracts a low-key crowd with occasional bursts of activity, especially when women's softball teams invade on Sunday afternoons for a post-game tipple. Although it retains a deserved reputation as an oasis for lesbians, most nights there's an eclectic mix of young and old, gays and straights, neighborhood regulars and curious visitors, most of them waiting to shoot pool at the red felt table. The interior sports blood-red walls decked out with old mirrors, masks, clocks, and Marilyn Monroe posters, not to mention a carved wooden statue of a Native American. There's a quiet outdoor patio/garden in back.

## ZEITGEIST
*199 Valencia St. (Duboce), (415) 255-7505*
*Daily 9am-2am*

This gritty outpost steadfastly remains the premier biker bar for the scuffed boots and pierced parts set. The City's *über* urban beer garden, underneath a freeway, boasts the highest number of motorcycles parked outside of any building in town other than a repair shop. (There is limited street parking, but plenty of sidewalk bike parking available.) Obviously the place can get a bit rowdy, but the friendly bartenders rarely lose control: their sign near the Playboy bunny skull above the bar reads Dropin—Drinkup—GET OUT! NO REFUNDS. In addition to killer Bloody Marys, there's a considerable selection of beers on tap, varying by season and subject to availability. A jukebox, a pool table, and two pinball machines round out the entertainment. For those who can't crawl home or don't have a place of their own, the bar advertises rooms for rent upstairs. One patron recommended Zeitgeist because it's the closest bar to his front door. Perhaps not a stunning tribute, yet it does speak to the neighborliness of the place.

★

## Late Night Eats

### ARABIAN NIGHTS $$
*811 Valencia St. (19th St./20th St.), (415) 821-9747*
*Tu-Th 6pm-11pm; F-Sa 6pm-midnight (happy hour light menu 3pm-8pm)*
Sure it's a lively nightspot, but the superb fare also deserves attention. Start with the delicious *baba ghanoush* (just the right consistency) or grilled quails as an appetizer; move on to the other-worldly "sultan's pleasure" (rack of lamb with herbs, couscous, and rice), the vegetarian plate of 40 thieves (hummus, falafel, and so on), or the excellent shish kebab with very large cubes of meat.

### BRUNO'S $$$
*2389 Mission St. (19th St./20th St.), (415) 550-7455*
*Tu-Th, Su 6:30pm-11pm; F-Sa 6:30pm-midnight*
Bruno's has been reborn as a soigné fifties-style supper club featuring cocktail-dress-clad hostesses, circular red vinyl booths, and the innovative cooking of chef James Ormsby. Start the evening with a martini and an order of oysters, then move on to braised lamb shank with truffled white-bean ravioli or delectable herb gnocchi with seared scallops and asparagus tips.

### EL FAROLITO ¢
*2777 Mission St. (23rd St./24th St.), (415) 826-4870*
*Daily 9am-2am*
*4817 Mission St. (Onondaga), (415) 337-5500*
*Daily 9am-1am*
At El Farolito, there's always a line, and it's no wonder. In addition to excellent tacos, burritos, and tamales served with awesome salsa fresca and spicy tomatillo-avocado salsa, you can get fresh-squeezed orange and carrot juice. There's plenty of seating, loud *banda* music on the jukebox, and a generally festive atmosphere. No credit cards.

### EL ZOCALO
*3230 Mission St. (Valencia), (415) 282-2572*
*M-F 11am-3am; Sa-Su 11am-4am*
*Zocalo* is the Spanish word for the bustling square of shops and cafés found at the heart of many Mexican towns, and this interesting Salvadoran twist on the cheap and tasty Mission taqueria lives up to its namesake with a large and loyal set of late-night regulars.

### GRANDEHO'S HIBACHI $
*3111 16th St. (Valencia/Guerrero), (415) 626-5022 or (415) 626-5023*
*M-F 11:30am-11pm; Sa-Su 11:30am-midnight*
This hole-in-the-wall eatery is a perfect choice for a group that can't decide on anything except bargain prices. The menu offers a limited selection of Chinese, Japanese, Thai, and Korean cuisine, with some passable renditions of each genre. The restaurant's convenient location and low prices make up for the less-than-immaculate interior offering limited table seating plus a few counter stools.

### LA RONDALLA $
*901 Valencia St. (20th St.), (415) 647-7474*
*Tu-Su 11am-3am*
When you spot the Christmas lights, you know you've found the right place. See bar listing. No credit cards.

### MAGIC DONUTS ¢
*2400 Mission St. (20th St.), (415) 824-3302*
Daily 24 hours

### MR. PIZZA MAN $
*3146 24th St. (Shotwell), (415) 641-0333*
*Daily 24 hours*
The mysterious Mr. Pizza Man must be good with a mound of dough because the pizza crust at this chain eatery is thick and excellent.

## NORTH BEACH PIZZA $
*4787 Mission St. (Excelsior), (415) 586-1400*
*M-Sa 11am-11pm; Su noon-11pm*
The celebrated chain of San Francisco pizza parlors is loud and energized, with lots of families and large groups in attendance. Toppings are sometimes hidden between the gooey cheese and chewy crust. The menu includes other Italian favorites, but stick to the pizza. Service can be rushed when the place is packed and lines are long. The chain has very efficient delivery.

## PANCHO VILLA TAQUERIA ¢/$
*3071 16th St. (Valencia/Mission), (415) 864-8840*
*Daily 10am-midnight*
Every out-of-town guest or newly minted resident loves the clean, white-walled dining room, the tasty chips and table sauces, the tantalizing aromas from the always-flaming grill, and the mile-long line of cooks and burrito assemblers. The menu is extensive, the burritos and tacos are understandably popular, and the combination plates, while more expensive than other places, are very good.

## RADIO VALENCIA $
*1199 Valencia St. (23rd St.), (415) 826-1199*
*M-Tu 5pm-midnight; W-Su noon-midnight*
See bar listing.

## SLOW CLUB $$
*2501 Mariposa St. (Hampshire), (415) 241-9390*
*M 7am-3:30pm; Tu-F 7am-11pm; Sa 6:30pm-11pm*
This chic, postindustrial café appeals to the artistic set that flocks here after hours to quaff Red Hook on tap and indulge in Niman-Schell burgers and fries. The Mediterranean-style food is uniformly well done, imaginative, and generously portioned.

## TAQUERIA CANCUN ¢
*2288 Mission St. (19th St./20th St.), (415) 252-9560*
*Daily 10am-1am*
A low ceiling, polished pine tables, and a huge *banda*-blaring jukebox give this busy taqueria an authentic cantina feel. Come here for super hot guacamole, and for one of the best vegetarian burritos in the city—a pastrylike tortilla crammed with tasty beans, rice, and half of an avocado. No credit cards.

## TAQUERIA SAN JOSE ¢
*2830 Mission St. (24th St./25th St.), (415) 282-0203*
*Daily 8am-1am*
*2839 Mission St. (24th St./25th St.), (415) 282-0283*
*Daily 8am-11pm*
When you're tired of taquerias serving bland heaps of undifferentiated filler, head to this pair of taquerias for a culinary awakening. The long list of well-prepared taco and burrito fillings includes the standard beef and chicken, plus authentic specialties such as *al pastor* (barbecued pork), chorizo sausage, tongue, and brain. The decor is typical taqueria: a spare, bright hall with tile floor, Formica tables, murals on the walls, and a loud jukebox. Cash only.

## TRULY MEDITERRANEAN ¢
*3109 16th St. (Valencia/Guerrero), (415) 252-PITA/7482*
*M-Sa 11am-midnight; Su 11am-10pm*
Roxie Cinema regulars and Mission barflies truly appreciate Truly Mediterranean—a tiny fast-food joint that serves up falafel, *shawerma*, and hummus. Aside from the comical counter staff, what makes this Middle Eastern food rise above the crop is the preparation: the sandwiches are filled, rolled burrito style, and then grilled briefly. A few stools inside and two tables outside, to watch the hipsters walk by.

# Lower Haight
# Upper Market
# Western Addition

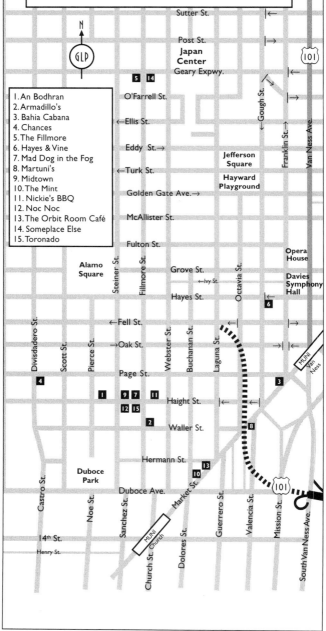

1. An Bodhran
2. Armadillo's
3. Bahia Cabana
4. Chances
5. The Fillmore
6. Hayes & Vine
7. Mad Dog in the Fog
8. Martuni's
9. Midtown
10. The Mint
11. Nickie's BBQ
12. Noc Noc
13. The Orbit Room Café
14. Someplace Else
15. Toronado

Sutter St.

Post St.
**Japan Center**
Geary Expwy.

O'Farrell St.

Ellis St.

Eddy St.

**Jefferson Square**

Turk St.

**Hayward Playground**

Golden Gate Ave.

McAllister St.

Fulton St.

**Opera House**

**Alamo Square**

Grove St.
Ivy St.

**Davies Symphony Hall**

Hayes St.

Fell St.

Oak St.

Page St.

Haight St.

Waller St.

Hermann St.

**Duboce Park**

Duboce Ave.

14th St.
Henry St.

Sutter St.
Post St.
Gough St.
Franklin St.
Van Ness Ave.
Steiner St.
Fillmore St.
Octavia St.
Divisadero St.
Scott St.
Pierce St.
Webster St.
Buchanan St.
Laguna St.
Castro St.
Noe St.
Sanchez St.
Market St.
Dolores St.
Guerrero St.
Valencia St.
Mission St.
South Van Ness Ave.

Church St.

MUNI Van Ness
MUNI Church

GLP

101

The center of the city is a diverse mosaic of neighborhoods with appropriately diverse bars and clubs. In the up-and-coming Lower Haight, the 1990s have brought a new youth culture reflected in the surreal decor of Noc Noc, the one-world vibe of Nickie's, and the studied toughness of Midtown. Over in the Western Addition, a Jazz Preservation District is trying to take seed, anchored by Someplace Else. And on Upper Market, the spirit of the Castro creeps toward the Bay in such fun spots as Martuni's and The Mint.

★

### ARMADILLO'S
*200 Fillmore St. (Waller), (415) 553-8953*
*Daily 4pm-2am*

A great place to slum—nice and dark, exceedingly dingy, and extremely smoky and loud. The pool table in the center of the bar is always in use. The jukebox blasts equal parts old heavy metal—Sabbath, Deep Purple, Led Zep—with a dash of soul (yes, that *is* Aretha Franklin following Ozzy Osbourne). The cast of characters is obligingly undershampooed and overtattooed. On a good night, the place feels like a bad-guy bar from any B-movie, but under its gruff exterior, Armadillo is soft and cuddly. They'll barbecue on the sidewalk on nice weekends, and a bottle of Pabst goes for $1.50. The bartenders are friendly, cry-on-my-shoulder types. Two caveats: Armadillo is perhaps the smelliest bar in San Francisco. Count on hair and clothes reeking upon returning home. Second, that block of Waller is a bit dodgy, so don't get too loose or you may get jacked on your way back to the car. *Note:* Armadillo's building recently suffered a fire and Armadillo's is trying to reopen (a benefit event was held at Hotel Utah to raise money). Call ahead.

### BAHIA CABANA
*1600 Market St. (Franklin), (415) 861-4202*
*Daily 10pm-2am*

There's an entire world of culture partying at this Brazilian thatched-hut restaurant-cum-nightclub. You'll find bikini-clad, samba-stepping women on Saturday nights (which feature great samba and pagode bands like Entre Nos), and Wednesdays a multi-orientation crowd grooves to the American-European progressive/house-techno music while downing *caiparinhas* (the Brazilian version of the margarita). Club Charisma brings the "100 percent ritmo" of salsa, merengue, and Latin house every Friday—if you want to get into step, stop in for free salsa lessons the night before. And there's always Tuesday night karaoke. In fact, it's a full-fledged, hard-core, dance-til-you-sweat party every night of the week.

## CHANCES
*298 Divisadero St. (Page), (415) 255-6101*
*Daily 5pm-2am*

Chances is a *terrible* name for a bar, conjuring up images of cheesy suburban dance clubs located in strip malls and featuring Singles Nights and sweet cocktails like Sex on the Beach. Which is too bad, because this Chances, owned and operated by Palestinian brothers Sean and Hank, is actually a relaxed, beer-oriented neighborhood hangout. Bright neon beer signs adorn the walls, rock and roll blasts from the jukebox, and pool tables, pinball, and Foosball constitute the diversions. In short, Chances is the type of place to shoot pool while swilling from a $2.50 happy hour pint of Rolling Rock. A mixed crowd of older neighborhood types and Lower Haight youth movement representatives dominate the crowd on weekdays, while weekends attract a more motley group.

## THE FILLMORE
*1805 Geary Blvd. (Fillmore), (415) 346-6000, show info;*
*(415) 346-3000, office*
*Open for performances only*

There are music venues, and then there are *legendary* music venues. The nondescript Western Addition brick building known as The Fillmore definitely falls into the latter category. Indeed, it is such an intrinsic part of San Francisco's musical and cultural history that it's hard to conceive of the '60s ever having happened without the psychedelic extravaganzas that occurred here: the Grateful Dead, Janis Joplin, Jefferson Airplane, and many more, all immortalized in photos and posters covering the walls. These days, post-seismic retrofit, the bilevel ballroom with great acoustics continues to draw big-time rockers on occasion (e.g., Tom Petty's twenty-night engagement), while providing an encouraging setting for young bands on their way up. Many shows are all ages, which brings out the teenagers in force, but don't plan on grabbing a drink for a too-young friend in this heavily enforced over-21-hand-stamps-required atmosphere. There are bars on both floors, with a sep-

---

### *My Favorite Bar*

**RADIO VALENCIA**
**by Windy Chien**

Although it isn't strictly a bar or a nightclub, I find myself at Radio Valencia most often because it's one of the warmest spots in the city. Up to three nights a week they feature well-chosen musicians (usually bluegrass or improv/avant/jazz) you don't find at any other joints. The decor is vintage chic (emphasis on "chic," mind you, as opposed to "tacky"). The service is extremely friendly and personable, and the food, well, Lanee's West African Peanut Soup is worth its weight in gold. The restaurant also functions as a "one-room radio station," featuring an ever-rotating, wonderfuly eclectic playlist (with a copy of the current list posted on every table) compiled by the owners, staff, or every so often a well-tuned-in customer. Highly recommended.

*Windy Chien is the owner of Aquarius Records in the Mission District.*

arate dining area on the second floor that offers decent pasta and fried foods to eat during the show.

## HAYES & VINE
*377 Hayes St. (Franklin/Gough), (415) 626-5301*
*M-Th 5pm-midnight; F-Sa 5pm-1am*

This elegant and welcoming bar is a real find for wine lovers. The interior is all curves, rich textures, and warm colors. The tomelike wine list includes not only the familiar names from California and France, but also harder-to-find wines from all over the world. Many are served by the bottle, glass, or taste. Each week a different flight of tastes (highlighting a different region or type of wine) is offered to the discerning clientele. Sit at the softly illuminated bar or one of the many cozy tables for two or four. Or, for truly optimal seating, head to the back room, which is made up of just one round, crushed-purple-velvet booth. Tuck yourself away with a couple bottles of *vino* and four or five of your favorite people, and you'll never want to come out.

## MAD DOG IN THE FOG
*530 Haight St. (Fillmore/Steiner), (415) 626-7279*
*Daily 11:30am-2am*

There's so much to say about Mad Dog in the Fog, it's hard to know where to begin. First off, it's the premier Anglophile bar in town, a virtual England-on-Haight. The entire huge space (well, most of it anyway) is decorated with bar towels trumpeting various brands of ale, soccer club banners, and other touchingly British souvenirs. Secondly, the beer selection is wonderful, with lots of dee-lish imports in bottles (including the sublime Boddington's and Old Peculiar) and a respectable number on tap as well. Add to that darts and a lovely back garden and you've got a dynamite destination. Seating is plentiful, and the front room is a no-smoking section with a big window that opens onto life in the Lower Haight. Perhaps the best feature of the Mad Dog, however, is the trivia game held every Monday and Thursday. The same guy has been running it for some time (apparently he makes his living at it; more power to him), bellowing out questions over the din of the bar in a sometimes incomprehensible Irish brogue. If all this isn't enough—and it certainly should be—stop by at 5:30 or 6 some morning during Mad Dog's legendary live satellite screenings of major British football matches. Stick your head in the door, if it's even possible, and be rewarded by the sight of dozens of sports-crazed British expats clutching pints of Guinness, screaming at the telly at the tops of their lungs, pissed out of their minds at 6 in the morning. Bloody good.

## MARTUNI'S
*4 Valencia St. (Market), (415) 241-0205*
*Daily 2pm-2am*

What was once a divey Dutch biker joint has been reborn as an upscale piano bar, complete with the requisite disposable-income crowd to justify its existence. It's a smartly dressed group of drinkers, too, comprising a mixed age demographic but generally skewing toward the thirtysomething crowd and gay men. The decor clearly aims to attract the younger element

## Swing Dancing

Until recently, those people who like to dance had been suffering through a bleak period. There were still leftovers from the '60s, expressing themselves no matter what the beat or style of the music, and a few self-abusive slam dancers were still caught in the '70s. In country towns, line dancing spread like Velveeta on a hot day, but it never took hold in the cities. Then, lo and behold, swing dancing, the favorite of boomers' parents and Xers' grandparents, caught fire. In San Francisco, where the vintage-clothing-and-cocktail crowd had been looking for the Next Big Thing, swing dancing now rages through town like an inferno.

Swing dancing looks deceptively simple, but don't let that fool you: it demands a lot from its practitioners, as anyone who has seen the movie *Swingers* can confirm. You have to learn the steps and be in synch with your partner or it's positively dangerous. (On a crowded dance floor, if you're inexperienced or you've had one too many drinks, it's a guarantee you'll slam into something or someone.) You need proper attire—baggy trousers or a skirt that really moves—and appropriate shoes are a must. (Spiked heels and combat boots won't do.) But the basics are easy enough to learn, and there's a great sense of accomplishment in doing it, not to mention all the fun you'll have. It's a seesaw ride, a swing, and the tunnel of love all in one.

### Where To Learn

**Fort Mason:** Wednesday evening classes; call (510) 549-3591 for details.

**Metronome Ballroom:** Potrero Hill, 1830 17th St. (DeHaro/Rhode Island), (415) 252-9000. Learn West Coast swing (there's East Coat swing, too, but when in Rome . . .) or lindy hop in a large, airy place near Showplace Square. Group and private lessons for couples and singles are offered days and evenings. The first class is free for new students. There are dance parties so that you can practice what you've learned.

**Renaissance Ballroom:** Tenderloin, 285 Ellis St. (Mason/Taylor), (415) 474-0920. Learn West Coast swing or the lindy hop in a big, old-fashioned studio near Glide Memorial Church. You can study privately or in a group. On Friday evenings, parties are held at which you can get used to dancing with other learners before you take on the real world.

**Work that Skirt:** Swing dancing taught at a variety of clubs and venues. Call (415) 664-6946 for information.

### Where to Dance

**Café du Nord:** Upper Market, 2170 Market (Church/Sanchez), (415) 979-6545. The ambience is perfect in this basement club that looks like a Swiss chalet on the outside and a speakeasy inside. There's a long bar, a front room with a small stage, a back room also with a stage, and tucked-away booths for tête-à-têtes. People here dress up. Free (after $3 to $5 cover) swing lessons are offered on Sundays from 8 to 9pm, and the band comes on at 9pm. The happy hour runs from 4 to 7pm, and there's no cover before 8pm.

**Hi-Ball Lounge:** North Beach, 473 Broadway (Montgomery/Kearny), (415) 39-SWING. Lots of red velvet but with animal motifs as well. The swingers wear retro clothing from the '30s through the '60s. A martini happy hour lasts from 5 to 9pm Fridays. Swing classes are held on Sundays, Tuesdays, and Wednesdays from 7 to 9pm at a reasonable $5 for each person or $7 for a couple per lesson.

**Lehr Brothers' Grill:** Nob Hill, 790 Sutter St. (Taylor/Jones), (415) 474-6478. Once called the Greenhouse, the Grill still looks like it, with many potted plants and a glass ceiling. Mondays, during what's called Swing Shift, free swing classes are offered from 7:30 to 8:30pm. Live swing music starts at 9pm, or at 10pm on Fridays.

of the symphony-and-opera set, with stylish wall sconces and flickering tableside candles, dark walls covered with a fancy slotted wood design, and plenty of noise-muffling carpeting. At the front-room bar, smartly dressed bartenders sling strong martinis, and in the back room, professional musicians tickle the ivories, take requests, and keep the good times rolling. (There are often jazz combos, too.) Come early to get a seat near the piano. Packed late in the evenings on weekend nights.

## MIDTOWN

*582 Haight St. (Fillmore/Steiner), (415) 558-8019*
*Daily noon-2am*

Midtown is a hip, casual study in red and black: red-and-chrome barstools and chairs, black-vinyl booths and café tables, and red plastic ashtrays. The concrete floor, pool table, and unframed mirrors suggest local dive, while the microbrews and cider on tap and good selection of top-shelf vodka and whiskey suggest a sophisticated cocktail palate. The Seattle sound—loud, driving, and very 1992—blasts from the stereo, and bartenders sport multiple tattoos and piercings. Patrons lean their skateboards against the bar, a variety of personalized bicycles lean against the walls, and a few dogs wander through, searching for their owners. On weekends the colorful crowd nearly spills out the picture windows onto Haight Street. The food selection is limited to a variety of individual-package chips. (It's Haight Street, after all, so you don't have to rely on the bars for food.) The attentive bartenders make a mean Bloody Mary (garnished with olives) and greet by name every other person who slides up to the bar.

---

**330 Ritch:** SoMa, 330 Ritch Street (off Townsend btwn. 3rd St./ 4th St.), (415) 541-9574. Select something from the full bar or on-tap beers before enjoying the free swing classes that precede the live swing music on Wednesdays. Come dance on Thursdays through Saturdays from 6 to 10:30pm. This place is beloved of the techno types who work in the area.

**Places for Swing Dancing if the Music Calls for It**

**Bimbo's 365 Club:** North Beach, 1025 Columbus Ave. (Taylor/ Chestnut), (415) 474-0365. You can't get more authentic atmosphere than at Bimbo's. It's been around since the 1930s. The gloriously plush bathrooms and telephone booths are must-sees. Free swing lessons are offered when the music calls for it.

**Bottom of the Hill:** Potrero Hill, 1233 17th St. (Texas/Missouri), (415) 621-4455. More laid-back than many other clubs, this rock-and-roll venue sometimes has swing bands and dancing.

**Coconut Grove:** Polk/Van Ness, 1415 Van Ness Ave. (Bush/ Pine), (415) 776-1616. This opulent club, which is trying so hard to come up with an identity for itself, has swing music and dancing on occasion.

**Deluxe:** Haight Ashbury, 1511 Haight St. (Ashbury/Clayton), (415) 552-6949. The black-leather booths and Formica tabletops make the Deluxe seem more like a swing kitchen than a swing ballroom. If a swing band is playing, there'll be dancing. Try Bloody Mary Sundays in the afternoon. The sounds of Frank Sinatra reign on Sundays at 9pm.

## THE MINT
*1942 Market St. (Duboce/Laguna), (415) 626-4726*
*Daily 11am-2am*

Ah, karaoke—one of Japan's most significant cultural gifts to the world. Sadly, most people associate karaoke night with drunk businessmen singing Beatles songs off-key or sorority girls screaming Lionel Ritchie's lyrics. In fact, the Japanese take karaoke performances *very* seriously, as a rare chance to reveal a different side of one's self, an approach rarely taken in America. Which is what makes the Mint so special. Not only is every night here karaoke night (otherwise there'd be little to recommend this nondescript place except for the side door connecting it to Hot n' Chunky Burgers), but those customers who take part, mostly gay men well-versed in camp and irony, respect the inherent seriousness in the art form. They choose their songs carefully. They find nuances in tempo and phrasing. They force the audience to rethink their assumptions and prejudices about music. Whether it's a German tourist singing "Strangers in the Night" or a young lesbian singing "Here Comes My Girl," there are always memorable moments being made at the Mint, and if you're too shy to go up on stage, don't worry—watching is almost as fun as taking the mike yourself. Anchor Steam and Sierra Nevada are among the beers offered on tap.

## NICKIE'S BBQ
*460 Haight St. (Webster/Fillmore), (415) 621-6508*
*Tu-Th 9pm-2am*

If Nickie's looks way too small on the outside to be a dance club, that's because it is. The small, grubby, bare-bones room consists of little more than the bar and a few leather-padded booths; when the typically vibrant and diverse young Lower Haight crowd shows up, the whole place is a dance floor, and it's one nation under a groove. Each night there are different DJs and sounds. Monday features Grateful Dead jams; Tuesday it's world beat (with renowned spin-ster cheb i sabbah); Wednesday it's funk; Thursday it's groove jazz, soul, and Latin; and Friday and Saturday it's full-on '70s funk and soul. Although some say a decline in the quality of the music mix has brought an end to the sardine-packed, sweaty-bodied days of yore, this remains an excellent place to shake your booty, and the cover charge is never more than five bucks. Wide selection of domestic and imported beers. Pool tables downstairs. Take to heart the sign that says "Be Nice or Leave."

## NOC NOC
*557 Haight St. (Fillmore/Steiner), (415) 861-5811*
*Daily 5pm-2am*

Noc Noc possesses what is arguably the weirdest interior of any bar in the city, which is saying a lot. The painted, papier-mâché-surfaced walls are covered with sections of aircraft sheet metal, hieroglyphics, and obscure images of scary creatures. Tiny, silent TVs hang from the ceiling, showing blank blue screens (perhaps it's a subtle dig at sports bars). Throw pillows and squat, cramped seats are scattered among the various nooks and crannies. Basically, it's Dr. Who meets Dr. Seuss in San Francisco's equivalent of the bar from *Star Wars*. After being

## The "Be-At" Line

The **Be-At Line** (626-4087) is a recorded telephone hotline that's updated daily. Usually read by a fast-talking, laconic, professional club goer, it features a rundown of the must-see gigs and happening dance nights going on at both well-known and obscure San Francisco clubs. For those interested in the burgeoning underground dance/rave scene, there are often references to "pirate line" phone numbers and inscrutable messages that will lead the knowledgeable in the right direction. It's a local call from San Francisco.

bombarded by all of these oddities, you'll find the tiny bar itself remarkably pedestrian and tame, featuring a small but solid beer selection, plus wines and pretzels. A DJ hidden behind a booth in the corner plays acid jazz and ambient music for the young, suitably hipster crowd. Come early if you don't want to end up standing all night.

### THE ORBIT ROOM CAFÉ
*1900 Market St. (Laguna), (415) 252-9525*
*M-F 7:30am-2am; Sa-Su 8am-2am*

Whether making your way toward the Castro from the downtown department stores or waiting for your UC Extension class to start, a visit to the Orbit Room will be time well spent. A dimly lit room with echoey acoustics (thanks to high ceilings and stone floors, walls, and furniture), this is Art Deco minimalism at its best. Plop a drink down at one of the inverted conical tables, pull up one of the squat, backless cylindrical seats, and then listen to the sounds from a funky, old jukebox (or from the odd live ensemble performance). There's a wonderfully cool doughnut-shaped bar as well, offering a range of salads, caffeine vehicles, and other treats in addition to the normal libations. (A word to the wise: the pints of hard cider on tap are the best in the City.) Not a gay bar per se, although it attracts a clientele with a gay sensibility and sensible people of all orientations. If you've ever lamented the demise of style, take the antique F-Market streetcar up to the Orbit Room.

### SOMEPLACE ELSE
*1795 Geary Blvd. (Fillmore/Webster), (415) 440-2180*
*M-Sa 2pm-2am; Su 1pm-midnight*

Most people spend much of their lives wishing they were someplace else, and if just some of those people stop by the mellow drinking/jazz space run by former New Yorker (but still diehard Yankee fan) Thomas Campbell-Reed, he'll be very happy indeed. Increasing numbers of young urbanites and neighborhood elders come to this high-ceilinged room to play at one of the two pool tables or sit on the mismatched furniture and play board games like Battleship and Sorry. The bar itself is a tiny metallic table that seats seven (if they squeeze) and from which the gregarious, discerning Campbell-Reed dispenses such exotic beers as Chimay from Belgium and Momba from the Ivory Coast. There's also seating in the adjoining alleyway for smokers, who are not allowed to light up inside. The upstairs balcony holds live jazz performances Wednesday to Friday nights and poetry readings on Monday. Bowls of popcorn or pretzels cost just two bits, and draft beers are only two bucks for ticket hold-ers who show their stub to that evening's show at the Fillmore or movie at the Kabuki theater.

## TORONADO
*547 Haight St. (Fillmore/Steiner), (415) 863-2276*
*Daily 11:30am-2am*

At first, this bar doesn't look like much—uninspired basic decor, a bunch of high tables and stools surrounding an aver-age-looking bar, with a smaller room in the back near the juke-box. Then you see the beer bottles along the walls. Then you see the taps. And *then* you see, above the bar, the Sign. For beer connoisseurs, it's the menu from heaven: more than forty differ-ent brews on tap, from Humboldt to Hopland, from lagers to bitters, all reasonably priced and served with care by the knowl-edgeable bar staff. Add to that various ciders, malts, and an equally impressive selection of bottled beers, and this is Beer Central. Come with friends and make it an evening of compare and contrast.

★

## Late Night Eats

### IT'S TOPS $
*1801 Market St. (Octavia), (415) 431-6395*
*Su-Tu 8am-3pm; W-F 8am-3pm, 8pm-3am; Sa 8am-3am*
One of the few remaining authentic diners in the City. Leather, stain-less steel, and Formica surfaces abound, there's booth and counter seating, and the helpings are large and very filling. Everything from steak and burgers to pancakes, waffles, French toast, and shakes.

### ZUNI CAFÉ AND GRILL $$$
*1658 Market St. (Gough/Franklin), (415) 552-2522*
*Tu-Sa 11:30am-midnight; Su 11am-11pm*
A die-hard temple of Mediterranean cuisine frequented by the artsy set, with a few advertising and business types mixed in. It looks very New Mexico, with an adobe fireplace, a long copper bar, and lots of serapes thrown about. Interesting preparations include house-cured anchovies with Parmesan and celery, or a divine whole roast chicken for two served with Tuscan bread salad. Slow service with a bad attitude unless you're a regular.

# ★ Haight Ashbury / Panhandle Cole Valley

The Haight-Ashbury has changed. The Summer of Love is over, Jerry Garcia is dead, and a Gap stands at that infamous corner known to hippies the world over. What remains from the old days are panhandlers begging for change, teen runaways offering "buds" and "doses," and a richness of street life distinct to this neighborhood (whatever you might think of it). There are a variety of quality joints (no pun intended) in the Upper Haight, from the cocktail-addled Deluxe to the simple Club Boomerang, the last outpost of live music on a street that was once teeming with it. Cole Valley, the Haight's more residential neighbor to the south, also has some pleasant, slightly more upscale bars. Overall, you could make a very interesting evening out of a pub crawl around this entire neighborhood.

★

## CLUB BOOMERANG
*1840 Haight St. (Stanyan/Shrader), (415) 387-2996*
*Daily noon-2am*

Boomerang is a stale Twinkie: tough on the outside but sweet in the middle. A dusty red awning and solid black doors welcome you to this Hell's-Angel-with-a-heart-of-gold bar—the last remaining live music venue in the upper Haight now that the I-Beam and Nightbreak are no more. Across the street from Murio's Trophy Room, Boomerang exudes the same sort of tough-love vibe if you're over the lounge scene and looking for a rough-around-the-edges club with live bands. It features hard-touring, hard-rocking acts all week long. The booking has been known to be skittish and last minute, so ask the doorman if he has a schedule of upcoming gigs—he may just tear the last copy down off the front door and hand it to you. Depending on the night and presumably the band, the cover charge ranges from $3 to $6, and all shows before 9pm are free. If you're not grooving on the likes of Fluke Starbucker, Solarcane, and Uberhund, the club also sports a full bar, pinball, and a pool table. (It may be one of the few places in town where you can be sinking an eight ball in an organized pool tournament while listening to a live band.) "Boom goes your weekend," as they like to say.

## DELUXE
*1511 Haight St. (Ashbury/Clayton), (415) 552-6949*
*Daily 4pm-2am*

Small, swinging, and smoky, with a beatnik attitude and a 1940s style—that's the Deluxe. Sit at the bar and chat up the hip, the groovy, and the not-necessarily-the-Haight-Street crowd. Stir your martini with an olive-clad toothpick. Sit back and let the sounds emanating from the tiny stage move you—owner Jay Johnson often does his best Frank Sinatra to the accompaniment of a jazz trio, or Steve and Patsy and other acts get the joint swinging and singing. You can also have a seat at a 1950s chrome tabletop and ask one of the friendly servers (who's working a 1940s fashion statement with peplum skirt, beehive

# Haight Ashbury
# Panhandle / Cole Valley

1. Club Boomerang
2. Deluxe
3. Finnegan's Wake
4. Gold Cane
5. Kezar Bar & Restaurant
6. Kezar Pub
7. Martin Mack's
8. Murio's Trophy Room
9. Persian Aub Zam Zam
10. Pig & Whistle
11. Storyville

hair, and three-inch pointy-toed pumps that would put Lucille Ball to shame) for a Cosmopolitan, a gin and tonic, or what some say is the best Bloody Mary in town. All told, a flashback San Francisco hot spot that's hip enough to make you hop.

## FINNEGAN'S WAKE
*937 Cole St. (Parnassus/Carl), (415) 731-6119*
*Daily 11am-2am*

Although located in an upscale university neighborhood, this roomy hangout is designed to make all feel welcome. There is no dress code (staff members don T-shirts), and aside from the inviting woodwork and lengthy bar counter, there are no decorations to commit it to any theme. With a harmonious blend of friendly locals, ex-hippies, and students, one might declare it a *Cheers* hybrid of sorts, only instead of Norm they have Norb, a local mover said to be good for an anecdote or two. Many favorites are on tap, such as Red Hook, Golden Bear, and Widemer Wheat. Half the bar houses pool tables, dartboards, pinball machines, and tables aplenty. Out back is a daytime patio with a Ping-Pong table and a barbecue that's fired up for Memorial Day and Labor Day. If there *is* any thematic connection with the James Joyce novel that spawned its name, it is that Finnegan's Wake unwittingly celebrates the sheer joy of living.

## THE GOLD CANE COCKTAIL LOUNGE
*1569 Haight St. (Ashbury/Clayton), (415) 626-1112*
*Daily noon-2am*

At the current location of this perennial Haight Street haunt, the bartenders have been turning out inexpensive mixed drinks (these days, $2.75) to the neighborhood for 20 years; at its previous address, just down the street, they served them for 40 years. And what a neighborhood! The Haight is infamous for its hippies, punksters, rambling youths, and been-around-the-block old-timers. At the Gold Cane, residents who actually saw the Jefferson Airplane perform live nurse their tumblers of scotch right next to cocktail-sipping British dandies who bum cigarettes from neohippies swilling microbrews. The long bar, which features school pictures of the owner's two sons, is separated by arches from two spacious rooms with unpretentious, cafeteria-style wooden tables. An enormous mounted moose head presides over the space, and even JFK makes an appearance over a corner booth. The jukebox is a testament to the musical heritage of the streets outside. Another bonus: Gold Cane is known for serving drinks with trivia napkins. Rumor has it this tradition may be expanded to include bar-top trivia games. While you wait for that day, grab a stool and listen to the owner spin one of his many intriguing tales.

## KEZAR BAR & RESTAURANT
*900 Cole St. (Carl), (415) 681-7678*
*Daily 5pm-2am*

Yuppies love the Kezar Bar & Restaurant because it's straight out of a glossy magazine ad: warm, inviting, and upscale, with enough bohemian quirks (like the skeleton figurines painted over the dark interior walls) to satisfy the rebel in them. Students love the Kezar because drinking here makes them feel like yuppies. Both camps appreciate the laid-back, no-sales-pitch atmosphere of the place, which is why many apparent first dates seem to occur here. Sadly, the wait staff can be anything from glacial to spacy; they have been known to take 10 minutes to serve a beer, after taking even longer to get the order. Anchor Steam, Sierra Nevada, and other microbrews are on tap, while sandwiches, salads, and great burgers are on the menu.

### KEZAR PUB
*770 Stanyan St. (Waller/Beulah), (415) 386-9292*
*M-Th 3pm-2am; F noon-2am; Sa-Su 10am-2am*

Originally a hangout for the 49ers, back when they played near-by at the old Kezar Stadium, the current incarnation of Kezar Pub was born in 1996. Walking in, you get a taste of nostalgia (historical sports photos and memorabilia) with modern California touches (microbrews on tap, well-chosen liquor, Golden Tee 3-D Golf video game). The long bar, low slat ceiling, and wooden chairs give the Kezar the feel of a club locker room without the locker-room smell. Two satellite televisions blare a variety of sporting events (hockey, basketball, and preseason football all at once!), while Patagonia-clad San Franciscans cheer for their alma maters or hometowns in between rounds of shots. Every conceivable beer label is offered either on tap or by the bottle. Pitchers are available—a good bet for groups and/or heavy drinkers—and there is usually a beer promotion in effect. Hearty California pub food—burgers, fried calamari—is served swiftly. The back room features a fireplace and two crowded pool tables. Most nights, the atmosphere recalls that of a well-behaved fraternity party. Expect lots of college sweatshirts.

### MARTIN MACK'S
*1568 Haight St. (Ashbury/Clayton), (415) 864-0124*
*Daily 10am-2am*

The Irish drinking establishment for the Upper Haight is a long, narrow joint divided into a front room, where the cheer-ful bar staff keeps those Guinnesses flowing, and the bright and airy dining room in back, which serves one of the largest, tasti-est, most artery-clogging Irish breakfasts around. (It's the per-fect place to stop after an evening of revelry and eat your way out of a hangover.) The bar is done up in the standard green-wall with wood trim, with stools and high tables near the street-facing windows so you can watch the hippies and tourists walk by. Sports and not much else are viewed on TVs at both ends of the room. Mostly this is just a nice neighborhood bar that attracts Irish and non-Irish in equal numbers.

### MURIO'S TROPHY ROOM
*1811 Haight St. (Shrader/Stanyan), (415) 752-2971*
*Daily noon-2am*

Think of the scene in *The Sure Thing* when John Cusack wanders into a local bar and buys a "trough of wine spritzer for cowboy guy," and you've got a good idea of Murio's Trophy Room. This bar is definitely not for the Cocktail Nation, but if you want to impress your friends with a local down-and-dirty dive where it only *looks* like you could get your ass kicked, then check it out. A filthy, green tile floor, mismatched bar stools, and men with long hair dominate the place, where the only indication of the '90s is the now-ubiquitous year-round Christmas lights hanging haphazardly from the ceiling. The somewhat-scary surroundings belie a heart of gold. Shouting orders at the doorman to toss out a rude, obnoxious drunk, the bartender (the one with the ponytail and lightning-bolt earring) may, in his next breath, render an erudite theater review while taking your drink order. Speaking of drinks, two mixed ones and a beer will set you back just $7.50, and the call bar is impressive. Murio's Trophy Room also offers a couple of video games, a pinball machine, two pool tables, a well-stocked jukebox, and a truckload of character.

## *Irish Bars*

**by someone who knows**

*Who knows Irish bars better than an Irishman? San Francisco resident Barry Roche, a native of Dublin, offers this subjective look at Irish bars in his new home:*

Faux or the genuine article? This is the dilemma facing the pub crawler seeking to quench their thirst in an "Irish" pub. Let's forget for the moment the problematic notion that anybody should *try* to attempt this feat some 6,000 miles away from Ireland. Some San Francisco bars make an honest, concerted effort to capture the sprit and ambience of an Irish pub. Some are hewn from chipboard rather than oak. Still others are under the impression that simply serving Guinness gets you there.

The working-class Irish pubs are predominately situated in the Richmond and the Sunset. **The Blarney Stone, Ireland's 32,** and the **Abbey Tavern** adorn Geary Boulevard. Generally one step up from spittoons, these places can be characterized by their homogenous clientele—male, blue collar, and nearly always first-generation Irish. Music and food can be served upon occasion, but they are essentially cheap and unpretentious. Leave the tie at home and don't bother asking for a Manhattan.

The faux Irish pubs are increasingly numerous: **The Dubliner** in SoMa and **Pat O'Shea's Mad Hatter** in the Richmond are two of the most notorious examples. These are nothing more than fratboy sports bars. I wouldn't edify their existence by any further comment except to say "don't."

If you really want to get close to the true Irish experience, though, I can warmly recommend **O'Reilly's** in North Beach, **An Bodhran** in the Lower Haight, **The Irish Bank** in the Financial district, and **Kate O'Brien's** in SoMa. Each of these pubs makes a genuine attempt to be as close as possible to the real thing. Apart from An Bodhran, they draw a mixed crowd of young Irish white collars and natives (if there actually are any in San Francisco). This engenders a lively mix, and on Fridays it's guaranteed that space will be hard to come by. The Irish Bank can claim the unique attraction of being able to let the crowd spill into the alleyway outside, a perfect solution for a balmy evening downtown. Most important, all of these places serve good Guinness, *the* measuring stick for any dyed-in-the-wool Irish pub. No matter if your bar is a rat's nest in every other respect, if your barman or barwoman can pull a good pint, he or she can be assured of making a living. Each of these bars also serves food, which is almost always good, especially the fare at O'Reillys. But when you're having a few pints, why spoil your appetite with food?

For all that they offer, however, none of these pubs can ever capture the true spirit of a real Irish pub. That can only be done on shores distant from these. When you get there, take out your map, find your way to Mulligan's of Poolbeg Street, and have a pint of plain for me.

## PERSIAN AUB ZAM ZAM

*1633 Haight St. (Clayton/Belvedere), (415) 861-2545*
*No set hours of operation*

Those wishing for a respite from the "peace and love" groove of the Haight-Ashbury are strongly advised to drop by this tension-filled, claustrophobic, windowless room dominated by a padded horseshoe bar. Owner and bartender Bruno, who has run this place forever, opens and closes when he feels like it and dispenses cocktails with the most terrifying demeanor west of the Citadel. When he's not busy throwing out newly arrived patrons whose looks rub him the wrong way, he's ridiculing your choice of drinks (if it's not a martini) while refusing the requests from neophytes to sit at the empty back tables. So why does anyone bother going here? Very strong drinks, for one. And of course, surviving the whole experience makes a great war story.

## PIG & WHISTLE

*2801 Geary Blvd. (Wood), (415) 885-4779*
*Daily 11:30am-2am*

Geary Boulevard is so darned long and heavily traveled that going from its downtown source to Ocean Beach is the city equivalent of driving cross-country. Dropped into this strained analogy, the Pig & Whistle becomes a kind of Midwest pit stop. A favorite of Richmond locals, this spot is a sure thing when looking for good beer (23 choices on tap, written on the giant blackboard behind the bar), great company (interesting neighborhood get-together of British and Irish expats, Inner Richmond preppies dressed in black, postheroin elder Haighstmen, and even a few bikers), and excellent bar food, especially the fish and chips and the banger roll (sausage sandwich). The bar has that unmistakable saloon look that comes from historic wood, while a side room holds a pool table for patrons' use. A stable of dedicated dart players gives the pockmarked boards steady use. A true pub, whether it's your ultimate destination or not.

---

### *BASS Tickets*

Many of the City's venues that present live music also have, alas, exasperatingly limited daytime box-office hours. If you are unable or unwilling to take time off to pick up tickets, you run the risk of showing up for an already-sold-out show when you arrive at the club on the night of the gig. No matter whether out of sheer laziness or sheer necessity, you can avoid this predicament with a telephone and a credit card by going through **BASS Tickets** (510-762-BASS). Think of them as the Bay Area's equivalent to Ticketmaster, Pearl Jam's nemesis ticket broker. As with most ticket brokers, be aware that you will pay dearly for the convenience. BASS charges not only for each "transaction" (one phone order), but also adds on a handling fee for *each ticket*. It is not unheard of to pay 30 percent or more of the cost of a single ticket in surcharges. (One of the contributors to this book actually ended up putting out $13.75 for an $8 ticket.) Service charges are somewhat less when purchasing tickets in person through a BASS outlet such as those at The Wherehouse or Tower Records, but you'll still probably feel royally screwed. People who are into the net can purchase tickets on-line through Ticketweb (http://www.ticketweb.com).

---

## STORYVILLE
*1751 Fulton St. (Central/Masonic), (415) 441-1751*
*Daily 5pm-1am*

Red velvet walls, black leather couches, gold deco sconces, glowing fireplaces, and old-time photos give Storyville the feel of the legendary jazz clubs of New York and the Fillmore. Here, African-Americans who had patronized the old joints mix with both jazz-loving professionals and younger people who are trying the supper club thing. (The crowd evolves as the evening progresses, starting older and getting younger.) There are two rooms: The Lounge in front is where, for the price of a drink, you can listen to the house band, including Don Pender and various others, play from 5pm until 8pm. The nonsmoking Showroom in the back offers both dining and the club's headliners. The acts are mostly solid, midlevel combos. The food celebrates the Louisiana kitchen with jambalaya, gumbo, and catfish on the menu, and a jazz brunch features eggs sardou, seafood omelets, and crayfish on brioche. Desserts include gooey chocolate pecan parfait and sweet potato crisp. No cover is charged most nights.

★

## Late Night Eats

### BAMBINO'S $
*945 Cole St. (Parnassus/Carl), (415) 731-1343*
*Su-Th 11am-11pm; F-Sa 11am-midnight*

Although they make plenty of tasty pizzas for pickup and delivery, Bambino's is also a good Italian restaurant in its own right, a cozy storefront with frilly lace curtains and virgin-white tablecloths. The enormous pasta servings (which follow the copious amounts of bread) are generally excellent, especially angel hair with sun-dried tomatoes, mushrooms, zucchini, and caramelized red onions.

### CHA CHA CHA $
*1801 Haight St. (Shrader), (415) 386-5758*
*Su-Th 11:30am-4pm, 5pm-11pm; F 11:30am-4pm, 5pm-11:30pm;*
*Sa 11:30am-4pm, 5pm-11:30pm*

You *will* have to wait for a table at this swinging Caribbean restaurant in the Haight, but it's a small inconvenience considering the quirky, palate-tingling food that comes out of the kitchen. Most items are tapas sized, so order a selection and share. Shrimp in creamy Cajun coconut sauce is sublime, as are fried plantains and just about everything else on the menu. The kooky, witch-doctorish decor adds to the experience.

### CHABELA ¢
*1805 Haight St. (Shrader), (415) 751-6204*
*Su-W 11am-midnight; Th-Sa 10:30am-2:30am*

A small, bright taqueria that could probably survive on overflow from Cha Cha Cha alone. (They actually swapped locations a few years ago.)

### CREPES ON COLE ¢
*100 Carl St. (Cole), (415) 664-1800*
*Su-Th 7am-11pm; F-Sa 7am-midnight*

Crêpes come with a variety of fillings, like curry, salsa, or tofu, or you can design your own plate. Exceptionally good "house potatoes" (home fries) accompany the thin pancakes. Portions are quite large, and it's a nice place to either grab a quick bite or pass a few hours.

## Late Night Eats

### ESCAPE FROM NEW YORK PIZZA ¢
*1737 Haight St. (Cole/Shrader), (415) 668-5577*
*Su-W 11:30am-midnight; Th 11:30am-1am; F-Sa 11:30am-2:15am*
Quick service pizzeria that serves up fairly faithful renditions of New York style pies—a thin, crisp crust; tangy tomato sauce, and a perfect layer of cheese.

### KAN ZAMAN $
*1793 Haight St. (Shrader), (415) 751-9656*
*M 5pm-11pm; Tu-Th noon-11pm; F-Sa noon-midnight; Su noon-11pm*
A reasonably priced Middle Eastern restaurant in the riotous Upper Haight, serving fine food amidst fake palm trees and exquisite murals, with floor seating on cushions available. For a novel dessert of sorts, head to the bar and try the apple-, honey- or apricot-flavored tobacco, which is smoked through hookahs. Diners on weekend evenings may be lucky enough to catch a free performance by a belly dancer.

### LUCKY PENNY $
*2670 Geary Blvd. (Masonic), (415) 921-0836*
*Daily 24 hours*
The best thing about the Lucky Penny is that you can park here without significantly raising your blood pressure. Things look less rosy once you're inside the restaurant; its under-$6 surf 'n' turf specials are reminiscent of the Las Vegas casino coffee shops one only frequents after losing one's life savings at the roulette table. Still, if you're up all night and hungry, the fries are actually good and the coffee is decent as well.

### MEL'S DRIVE-IN $
*3355 Geary Blvd. (Parker/Stanyan), (415) 387-2244*
*Su-Th 6am-1am; F-Sa 6am-3am*
Mel's is part of the movement to recapture the glory of the '50s, with coin-op jukeboxes at every table and a menu with favorites like meat loaf sandwiches and bread pudding. A popular late-night hangout, especially with teens, Mel's is perfect for a milk shake after the movies and is a fun place to go with a group. Be sure to save room for dessert. No credit cards.

### MR. PIZZA MAN $
*3409 Geary Blvd. (Stanyan), (415) 387-3131*
*Daily 10am-4am*
The mysterious Mr. Pizza Man must be good with a mound of dough because the crust on the pizza at this chain eatery is thick and excellent. If you're feeling gourmet, they offer a number of interesting topping options; the artichoke heart pizza is particularly good.

### TAQUERIA EL BALAZO ¢
*1654 Haight St. (Clayton), (415) 864-8608*
*Su-Th 10:30am-11pm; F-Sa 10:30am-1am*
A brightly colored taqueria that has ample seating for its hip (and hippie) clientele. Choices include the usual tacos, burritos, and quesadillas, but the specials are noteworthy, including Bob's Burrito (with garlic, zucchini, and mushroom) and Jerry's Burrito (with fresh tender cactus and Mexican goat cheese). Even with a fresh fruit drink, it's hard to spend more than five dollars on a filling meal. No credit cards.

The center of gay life in the city, the Castro is obviously notable for the plethora of gay bars scattered at or near the intersection of Castro and 18th streets. You'll know they're nearby: the house music will be pumping, the dance floors will be packed, and men in leather or men in drag will be as common as the fog in summertime. Some clubs are frenetic meat markets, the same-sex equivalent of the Triangle in the Marina; others are more mellow hangouts for longtime couples and good friends. There are also plenty of bars and clubs that have clientele of all sexual orientations, especially along Market Street closer to Church Street. Noe Valley, better known for its family-friendly character than its nightlife, still offers a few cozy and quirky bars (the Dubliner and O'Greenberg's, respectively) that predate the onslaught of gentrification. No matter what your preference, the Castro and Noe Valley have plenty of neighborhood bars that make even the first time visitor feel right at home.

★

### THE BADLANDS
*4121 18th St. (Castro/Collingswood), (415) 626-9320*
*Daily 11:30am-2am*

Badlands offers a back-to-basics course for students of gay bars. The lights are low, the space is cavernous, and the purpose is clear: meeting Mr. Right—and pronto. All the old standards are in place: pool tables, western memorabilia, crates of empties that double as furniture. And if you get bored with the crowd, you can entertain yourself by examining the collection of real gay vanity license plates displayed on the walls. Most significantly, Badlands can be credited with leading the charge in the revival of Sunday afternoon beer busts. Often imitated but never duplicated, this bust remains the most popular (literally wall-to-wall men, with a fresh supply lined up outside) and the most economical ($1.25 bottles) in the neighborhood. If you've been wondering where you can drink on Sundays on the cheap while jammed into a room that shrieks "pectorals," walk no farther than Badlands.

### THE CAFÉ
*2367 Market St. (Castro), (415) 861-3846*
*Daily 12:30pm-2am*

A rock-solid institution of the Castro nightclub scene since its days as Café San Marco in the early eighties, The Café continues to be the destination of choice for the twentysomething gay male crowd. Lesbians have been known to cry foul that gay men have taken over a bar that was largely their turf until the mid-'90s, and some straights decry the bar's "no straight kissing" policy (quickly renamed a "no deep kissing by anyone" policy when the bar was recently charged with discrimination). Nonetheless, both lesbians and straights are still found here in large numbers early in the evening; later on the crowd becomes almost exclusively male and gay. The large, generic-looking two-story nightclub is divided into various sections—a

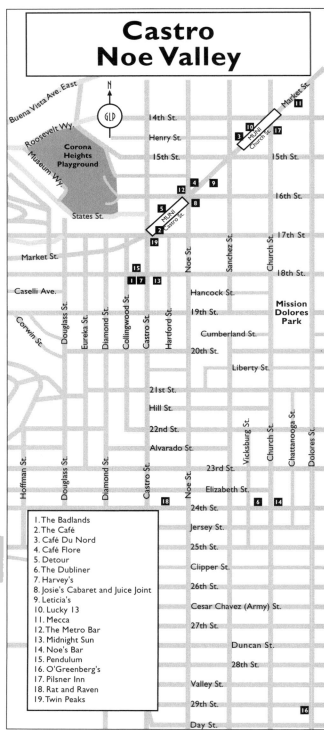

# Castro
# Noe Valley

N

GLP

Buena Vista Ave. East

Roosevelt Wy.

Museum Wy.

Corona Heights Playground

States St.

Market St.

Caselli Ave.

Corwin St.

14th St.

Henry St.

15th St.

Market St.

**[11]**

**[10]** **[3]** MUNI Church St. **[17]**

15th St.

**[4]** **[9]**

**[12]**

**[8]**

**[5]** MUNI

**[2]** Castro St.

**[19]**

16th St.

17th St

18th St.

**[15]**

**[1]** **[7]** **[13]**

Hancock St.

19th St.

Cumberland St.

20th St.

Liberty St.

21st St.

Hill St.

22nd St.

Alvarado St.

Mission Dolores Park

Hoffman St.

Douglass St.

Eureka St.

Diamond St.

Collingwood St.

Castro St.

Hartford St.

Noe St.

Sanchez St.

Church St.

Corwin St.

Douglass St.

Diamond St.

Castro St.

Noe St.

Vicksburg St.

Church St.

Chattanooga St.

Dolores St.

**[18]**

23rd St.

Elizabeth St. **[6]** **[14]**

24th St.

Jersey St.

25th St.

Clipper St.

26th St.

Cesar Chavez (Army) St.

27th St.

Duncan St.

28th St.

Valley St.

29th St.

Day St.

**[16]**

1. The Badlands
2. The Café
3. Café Du Nord
4. Café Flore
5. Detour
6. The Dubliner
7. Harvey's
8. Josie's Cabaret and Juice Joint
9. Leticia's
10. Lucky 13
11. Mecca
12. The Metro Bar
13. Midnight Sun
14. Noe's Bar
15. Pendulum
16. O'Greenberg's
17. Pilsner Inn
18. Rat and Raven
19. Twin Peaks

dance floor, two pool tables, the bar, and a balcony that commands a prime view of the corner of Market and Castro below—with each attracting its own clique. Monday night is $1.25 domestic beer night and Tuesday is half-price well drinks night, but regulars still swear the best night to go is Thursday, when the weekend hasn't yet drawn the out-of-towners, but the city boys are out and about.

## CAFÉ DU NORD

*2170 Market St. (Church/Sanchez), (415) 979-6545*
*Daily Su-Tu 6pm-2am; W-Sa 4pm-2am*

Café Du Nord is a throwback to the days of dining and dancing, when martinis were clear, everyone smoked cigarettes, and "vintage clothing" meant hand-me-downs. There's a comfortable, well-used feeling about the nightclub: everything has a charming patina of wear, with no glitz or pomp or new paint to be seen. Dusty red velvet abounds as you descend the dramatically steep stairs into the spacious-yet-cozy bar. Beyond the bar is a smallish room, with little white-clothed tables and a stage in front of a real dance floor that gets plenty of use. There's music seven days a week in a delightfully wide range of styles. Learn to salsa dance for free on Tuesdays with Benny Velarde, enjoy the musical stylings of such retro swing acts as Lavay Smith and the Red Hot Skillet Lickers on Saturdays, and occasionally hear such legendary bluesmen as Charles Brown. Cover charge is unusually modest, $3 Sunday through Thursday and $5 on the weekends, with no cover before 8pm. Cocktails are $2 during happy hour (4-7pm daily). If you need a place to bring a date for dinner or to show off your Palm Beach suit, Café Du Nord should be on your A list.

## CAFÉ FLORE

*2298 Market St. (Noe), (415) 621-8579*
*Su-Th 7:30am-11:30pm; F-Sa 7:30am-midnight*

Although it is not a club, the triangular Café Flore definitely maintains enough of a scene to rival one, thanks to the overflow of humanity that makes waiting for a table a true test of patience. (If a wait turns up nothing, introduce yourself to someone with an extra seat.) The dark-stained woods of the interior call to mind an alpine cabin, while the leafy outdoor patio, protected from the wind by a glass wall, is one of the City's most celebrated hangouts. Complete with everything from alcoholic drinks to iced coffee to squid over pasta, this is an ideal spot to sit back and watch the Castro walk by. With everyone from flaunting body builders to lesbian punks (it isn't nicknamed Café Hairdo for nothing), Flore contains its own minidrama, so keep your eyes and your ears open for the ultimate in free entertainment, even if you don't know who the players are.

## DETOUR

*2348 Market St. (Noe/Castro), (415) 861-6053*
*Daily 2pm-2am*

The Detour is a neighborhood fixture, site of the nightly "sidewalk sale." That's the term for the outdoor mingling that occurs just after last call and the mass exodus from the bars—the time when expectations, standards, and just about every-

## Gay Bars of Special Interest

### THE PENDULUM
*4146 18th St. (Collingswood/18th St.), (415) 863-4441*
*Daily 6am-2am*
This bar caters to African-American gay men and their friends. It is very popular and plenty of fun, with patrons and music spilling out onto the sidewalk.

### ESTA NOCHE
*3079 16th St. (Valencia/Mission), (415) 861-5757*
*Su-Th 1pm-2am; F-Sa 1pm-3am*
Not surprisingly, this Mission gay bar—the best in the neighborhood—draws a mainly Latino crowd who absolutely must dance to the latest, hippest salsa (mixed with disco and 80s music on the weekends). Order a Corona (in Spanish) and check out the drag show.

### N'TOUCH
*1548 Polk St. (California/Sacramento), (415) 441-8413*
*Daily 3pm-2am*
This is traditionally the City's most popular hangout for Asian-American gay men. Check it out, and along the way, stop off at the other Polk Street venues, some dating from the era when Polk Street was the gay part of town and the Castro was just somebody's cow pasture.

thing else are cast aside in hopes of one more chance at meeting Mr. Right's evil twin, Mr. Available. Very dark and very crowded, this bar-dance club features the rarely utilized motif of chain-link fencing as decor (and the even less frequently seen but amazingly convenient feature of an ATM right at the bar). The music you'll hear varies from night to night depending on the evening's theme, but it never deviates much from one of those Castro mainstays that sounds like a "Jeopardy" category, such as Techno and Music from the '80s. Go-go boys pack the place on Saturday nights—well worth the sore neck on Sunday, especially if there's someone there to massage it. Incidentally, the messages in the laser display may be subliminal, but the messages from the other patrons certainly won't be.

## THE DUBLINER
*3838 24th St. (Church/Vicksburg), (415) 826-2279*
*M-F 1pm-2am; Sa-Su 10am-2am*
Although unapologetically Irish (see the occasional wall poster announcing a benefit dance for fellow countrymen facing extradition to England "for their part in the Irish freedom struggle"), the folks behind and bellied up to this Noe Valley bar make everyone feel at home. The crowd ranges from paint-splattered construction workers to wool-suited lawyers, fresh-faced twentysomethings to silver-haired mums stopping by for a postshopping, presupper cocktail. Maybe it's the Irish blood, but the bartenders here distinguish themselves with their ability to draw a Guinness properly and to remember a face, if not a name. The barstools are plentiful, and the jukebox is stocked with everyone from the Chieftains to Bob Marley to Patsy Cline. If you're so inclined, even a wine drinker can find a suitable glass of red here for only $3.50. If

you've had one of those days, take the J-Church to 24th Street. The Dubliner, a settling pint of Guinness, and a lift in your spirits are all less than a block away.

## HARVEY'S
*500 Castro St. (18th St.), (415) 431-4278*
*Su-Th 10am-2am; F-Sa 9am-2am*

Harvey's sits smack dab in the center of gay San Francisco, and yet it is much more the calm eye than the storm. In its most recent—and best—incarnation, this infamous bar, formerly known as the Elephant Walk, is almost like a gay Planet Hollywood, although the photos and memorabilia pay tribute to gay civil rights hero Harvey Milk and the many others who have followed his lead rather than a bunch of Tinseltown celebs. The wide, bright windows are ideal for watching the Castro Street scene unfold outside. Meanwhile, inside is one of the few places where gay men and women of all ages can find a friendly, low-key spot to mingle. Check out the drink specials on Sunday afternoons, as well as a full schedule of live music and dance. Harvey's is also one of the few places around to feature a full-scale bar menu: so handy, so glamorously European. Snag a seat at said bar, where a bevy of adorable lesbian bartenders set new standards for good service.

## JOSIE'S CABARET AND JUICE JOINT
*3583 16th St. (Market/Noe), (415) 861-7933*
*Daily 9am-11pm*

This colorful neighborhood institution combines a small but amazingly well-stocked daytime café—breakfast, lunch, and dinner daily from 9:30am to 7pm—and the Castro's best-loved nighttime local stage. In its evening cabaret guise, Josie's features gay comedy and theater, from high drama to high camp, with cover charges that vary with the performance or event. While performances span the talent range, great ones occur often enough, and less acclaimed ones always have at least something to offer in the way of entertainment. (If you want to see a performance with an unobstructed view, get here early for a good seat. If you don't, you'll be sitting in the balcony and hearing the show but seeing a support beam.) The price of admission is reasonable, rarely over $10, and it's only $5 for the open-mike comedy on Monday nights. The staff is awfully nice and will wait on you toe and heel with a smile. (Don't be intimidated by their Haight Street fashion sense.) And although this is called a juice joint, rest assured that draft beer is also served. On a sunny day, check out the back patio, have a mimosa, and soak up those rays.

## LETICIA'S
*2247 Market St. (Sanchez/Noe), (415) 621-0441*
*Su-Th 11am-11pm; F-Sa 11am-midnight*

The bright, tropical orange exterior of Leticia's may remind some folks more of Miami's South Beach than San Francisco's Upper Market, but the spirit of this bar-restaurant is strongly rooted in Castro exuberance. The enormous interior is done up in a playful decor: plush carpeting, scores of huge potted plants, seashell sconces, a row of Diego Rivera copies, faux-stone-and-brick moldings, and plenty of leather banquettes for large parties. The bartenders, many of whom sound like Desi Arnaz, Jr., are friendly and professional in their dress shirts and ties. The crowd is mostly neighborhood folks, many of whom are apparently working odd shifts, if they work at all. That's the only explanation for the 3pm to 5:30pm happy hour, when well drinks are $2 and margaritas are twice that. If you can't make it that early, the other option is to show up very late, after the diners have left and the drinkers return in force. Bottled Budweiser is available for the beer people.

## LUCKY 13

*2140 Market St. (Church/Sanchez), (415) 487-1313*
*M-F 4pm-2am; Sa-Su 2pm-2am*

If you're not put off by the imposing Germanic red-and-black facade, Lucky 13 is a very happening hangout spot. Long and narrow inside, lit only by red bulbs (give your eyes time to adjust), it sports upper-level seating along two walls, great for people-watching and snide-comment-making while rockers and Peg Bundy look-alikes meander below. The drink selection—28 beers on tap, more than 40 bottled brews, a wide variety of single-malt scotches, and a full bar—is sure to impress connoisseurs. A superlative jukebox provides a mix of punk, heavy metal, and straight-ahead classic rock. Yes, there is a pool table. One dollar off all draft beers during happy hour (until 7pm).

## MECCA

*2029 Market St. (Church/Dolores), (415) 621-7000*
*Su-W 5pm-midnight; Th-Sa 5pm-1:30am*

Who would have guessed that one of the City's hippest, most-crowded spots would be thriving in the neon shadow of the Market Street Safeway? Come here any weekend night and you'll see a beautiful crowd, well dressed and well financed (at least enough to support a couple of ultraprofessional parking valets standing at attention outside). Both straight and gay sidle up to what may be the best-looking bar in the city. The huge oval island, the centerpiece of this high-ceilinged industrial interior, has touches of retro elegance (think heating vent meets velvet curtain). Meanwhile, the restaurant, for once, is actually relegated to background status in this heady social scene, with tables tucked into corners and lining the edges of the room. While the kitchen opened to rave reviews, in general people don't come here to eat. They come to be seen, drink in hand, lookin' good.

## THE METRO BAR AND RESTAURANT

*3600 16th St. (Market/Noe), (415) 703-9750*
*M-F 2:30pm-2am; Sa-Su 1pm-2am*

Perched above the triangular intersection of Market, Noe, and 16th Street, Metro is the solution to some of life's intractable problems. Looking for a gay space that's not deafening or crowbarred full of people sporting attitude? Also looking for great Asian food in the heart of the Castro? The Metro comes through on both counts. It's a bright, fun space that boasts an outdoor balcony full of vivants enjoying the weather (when appropriate) and Market Street passersby (year-round). The Sunday beer special offers a civilized alternative to the insanely jammed Sunday beer busts elsewhere, while the Metro's margarita, a special on

Thursdays, is the best-kept secret in the Castro. (In fact, it may be the only secret that's kept in the Castro.) Lovers of campy TV will enjoy Monday nights when *Melrose Place* is screened for the crowd. Great gay bar, great restaurant, great fun all under one roof—how very San Francisco.

## MIDNIGHT SUN

*4067 18th St. (Hartford/Castro), (415) 861-4186*
*Daily noon-2am*

The Midnight Sun should be Stop Number One on any self-respecting tour of gay San Francisco. A video bar that mixes campy comedy and up-to-the-moment televised tunes, it pulls in a tightly packed crowd of friendly, attractive men. With live transmissions of the most popular television programs, this place is assured of being crowded nearly every day of the week. From *Melrose* Mondays to *Simpsons* Sundays, with *Ellen* (of course) in between, great music, great television, and great opportunities to strike up conversations are inevitable. Although the halcyon days of *Golden Girls* and *Designing Women* are behind us, the Midnight Sun remains one of the premier gay man's spots in the City. Helpful hint: Before you lose your heart to Mr. Right, check to see if he's a regular for show-tune Tuesdays.

## NOE'S BAR

*1199 Church St. (24th St.), (415) 282-4007*
*M-F 10am-2am; Sa-Su 8am-2am*

A perfectly serviceable neighborhood corner bar, Noe's has a great video golf game and an above-average collection of serious reprobates, most of whom can be found drinking up their pension and disability checks. It's a sports bar on weekends, especially when the Niners are playing. The rest of the time, grab a stool at the bar or a seat at a table by the window and nurse a drink while you observe the scene. The old-timers are good entertainment if you like loud bantering, since someone here always has an opinion (usually involving the gentrification of the neighborhood) and will announce it boldly enough for everyone to hear. If you're hungry, the newly opened CyBelle's pizza, with a full dinner menu, is just steps away through a connecting door.

## O'GREENBERG'S

*1600 Dolores St. (29th St.), (415) 695-9216*
*Daily 10am-2am*

Although it's a couple of miles long and a major thoroughfare, there's only one bar to be found along leafy Dolores Street, and it's been there for over 70 years. Formerly known as the Woods, the name changed one boozy Saint Patrick's Day 20 years ago when Greenberg, the owner (who at the time was Noe Valley's bar tycoon, running most of the popular 24th Street establishments), had an Irish version of his name printed up on the staff's aprons and the moniker just stuck. It's an airy sports bar with redwood walls, five TVs, and dartboards in back. Craig, the veteran bartender, cheerfully reports that the crowd is mostly thirty- and fortysomethings who grew up within shouting distance of St. Mary's Church a block away. The new generation of drinkers coming here from the Mission are, in Craig's words, "nice, quiet kids."

## PILSNER INN

*225 Church St. (Market/15th St.), (415) 621-7058*
*M-F 9am-2am; Sa 7am-2am*

The Pilsner Inn may seem like a gay hangout, with its rainbow flags outside and 1980s dance mix playing on the sound system inside (e.g., songs from Erasure), but the creeping tide of rockin' Mission Kids even infiltrates here, especially on weekends. Weeknights are still the domain of the older, leather-wearing constituency, but whatever your sexual orientation, you'll feel welcome most anytime. There's a great beer garden in back where you can bring your pint and stare up at the stars. ("No drugs or you'll be 86ed" reads a sign, so be warned.) Inside, seating options are limited, but since this is a starter bar, you should be able to snag a stool at the long bar or a seat at one of the few tables as the night progresses and patrons move on to other joints. Games include pinball, pool, darts, and video games. Sixteen beers on tap, not to mention penguins painted on the walls.

## RAT AND RAVEN

*4054 24th St. (Noe/Castro), (415) 285-0674*
*Daily noon-2am*

Even family-oriented Noe Valley, where preschoolers often outnumber adults on the sidewalk, has to get a little wild sometimes. The Rat and Raven is clearly geared toward the neighborhood's younger adults and DINKS (double income, no kids). On any given night, Soundgarden is blasting from the jukebox, the bar is a sea of Doc Martens and plaid shirts, and glasses of obscure Belgian ales or the hottest new microbrew cover the rows of high tables. With beer bottles and beer towels lining the walls and exposed beams of this dark, long room, it feels a bit like a European beer hall. That changes on Sunday nights, when all conversation stops and attention is turned firmly toward the large-screen TV and the newest episode of *The Simpsons*. (Interrupt this religious ceremony at your peril.) A dart board and a pool table are in the back, and a charming outdoor patio is inviting on the occasional warm night. Kudos to the bar staff for offering pitchers of their best brews at reasonable prices.

## THE TWIN PEAKS

*401 Castro St. (17th St./Market), (415) 864-9470*
*Daily noon-2am*

Perched at the intersection of Castro and Market, Twin Peaks was the first gay bar to offer something that, at the time, was radical beyond comprehension: big, clear windows opening right onto the street. Yes, gasp, people could see exactly who was in there. Decades later, the bar is just as proud and defiant, and still basking in the sunlight its patrons have a right to. In stark contrast to the often-manic energy of this neighborhood's other bars and clubs, Twin Peaks draws a much older, mellower crowd that enjoys the friendly, homey atmosphere. A bar, a balcony area, and plenty of comfortable café-style seating along the famous picture windows are all perfect for watching the world wander by. This is a mixed crowd of gays and lesbians, a place to hang out with old friends and, inevitably, make new ones.

★

## Late Night Eats

### BAGDAD CAFÉ $
*2295 Market St. (16th St.), (415) 621-4434*
*Daily 24 hours*
With its huge street-level windows and central Castro location, the 24-hour Bagdad Café is the perfect place for watching drunk people (or for drunken people-watching, as the case may be) over a plate of classic diner food.

### CAFÉ FLORE $
*2298 Market St. (Noe), (415) 621-8579*
*Su-Th 7:30am-11:30pm; F-Sa 7:30am-midnight*
See bar listing.

### CHOW $/$$
*215 Church St. (14th St./Market), (415) 552-2469*
*Su-Tu 11am-10pm; W-Sa 11am-midnight*
Moderate prices, a pumped-up, lively crowd, and a menu that spans the globe while offering certain essential old favorites (strawberry shortcake is a specialty) make this new Castro eatery worth a late-night glance.

### ESCAPE FROM NEW YORK PIZZA ¢
*508 Castro St. (18th St./19th St.), (415) 252-1515*
*Su-W 11:30am-1am; Th-Sa 11:30am-2am*
Quick service pizzeria that serves up fairly faithful renditions of New York style pies—a thin, crisp crust, tangy tomato sauce, and a perfect layer of cheese.

### HAPPY DONUTS ¢
*3801 24th St. (Church), (415) 285-5890*
*Daily 5am-2am*
The place to go if you're looking for a fresh-out-of-the-oven donut, cinnamon roll, or croissant. It's the safest place in town, too, given that there's probably at least one police officer there at any given moment.

### HOT 'N' HUNKY ¢
*4039 18th St. (Hartford/Sanchez), (415) 621-6365*
*Su-Th 11am-midnight; F-Sa 11am-1am*
The name of this little pink burger joint aims to describe the food as well as the clientele. If the thick and cleverly named burgers (the "Miss Piggy" bacon cheeseburger is an example) somehow don't put you in a good mood, you can head down the street to the Midnight Sun for a rousing night of music and TV.

### LETICIA'S $
*2247 Market St. (Sanchez/16th St.), (415) 621-0441*
*Su-Th 11am-10:30pm; F-Sa 11am-midnight*
The food is unmemorable—the black bean mole is a safe bet—and service comes with an attitude. In short, come for the convivial atmosphere, but go to the Mission for authentic Mexican specialties.

### MARCELLO'S PIZZA $
*420 Castro St. (Market/17th St.), (415) 863-3900*
*Su-Th 11am-1am; F-Sa 11am-2am*
Feta cheese is about as good as you can get as pizza innovations go, and Marcello's does it right. They serve slices and whole pizzas with unusual combinations of toppings, and they're just across from the Castro theater, great for a post-show, pre-Castro bar crawl bite.

## Late Night Eats

### MIYABI JAPANESE CUISINE $
*251 Church St. (Market), (415) 861-0447*
*M-Sa 5pm-1am; Su 5pm-10:30pm*
1980s pastels cover the walls of this Japanese restaurant, one of the few in town that is open late. It probably won't ever be in a Michelin Guide, but the inexpensive sushi is a definite plus.

### ORPHAN ANDY'S $
*3991-A 17th St. (Castro), (415) 864-9795*
*Daily 24 hours (closed Thanksgiving and Christmas)*
This is true diner cuisine, where you can get crispy fries, juicy burgers, pancakes, or eggs at any hour. Vinyl booths and a jukebox complete the picture. All-night service in the heart of the Castro means there can be a line after club closing time on the weekends. Cash only.

### PASTA POMODORO $
*2304 Market St. (Noe/Castro), (415) 558-8123*
*M-Th 11am-11pm; F-Sa 11am-midnight; Su noon-11pm*
Large servings of pasta at incredibly cheap prices—it's a concept that has made this citywide Italian restaurant chain very popular among those with big appetites and light pockets. Service is usually lightning quick yet still pleasant. Cash only.

### POZOLE $
*2337 Market St. (Castro/Noe), (415) 626-2666*
*M-Th 4-11pm; F-Sa noon-midnight; Su noon-11pm*
One of the most visually intriguing eateries around: the walls are painted in colorful cartoon hues, plaster figurines sit atop pillars, and dressed-up skeletons hang on the walls. As for the Mexican food served within, it looks great and tastes pretty good, too. Try the chicken-filled burrito Mexicano or the cactus-filled burrito Californiano; both are part of the menu devoted to low-fat dishes. No credit cards.

### SAUSAGE FACTORY $/$$
*517 Castro St. (18th St.), (415) 626-1250*
*Daily 11:30am-12:30am*
Family-style restaurant that serves up traditional Italian food, with exceptional (and exceptionally large) pizzas. The garlic bread is very good, too.

### SLIDER'S $
*49 Castro St. (18th St./Market), (415) 431-3288*
*Su-Th 11am-11pm; F-Sa 11am-3am*
Look for the char-broiled burgers cooking on the rotating grill by the window, and you'll know you've found this meat eater's heaven. Self-serve condiments bar so you can truly have it your way. Also serves chicken sandwiches, hot dogs, and the like.

### SPARKY'S $
*242 Church St. (15th/Market), (415) 621-6001*
*Daily 24 hours*
Whether you're a true hipster or you just like to observe the irony of them clomping around a typical diner in Docs or platform shoes, head to Sparky's at a late hour and suck up the trendiness of it all. Or you can avoid the whole scene and call for delivery.

Out in the Richmond and Sunset, also known as The Avenues, things are a whole lot quieter than in the rest of the City. The pace of life is slower. The straightforward neighborhood bars constitute virtually all the nightlife. The dearth of clubs is a testament to the fact that if people go out here at all, they go out primarily to drink with a small group of friends or just to say hello to their neighbors. (This may explain why the majority of the city's Irish bars are located in these neighborhoods.) The rare live-music club, like Last Day Saloon, programs such mainstream rock or blues that they prove the point about the area: if you want the experimental, head for SoMa or the Mission; if you want simple, down-home joints to keep you warm when the inevitable fog rolls in, come on out here. Drinks are cheaper and the attitude quotient is far lower, too. Similarly, the bars that dot West Portal's main drag are small, familiar dives whose sounds provide the only evidence of life after the neighborhood movie theater shuts down for the night.

★

## ABBEY TAVERN
*4100 Geary Blvd. (5th Ave.), (415) 221-7767*
*Daily 1pm-2am*

There's always a dull roar rising from the corner of Geary and 5th Avenue, where the Abbey lies. One big room of bland decor that mimics the Avenues Aesthetic, it's an easy place to grab a drink before or after dinner. Fun and games here is made up of a single pool table and two large-screen TVs tuned to sporting events or the latest sitcom, depending on the crowd, which is skewed toward older folks, the working class, and the Irish. No food is served, but it seems kosher to bring in your own since the bartenders themselves are often munching on a pizza behind their posts. If this is your last stop for the evening, don't miss the gumball machine at the door offering "Cover Alcohol Breath" gum.

## THE BEACH CHALET BREWERY
*1000 Great Highway (Fulton/Lincoln), (415) 386-8439*
*Daily 11:30am-midnight*

The Beach Chalet, the combination visitors center and brew pub at the outer edge of Golden Gate Park, recently reopened after lying vacant for years. The owners have overhauled the broad-columned rectangular building, creating a beautiful art deco interior with a wavy ceiling pattern, exposed wooden beams and light woods, plus giant plate glass windows affording a spectacular ocean panorama. Seating options abound in the spacious bar area: choose from the long bar with the giant copper brewing tanks behind it, the high tables in the corner, the wicker chairs facing the ocean, or the long benches that separate the bar from the restaurant seating. Although the bar serves plenty of liquors and bottled beers, the spotlight is on the five brews made on the premises, from the light and fruity Churchyard Pale Ale to the medium Pacific Porter. Before or after drinks, head downstairs to the visitors center, past the mosaic tiles and the carved wooden banister, to see the beautifully restored WPA-era murals of San

# Richmond / Sunset West Portal

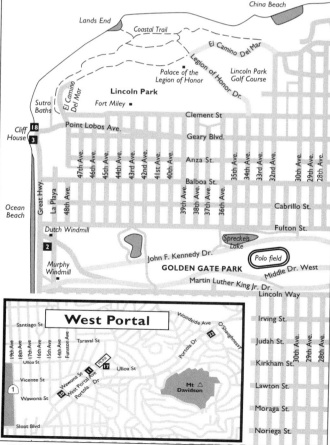

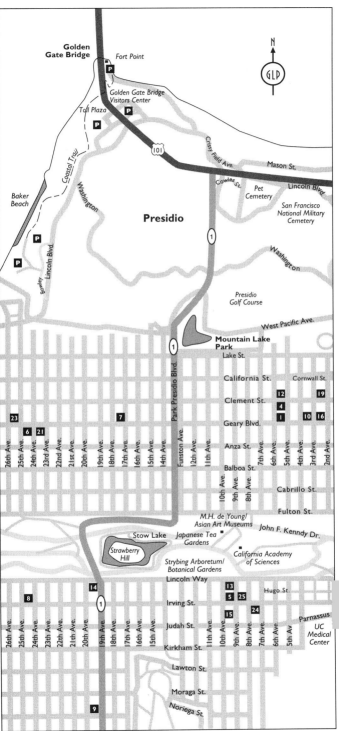

Francisco workers and the scale model of Golden Gate Park. With an unimpeded view of Ocean Beach and the vast Pacific, the Beach Chalet has already become a destination for plenty of well-scrubbed suburbanites, tourists, and well-to-do thirtysomething professionals: reservations are essential at the restaurant, and the bar is packed on weekend afternoons with a sporty, post-softball crowd. But if you don't have a car, it's one long MUNI ride to reach this windswept spot along the Great Highway.

## BEN BUTLER BAR
## PHINEAS T. BARNACLE

*Cliff House, 1090 Point Lobos Ave. (Great Highway), (415) 386-3330*
*Ben Butler Bar: M-Th 11am-1:30am; F-Su 9am-1:30am*
*Phineas T. Barnacle: Daily 10am-1:30am*

These are the two most westerly bars in the entire city. That should be readily apparent upon entering their host building, the venerable Cliff House, an ugly-on-the-outside/pretty-on-the-inside tourist haunt that hangs precariously over the Pacific and whose large back windows provide a sweeping view of the water from Pacifica to Marin. The Ben Butler is the ritzier of the two, an elegant Victorian interior of plush carpeting, molded copper ceilings, and low-slung oak tables. Drinks are predictably expensive and include the house specialty, the Ocean Beach (vodka, peach schnapps, cranberry juice, and pineapple juice). Appetizers such as calamari are also available. Phineas T. Barnacle is a dowdier joint with a nautical theme that may remind you of a ride at Disneyland. It's an A-framed room done up in dark woods and brass railings, with more limited window seating that primarily offers views of the Marin Headlands in the background and the Sutro Baths in the foreground. The TV is tuned to sports, though heaven knows why anyone would come all the way out here just for that.

## THE BITTER END

*441 Clement St. (5th Ave./6th Ave.), (415) 221-9538*
*M-F noon-2am; Sa-Su 10am-2am*

A local favorite, The Bitter End boasts a young, cheerful multi-ethnic crowd. A long, narrow room features plenty of table seating warmed by a working fireplace, a saloon-style bar covered with sports paraphernalia, a mounted deer's head, and a suit of armor at the foot of the stairs to the second floor. Pool tables are on both levels, and the enormous big-screen TV, possibly the largest in existence, is always tuned to whatever notable game is being broadcast. Although crowds are common here, notably on weekends, their members tend to be settled folks without that palpable sense of desperation that hovers over meat-market bars. In other words, you can drink in relative peace, notwithstanding the din emitting from the cranked-up jukebox. Newcastle, Red Hook, and other tasty beers on tap, served by a congenial staff.

## BLACK THORN

*834 Irving St. (9th Ave./10th Ave.), (415) 564-6627*
*M-F 4pm-2am; Sa-Su 1pm-2am*

This authentic Irish pub is full of ex-pats knocking back pints and having great "crack" (fun, not cocaine). With its low ceilings, dim lighting, and painted wooden horseshoe-shaped benches, this is the truest Irish pub in the Sunset. Stouts like Murphy's and Guinness are on tap, pictures of Ireland line the walls, and the color scheme is strictly green and white. On Thursday nights, there's a comedy act, and on Friday nights traditional Irish bands hold forth. Saturday nights a crowd packs the small dance floor, grooving to the electronic/ambient dance beat (just keep your distance from the dartboards).

## BLARNEY STONE
*5701 Geary Blvd. (24th Ave.), (415) 386-9914*
*Daily 2pm-2am*

As far as friendly Irish pubs in the Richmond are concerned, this is the pick of the litter. The one-room, salon-style bar is shrouded with sports paraphernalia, beer posters, and street signs from overseas. According to the congenial barkeep, the Blarney Stone offers "the best pint of Guinness in town." (Of course, a similar claim can be had for the asking at dozens of Irish bars in the City.) A few other quality imports are on tap. The televisions are always tuned to the game of the moment, which is international soccer whenever possible. Six high tables and the long bar provide ample places to sit, except on Saturday and Sunday nights when the bar is transformed into a rollicking disco dance club packed with local folks. The chef serves up a mean plate of curry fries and above-average fish-and-chips and burgers.

## THE COOPERAGE
*5320 Geary Blvd. (17th Ave./18th Ave.), (415) 386-2469*
*Daily 6am-2am*

The jewel of this compact sports hive is the digital display monitor that tirelessly trickles out the scores of all ongoing games, making it possible to follow your favorite team as if it were a company's stock, watching its fortunes rise and ebb as the clock ticks away. In addition, two televisions flank each side of the bar and another peers down from the opposite wall. This is essentially ESPN with a liquor license, and if you drop by and tune in you will find yourself among a chattering throng of comfortably attired locals who have found their Richmond haunt. A gas fireplace stands opposite the bar, and a pool table and dartboard are housed at the back; if you're quick, you can get in a game before the commercials are over.

## DURTY NELLY'S IRISH PUB
*2328 Irving St. (24th Ave./25th Ave.), (415) 664-2555*
*M-F 11am-2am; Sa-Su 10am-2am*

Durty Nelly's is a noteworthy emerald green daub on the canvas of the Irish scene. Informal and unpretentious, it offers plenty of Guinness, a tasty Irish stew, and some of the richest brogue in the Sunset. Depending on your disposition, you may be intimidated or delighted to discover most of the staff and the clientele are from Ireland (not that this is a rarity in a city seemingly full of transplants from the old sod). An unglazed terra-cotta tile floor, a brick fireplace, and a rich assortment of antiques, curiosities, and books evoke an aura of bygone days. A state-of-the-art CD jukebox benevolently embraces the modern. Evenings are chummy and convivial, with sing-alongs on Tuesdays (bring an instrument, sing, or just listen). Don't miss Trivia Quiz Thursdays (9pm), where the stakes are as high as the spirits. No cover.

## Darts

Nowadays, it seems like almost every bar in town is the proud host to a special—and by no means rare—breed: men and women throwing tiny, sharp, pointed objects at a round board on a wall several feet away. Whether you've been including a game of darts in an evening of drinking ever since you got your first fake ID, or your experience has been limited to throwing darts at the photograph of someone who has made you furious, there are lots of places in San Francisco for players of any level to down a few and throw a few. Here are some of the best, followed by a brief primer on playing and some vital places for those who take up the sport.

### Where to Play

A sampling of bars with dart boards; there are many more (see index at the back of the book).

**Black Thorn Tavern:** Sunset, 834 Irving St. (9th Ave./10th Ave.), (415) 564-6627

**Bloom's Saloon:** Potrero Hill, 1318 18th St. (Texas/Missouri), (415) 861-9467

**Eagle's Drift In:** Sunset, 1232 Noriega St. (19th Ave./20th Ave.), (415) 661-0166

**Edinburgh Castle:** Tenderloin, 950 Geary St. (Larkin/Polk), (415) 885-4074

**Ireland's 32:** Richmond, 3920 Geary Blvd. (3rd Ave./4th Ave.), (415) 386-6173

**Mad Dog in the Fog:** Lower Haight, 530 Haight St. (Fillmore/Steiner), (415) 626-7279

**Pig and Whistle:** Panhandle, 2801 Geary Blvd. (Wood), (415) 885-4779

**South Beach Billiards:** SoMa, 270 Brannan St. (1st St./2nd St.), (415) 495-5939

**Union St. Ale House:** Cow Hollow, 1980 Union St. (Laguna/Buchanan), (415) 921-0300

### How to Play

Just ask the bartender for a set of darts. At some places you'll have to leave collateral, such as a driver's license. If you have a choice of boards, select one that has less wear. (Darts don't stick properly in worn-out boards.) Some of the best games include:

*Around the World*: This is such an easy game that there's no need to keep score. Just throw three darts, one at a time, trying to hit any part of the wedge under number 1; after hitting that wedge, continue on in numerical order to 20. After throwing your three darts, remember which was the last number you hit. Then the next player gives it a try. After hitting 20 it's time to attempt the bull's-eye. This is where it gets challenging for a beginner.

*Cricket*: You have to hit numbers 20, 19, 18, 17, 16, and 15 three times each. If your dart lands in either large black part of the wedge, it counts for one of that number. If you hit the outer band in the wedge, it is worth two of that number. If you hit the inner band, it's worth three, and you don't have to hit that number any more. If you hit any of the numbers that you have already completed, you take those as points for extra credit, adding them up on the chalkboard.

*Tactics*: This is more difficult. It is just like cricket, only the darter calls out the number he or she expects to hit, and if the number is missed, no points are scored.

## IRELAND'S 32

*3920 Geary Blvd. (3rd. Ave./4th Ave.), (415) 386-6173*
*M-F noon-1:30am; Sa-Su 10am-1:30am*

First things first: it is *not* a good idea to walk in here waving the Union Jack. This is the IRA/Sinn Fein pub of record in San Francisco, as the historical paraphernalia scattered everywhere will attest. Politics aside, it serves up drink, food (from their *cistin),* and live music seven nights a week. Irish breakfasts (with real soda bread), pub grub such as shepherd's pie, and dinner specials such as bacon and cabbage are all available from the kitchen at some point during the day. There's no cover charge to see the varied musical offerings, which range from rock to traditional Irish, with open mike and acoustic nights as well. TV watchers can tune into live broadcasts of international sporting events—from Gaelic football to boxing—on satellite. The bileveled room also accommodates darts, pool, and an eclectic jukebox. The crowd is a mix of generations, although it definitely skews towards middle-aged and older, so it should come as no surprise that the favorite drink here is Guinness. If you're homesick, or just infatuated with modern Celtic culture, Ireland's 32 is a good place to scratch your itch.

## JOXER DALY'S

*46 West Portal Ave. (Ulloa/Vicente), (415) 564-1412*
*Daily 10am-2am*

Yet another pleasant and inviting Irish neighborhood pub, done up in the authentic black-and-tan hues of the Old Country, with a high ceiling, sparse-yet-tasteful wall hangings, and plenty of wood trim all about. Frequented by neighborhood folks and Irish nationals, there's plenty of room here to spread out at the bar and enjoy a pint of Guinness on tap while cursing the Giants on TV. Other bonuses include darts, a Britpop jukebox, and a blackboard (with chalk) in the men's loo.

---

### Clubs

**Golden Gate Darting Organization,** (415) 731-8107. About 125 members get together for darts on Thursday evenings at various bars. Call for locations and information.

**San Francisco Dart Association,** (415) 781-7332. Roughly 400 members play darts on Wednesdays at 34 San Francisco pubs. The SF Dart Association also publishes *Chalk Talk,* a dart magazine.

### Supplies

**Patricia Miller,** (415) 731-8107. Dart supplies are offered at roughly 15 percent off suggested retail prices. Mrs. Miller also offers retipping.

**Gamescape,** 333 Divisadero St. (Page/Oak), (415) 621-4263. This game store offers a wide range of darts and dart supplies. Open M-Sa 10am-7pm; Su 11am-5pm.

### Lessons

**Patricia or Ed Miller,** (415) 731-8107. If you don't have the nerve to learn darts in front of a barful of strangers, you can have a private lesson or two with the woman ranked 15th in the nation among female darters. Select your favorite pub and she'll meet you there during off-hours to give you a few pointers.

## LAST DAY SALOON
*406 Clement St. (5th Ave./6th Ave.), (415) 387-6343*
*M-F 2pm-2am; Sa-Su noon-2am*

Like a beacon, the Last Day Saloon's bright and hopping two-story interior draws in nightlifers adrift in the black quiet. The downstairs is straightforward sports bar, with longtime neighborhood residents drinking pints, listening to the jukebox, watching the pro league game of choice on TVs, and waiting for a turn at the pool tables. Upstairs, a sprawling room with tables in back and a sizable stage in front hosts the bands. The booking policy brings in lots of different types of mainstream music, from blues and rock to funk. Headlining weekend acts usually fill the room, while mostly just FOBs (Friends of the Band) turn up for the casual, less-crowded weeknights. History buffs will enjoy the wall covered with the names of the acts who have graced the stage. Yes, even Foghat once played here. Anchor and numerous other beers are on tap. There's a cover charge for the music.

## LITTLE SHAMROCK
*807 Lincoln Wy. (9th Ave./10th Ave.), (415) 661-0060*
*M-F 3pm-2am; Sa-Su 1pm-2am*

Established in 1893, the Little Shamrock is the oldest Irish bar in the city as well as a wonderfully inviting place within walking distance of the Haight and the Inner Sunset, located directly across the street from Golden Gate Park. You might have the distinct sensation that you're paying a visit to someone's gracious home, from the bed of flowers outside the front windows to the sofas and love seats and cluttered-attic decor inside. The cheerful atmosphere encourages lingering, perhaps near the cozy fireplace on a cold night. Be warned that darts are taken *very* seriously here, and denizens of the clubby darts room, with its array of league trophies, do their best to intimidate neophytes. The rest of the crowd is very easygoing, however, and includes a nice mix of folks from different neighborhoods and different ages. Yes, they serve Guinness.

## MOLLY MALONE'S
*1849 Lincoln Wy. (20th Ave.), (415) 681-3820*
*M-Th 2pm-2am; F-Su 10am-2am*

Located across from Golden Gate Park, Molly Malone's is part of the strong Irish bar scene in the Inner Sunset. Walk up to the classy brass-railing-and-wood bar, grab a Guinness on tap, pick out a tune on the CD jukebox, and then head for the back room warmed by a fireplace. There's a pool table there where you can match wits with Ireland's finest. After an evening at Molly's, you'll feel like you're at the heart of Dublin.

## MUCKY DUCK
*1315 9th Ave. (Judah/Irving), (415) 661-4340*
*Daily 11am-2am*

When the crowds and the trendiness of the Inner Sunset are getting to be too much, head for the Mucky Duck, a nice Irish bar that turns up the Neil Young-laden jukebox loud enough to drown out the loudest drunk. The decor is decidedly un-hip, just a few tables and a few stools, but there's a good selection of microbrews on tap, a pool table, popcorn, and more 49ers memorabilia on the walls than you could shake a stick at.

## PAT O'SHEA'S MAD HATTER

*3848 Geary Blvd. (2nd Ave./3rd Ave.), (415) 752-3148*
*Daily 11am-2am (opens at first kickoff during football season)*

Despite the intimidating sign hanging by the front door that reads We Cheat Tourists and Drunks, Pat O'Shea's is packed every night with an abundance of drunks and perhaps even a few tourists. Here, at the quintessential sports bar, televisions turned on to sports events occupy every nook and cranny, there are 25 beers on tap (microbrews and a few imports), and some first-rate bar food is served. Live bands play Friday and Saturday nights and for special occasions. The crowd varies from Inner Richmond locals to yuppies looking for some good clean preppie fun to die-hard sports fans who salivate at the word *playoffs*. The business lunch crowd is made up of extremely faithful neighborhood folk, and the staff prides itself on serving outstanding dishes from prime rib to pasta. St. Patrick's Day is the biggest attraction of all, with a "party line" that wraps around the corner.

## THE PHILOSOPHER'S INN

*824 Ulloa St. (West Portal/Claremont), (415) 753-9554*
*Daily 8am-2am*

Philosophers, out in West Portal? Hey, you'd be philosophical too if you had to take public transportation to and from downtown each day. This yellow-lit refuge, located mere steps from the MUNI turnstiles, is a convenient stopping-off point for downing a pint and ruminating over your lot in life. Caricatures of philosophers hang on the red-velvet wallpaper, enigmatically observing the barflies, which include lots of friendly older drinkers who aren't shy about engaging you in conversation. The pool table in back attracts the younger generation. Budweiser is the only beer available on tap.

## PLOUGH & STARS

*116 Clement St. (2nd Ave./3rd Ave.), (415) 751-1122*
*M 4pm-2am; Tu-Su 2pm-2am*

A favorite with the Irish lads and lassies residing in the Richmond, the Plough & Stars is an authentic re-creation of an Eire pub. The dim lighting, sparse decoration, and unobtrusive stage at the back will remind any former backpacker of a rural County pub. Seating options include long, narrow, communal tables of dark wood as well as the crowded bar. A mellow, ruddy-faced crowd enjoys pool, darts, and Guinness, with traditional Irish folk music playing nightly at 9:15 (there's a $4 cover charge except on Sundays). The bartenders are charming, and their thick brogue becomes easier to understand after a few pints. Asthmatics should bring their inhalers, as it can get quite smoky here. Anti-smokers should find another bar.

## TK'S

*328 West Portal Ave. (14th Ave.), (415) 566-9444*
*Daily 10am-2am*

Sure, lots of bars have dartboards, but how many sell a wide range of dart accessories from behind a locked glass case, treating them like 24-carat jewels? TK's does, for one. This run-down cubbyhole of a space, reminiscent of a 1970s rec room, features walls plastered with old black-and-white photos of prizefighters

## Late Night Eats

### BROTHER'S KOREAN RESTAURANT $
*4128 Geary Blvd. (6th Ave./7th Ave.), (415) 387-7991*
*Daily 11am-3am*
From the excellent *kimchee* to the wood-fired hibachi barbecue at your table, eating is a sweaty yet delicious experience at this authentic Korean barbecue house, a favorite among the local Korean community. The restaurant is known for its necessarily powerful ventilation system.

### EBISU $$
*1283 9th Ave. (Lincoln/Irving), (415) 566-1770*
*M-W 11:30am-2pm, 5pm-10pm; Th-F 11:30am-2pm, 5pm-midnight; Sa 5pm-midnight*
Top-notch sushi has made this bare-bones eatery a local favorite; expect a line most nights. Friendly, boisterous sushi chefs entertain the crowd at the sushi bar where the long list of daily specials is in plain view.

### GIORGIO'S PIZZERIA $
*151 Clement St. (3rd Ave.), (415) 668-1266*
*Su-Th 11:30am-11pm; F-Sa 11:30am-12:30am*
When the abundance of Asian eateries in the Richmond doesn't suit your fancy, Giorgio's offers huge salads and unexceptional traditional pizzas. Its tavern-like atmosphere will let you remain safely in a bar mentality when you're out drinking.

### MBE RESTAURANT $
*239 Clement St. (3rd Ave./4th Ave.), (415) 221-8883*
*Su-Th 11am-1am; F-Sa 11am-3am*
A simple storefront restaurant with bright lights and lots of mirrors. Serves up tasty noodle dishes, especially the pan-fried ones with chicken or pork.

### MILANO PIZZERIA $
*1330 9th Ave. (Irving/Judah), (415) 665-3773*
*Daily 1pm-1am*
In the never-ending search for true New York–style pizza in San Francisco, many people feel that this Sunset spot comes awfully close. Sandwiches, salads, main dishes, and pastas are also available. Delivery until midnight.

### PASTA POMODORO $
*816 Irving St. (9th Ave./10th Ave.), (415)566-0900*
*M-Sa 11am-11pm; Su noon-11pm*
Large servings of pasta at incredibly cheap prices—it's a concept that has made this citywide Italian restaurant chain very popular among those with big appetites and light pockets. Service is usually lightning quick yet still pleasant. Cash only.

### TART TO TART ¢
*641 Irving St. (8th Ave./9th Ave), (415) 753-0643*
*Daily 6am-2am*
This tiny bakery and coffee house dates back to the days before the Sunset became trendy, when all it had to offer were a few drugstores and a certain goofy charm. That charm lives on in Tart to Tart, a hangout that attracts an odd combination of stressed-out UCSF students, local skateboard punks, and late-night bargoers. They make a mean hot apple cider, and the pastries are usually excellent.

### VIDEO CAFÉ $
*5700 Geary St. (21st Ave.), (415) 387-3999*
*Daily 24 hours*
Provided you don't find the idea of dining in the middle of what is essentially your neighborhood Blockbuster a bit too bizarre even for the wee hours, the Video Café is an interesting place to munch on diner food while watching videos within a late-night delirium.

and a ceiling whose cracks reveal a clearly musty attic. The crowd runs the gamut from middle-aged folks without tattoos to middle-aged folks with tattoos, most of whom sport black Harley T-shirts. You'll also see lots of smokers who apparently have been addicted to nicotine for quite a while. The bar opens in the morning for the benefit of those who need a little pick-me-up before the hellish MUNI commute downtown.

## TOMMY'S MEXICAN RESTAURANT

5929 Geary Blvd. (23rd Ave./24th Ave.), (415) 387-4747
Daily 11am-midnight

It's always a party at Tommy's. Although the bar-restaurant is located out in The Avenues, it's best to take a cab for two reasons: parking is impossible, and once you get there you'll probably overindulge, since Tommy's is known for having the best margaritas this side of the Texas border. In fact, the restaurant even has a frequent drinkers club of sorts, where members can taste and sample the crème de la tequila. Surprisingly, the Yucatán-style Mexican cuisine is good, too, even without margaritas clouding your judgment. Family owned since 1965, Tommy's has proved its staying power in this predominately Asian neighborhood.

## TOWER LODGE

689 Portola Dr. (Fowler/O'Shaughnessy), (415) 564-9501
Daily 10am-2am

Like many of the cocktail bars located in the oft-forgotten "outer" neighborhoods, Tower Lodge eschews all the superfluous refinements and subtleties of trendier joints. A first-timer walking in may feel momentarily like the new sheriff in town. A wooden sign reading Castaways hangs above bartender Ed's medieval cash register, a quirky epithet that appears to wink at the equally quirky die-hards, mostly male, idly engaged in their customary offhand banter. The sallow walls are studded with an abundance of beer mirrors, and a neglected upright piano broods inconspicuously in the shadows. In the way of amusements, there are dartboards, pinball machines, a shuffleboard table, a pool table, and a video arcade game (golf). While it boasts being the highest cocktail lounge in the city next to the Carnelian Room, there are no windows. Alas, even if there were, a panoramic view wouldn't be possible.

## TRAD'R SAM'S

6150 Geary Blvd. (25th Ave./26th Ave.), (415) 221-0773
Daily 10am-2am

When the South Pacific of common myth comes calling, and the over-the-top Tonga Room is not in your plans, there's always Trad'r Sam's. The Richmond home of umbrella drinks, the Trad'r serves a mean Blue Hawaiian and other exotic concoctions, from the Singapore Sling and the Moscow Mule to the New Orleans Fog Cutter. There's a horseshoe bar in the center of this smallish room, with bamboo-framed, floral-print sofa booths against the walls. Princess chairs await the lucky few, who generally hog them for the entire night (rent them to friends while those lucky few are using the WC). Sadly, the South Seas warmth doesn't carry over to the surly staff: not even a big tip conjures a smile. Drinks run close to five bucks except during happy hour (Sundays to Thursdays 4pm to 7pm). Free popcorn and bags of potato chips are the only means of sustenance here. Guys, don't forget your white slacks and loafers.

## THE WISHING WELL

*603 Irving St. (7th Ave./8th Ave.), (415) 731-6433*
*Daily 10am-2am*

Now that the wonderful Embers Bar a few doors down has been replaced by a Pluto's Restaurant (continuing apace the Marina-ization of the Inner Sunset), this worn but welcoming neighborhood space is one of the last remaining links to an earlier, simpler time, when the Niners played at Kezar Stadium and before microbrews took the city by storm. Beers here don't get too adventurous beyond Michelob and Budweiser, and the clientele is older and full of Irish ex-pats. The yellowed walls, faded dark rug, oversized chairs, tacky fireplace, and old player piano make this place a comfortably shabby hangout. Big picture windows face onto Irving Street, and since the bar is rarely crowded, it's a good place to sip a beer and catch up with friends. Take to heart the sign that warns: "If you're thin-skinned, don't come in."

## YANCEY'S SALOON

*734 Irving St. (8th Ave./9th Ave.), (415) 665-6551*
*Daily noon-2am*

This huge saloon is so sprawling it's a wonder it takes up just one ZIP code. Filled with comfy chairs, cushy antique sofas, and big wooden tables (a few of which approach King Arthur-esque proportions), the interior is illuminated by Tiffany lamps and bristles with more hanging plants than the average greenhouse. There's also a long bar serving a good selection of draft beers (including the masterful Boddington's) and cozy seating by windows that open up on those rare windless and fog-free Sunset evenings. An entirely separate area is devoted to darts. Pub grub is readily available, and there's a PA system that calls the names of folks waiting for a table at PJs Oyster Bar across the street. The crowd tends to be mostly UCSF and USF students, along with young, well-dressed locals. Live music Saturday nights.

★

# SPECIAL FEATURES INDEX

# BAR & CLUB INDEXES

## DANCING

## HOUSE/TECHNO MUSIC

# FOOD & DRINK

## FULL MENU AND/OR RESTAURANT

## SNACKS

## MICROBREWS

# GAMES & DIVERSIONS

## POOL TABLE(S)

## DARTS

## OTHER GAMES

## SPORTS ON TV

# OTHER FEATURES

## GAY & LESBIAN

## OUTDOOR SEATING

## ROMANTIC

## THEME BARS/ NOTABLE DECOR

## ALPHABETICAL

## MAPS

## SIDEBARS

# DID YOU ENJOY THIS BOOK?

Good Life Publications produces high-quality guides to Northern California. Our books are available in bookstores throughout the region. You may also order directly. Here is a list of current titles.

---

## GOOD LIFE SAN FRANCISCO NIGHTLIFE GUIDE
A hip, lively resource for exploring San Francisco's varied nightlife, from concert halls to beer joints, gay clubs to wine bars. $9.95

## GOOD LIFE SAN FRANCISCO RESTAURANT GUIDE
A complete reference to the Bay Area's top restaurants. Includes over 700 reviews, star ratings, convenient indexes, and maps. $10.95

## GOOD LIFE SAN FRANCISCO RESTAURANT MAP
An ingenious combination: a pocket-sized guide to San Francisco's top restaurants in a handy folding laminated map all in one. $5.95

## GOOD LIFE SAN FRANCISCO BUDGET GOURMET
More than a guide to cheap eats, we tell you where to find great food at terrific prices throughout the Bay Area. Includes over 600 reviews, star ratings, convenient indexes, and maps. $9.95

## GOOD LIFE SAN FRANCISCO INSIDER'S GUIDE
A comprehensive sourcebook for Bay Area living, perfect for new-comers or visitors looking for a local view of the Bay Area. $14.95

## GOOD LIFE PENINSULA & SAN JOSE INSIDER'S GUIDE
The only comprehensive recreation and entertainment guide to Silicon Valley and the Bay Area. Perfect for newcomers. $12.95

## GOOD LIFE PENINSULA & SAN JOSE RESTAURANT GUIDE
The only restaurant guide for the SF Peninsula, San Jose, and Silicon Valley, with over 600 reviews, indexes, and maps. $10.95

## GUIDE TO THE GOOD LIFE IN BERKELEY
The only comprehensive guide for Berkeley and theEast Bay. $7.95

---

Ship To _____

Street/P.O. Box _____

City _____ State _____ Zip _____

Phone _____

Title                          Quantity  X  Price
_____ = _____
_____ = _____
_____ = _____

Subtotal                                    = _____

CA Residents add 7.5% Sales Tax             = _____

Postage: $2 for first book, $.50 each additional  = _____

**TOTAL**  (Checks to Good Life Publications)  = _____

Credit Card # _____

Visa ___  MC ___  AMEX ___  Exp. Date _____

Signed _____

---

**To order, send form to GOOD LIFE PUBLICATIONS
580 Washington St. #306, San Francisco, CA 94111
or call toll-free (888) 989-GOOD**